Living with China

THE AMERICAN ASSEMBLY was established by Dwight D. Eisenhower at Columbia University in 1950. Each year it holds at least two nonpartisan meetings that give rise to authoritative books that illuminate issues of United States policy.

An affiliate of Columbia, the Assembly is a national, educational institution incorporated in the state of New York.

The Assembly seeks to provide information, stimulate discussion, and evoke independent conclusions on matters of vital public interest.

CONTRIBUTORS

JULIA CHANG BLOCH, United States-Japan Foundation

HARRY HARDING, George Washington University

DAVID M. LAMPTON, National Committee on United States-China Relations

KENNETH LIEBERTHAL, University of Michigan

MICHAEL B. McELROY, Harvard University

SAM NUNN, United States Senate

CHRIS P. NIELSEN, Harvard University

MICHEL OKSENBERG, Stanford University

DOUGLAS H. PAAL, Asia Pacific Policy Center

DWIGHT H. PERKINS, Harvard University

EZRA F. VOGEL, Harvard University

THE AMERICAN ASSEMBLY
Columbia University

Living with China

U.S./China Relations in the Twenty-First Century

EZRA F. VOGEL
Editor

W. W. NORTON & COMPANY
New York   London

For information about permission to reproduce selections from this book, write to
Permissions, W. W. Norton & Company, Inc., 500 Fifth Avenue,
New York, NY 10110.

The text of this book is composed in Baskerville
Composition and manufacturing by the Haddon Craftsmen, Inc.

Library of Congress Cataloging-in-Publication Data
Living with China : U.S./China relations in the twenty-first century / Ezra F.
    Vogel, editor.
        p.   cm.
    Includes bibliographical references and index.
    ISBN 0-393-04540-4. — ISBN 0-393-31734-X (pbk.)
        1. United States—Foreign relations—China.   2. China—Foreign relations—
    United States.   3. United States—Foreign relations—China—Forecasting.
    4. China—Foreign relations—United States—Forecasting.   I. Vogel, Ezra F.
    E183.8.C5L58   1997
    327.73051—DC21   97-2333
                                                                        CIP

W. W. Norton & Company, Inc., 500 Fifth Avenue, New York, N.Y. 10110
http://www.wwnorton.com

W. W. Norton & Company Ltd., 10 Coptic Street, London WC1A 1PU

1 2 3 4 5 6 7 8 9 0

Contents

Preface

When The American Assembly decided in June 1995 to undertake a project on U.S.–China relations, there were several assumptions on which most experts agreed:

1) China would become one of the three largest economies in the world early in the 21st century, perhaps the largest by the middle of the next century. /

2) China could well become the most important country to the U.S., for better or for worse, more important even than Japan, Mexico, Canada, or Russia.

3) The United States had no agreed consensus on what its long-term interests were concerning China.

4) U.S. policy had been a collection of separate responses to specific crises and circumstances—and television images. Policies were often contradictory, and not part of an overall strategy to advance U.S. interests.

5) China was seen by some people more as a potential adversary than a partner. In history, the emergence of a new global power has often brought not only economic challenge, but also threats

of instability and war. If China became an adversary rather than a responsible member of the international regime, the United States would find it increasingly difficult to resolve a wide range of global, regional, and bilateral problems, increasingly difficult to resolve urgent domestic problems postponed by the cold war, and might well find itself in a new and destructive cold war, but this time with China as adversary. It is extremely desirable to find a way of bringing China into its new role without war or instability, and as a responsible member of the international regime, with a stake in its success.

Although there were beginning signs of improvement in China–U.S. relations starting in mid-1996 (though mostly in symbolic gestures and especially concerning high-level contacts and visits), these five assumptions were still valid as this book was being prepared.

Sensing that China represented the most critical foreign policy issue on which the United States needed to develop a comprehensive strategy and national consensus, The American Assembly, created by President Eisenhower to develop consensus on vital policy issues, decided to undertake an unusually comprehensive four-phase multiyear project. This volume represents the papers developed for use as background for an American Assembly of national leaders and experts who met from November 14th to 17th of 1996, one week after the presidential election, to prepare a consensus report, which can be found in this volume, to the new administration.

This U.S.–China Assembly was co-chaired by Senator Sam Nunn, whose speech to the Assembly is included as the final chapter of this book, and by John Whitehead, deputy secretary of state under George Shultz during the Bush administration. Ezra Vogel, Henry Ford II professor of the social sciences and director of the Fairbank Center for East Asian Research at Harvard University, was the program director. The Arden House Assembly was addressed by our co-chairs and by Brent Scowcroft, former national security advisor to President Bush, and a former trustee of The American Assembly.

The four phases of the Assembly's China program are as follows:

Phase I was a visit by an Assembly delegation for consultation at the highest levels in China and six of its neighbors: Hong Kong, Taiwan, Japan, South Korea, Indonesia, and Singapore. In China meetings were held with President Jiang Zemin; Vice Premier Zhu Rongji; Xiao Rong, daughter of Deng Xiaoping and head of the Association for Relations across the Taiwan Strait; Wang Daohan, former mayor of Shanghai and mentor to Jiang Zemin; Liu Huaqiu, director of the State Council on Foreign Affairs; many other senior government officials; and a wide range of scholars and experts on the United States. Our host in China was the Chinese People's Institute for Foreign Affairs, a quasi-government entity organized by then-Foreign Minister Zhou En-Lai in 1949 to establish contact with important nongovernment individuals and organizations from major countries. Similar meetings were held in the other six countries. Following two weeks of meetings, at which drafts of the chapters in this volume were discussed, all of the chapters were substantially rewritten for use in the Arden House session, and for this publication. Frequent references in this volume to conversations in June of 1996 relate to this trip. Leonard Woodcock, the first U.S. ambassador to the People's Republic of China, led the Assembly delegation, which included all but one of the authors of chapters in this book. A copy of that report is available at no cost from The American Assembly and on the Assembly homepage: (http://www.columbia.edu/cu/amassembly/).

Phase II was the Arden House meeting for which this volume was produced. Sixty-one American leaders, representing a wide range of constituencies and interests concerning China, met for four days to develop a statement on U.S. long-term national interests concerning China, and to make specific policy recommendations aimed primarily at the incoming second Clinton administration.

Phase III will be a bilateral U.S.–China Assembly, probably to be held in 1997, at which the approximately sixty participants will be divided equally between China and the U.S. This Assembly will seek common ground on which to base improved U.S.–China relations. It is being organized with the Pacific Council on International Policy (PCIP), the west coast affiliate of the Council on Foreign Relations.

Phase IV will be a series of programs organized in cooperation with The American Assembly by groups across the United States, and quite possibly in mainland China and Taipei. For example, there was a regional Assembly at the U.S. Air Force Academy in February 1997; in Seattle for the Western region of the U.S., organized by the Washington State China Relations Council and the PCIP; in Houston, organized by the Asia Society; in Atlanta, organized by The Carter Center of Emory University. Other cities, including San Francisco and Honolulu, and other organizations are considering additional Assemblies. Each regional Assembly will issue its own report, which will also be available to the public.

The American Assembly is grateful to those organizations and individuals who, by their generous contributions, made this program possible:

Major Funders
    The Starr Foundation
    The Henry Luce Foundation
    AT&T
    The Ford Foundation

Funders
    General Motors
    The Boeing Company
    Cargill
    Motorola
    DuPont

Contributors
    Springfield Holdings
    Mortimer B. Zuckerman
    Albert Kunstadter Family Foundation
    ChinaMetrik

As in all publications of The American Assembly, the views are those of the individuals writing each chapter and do not necessarily reflect the views of the Assembly nor of any of the organizations and individuals listed above.

The American Assembly believes that this volume honors the founding mandate of President Dwight D. Eisenhower "to illuminate public policy." It is our hope that it will serve well the citizens in both China and the United States who seek ways to create a more constructive relationship between our two countries, and will help American political and thought leaders to create a coherent long-term vision of the policies needed to advance America's national interests and values.

> Daniel A. Sharp
> President
> The American Assembly

Living with China

Introduction:

How Can the United States and China Pursue Common Interests and Manage Differences?

EZRA F. VOGEL

When clear national purposes collapsed in the United States at the end of the cold war, no consensus remained to counterbalance either the appeals of special interest groups or the images projected by the media, both of which gained greater prominence in the ensuing policy vacuum. Interest groups and television stories, no matter how quixotic and inconsistent with overall U.S. priorities, are now able to shape national policy. Can we not articulate new national goals against which to measure the arguments of pressure groups and the impressions conveyed by the latest scene on the nightly news?

The American Assembly meeting in November 1996, from which

EZRA F. VOGEL is director of Harvard's Fairbank Center for East Asian Research and the Henry Ford II Professor of the Social Sciences at Harvard University. He served as the Clinton administration's national intelligence officer for East Asia from August 1993 to August 1995. He has published *The Four Little Dragons: The Spread of Industrialization in East Asia, One Step Ahead in China: Guangdong under Reform*, as well as numerous other books and articles concerning Chinese domestic and international affairs.

this volume derived, was based on four premises: (1) that interested and informed citizens representing groups with different perspectives can help forge a consensus of overall long-term U.S. national interests; (2) that such an effort can help political leaders steer a steady course benefiting the nation as a whole; (3) that the current suspension of U.S.–China tensions provides a window of opportunity for constructive discussions to improve relationships; and (4) that relations with China are critical for U.S. foreign policy interests in the twenty-first century. The importance of Haiti, Somalia, Bosnia—even of the Middle East and Russia—is likely to pale in the long run by comparison with China, the nation that may well rank with the United States as the other leading power in the world in the years to come.

The Rise of China

China, with proud aspirations that draw on 2,200 years of continuous political history, a rich civilization, and the world's largest population, is already beginning to act as if it were the major power it is likely to become. And other countries, anticipating China's rise, are beginning to accommodate its wishes or seek alliances to resist possible Chinese pressures.

China is not yet a superpower. Even measured by purchasing power parity, the Chinese economy lags far behind the U.S. economy. Measured by current exchange rates, which help define a nation's international economic leverage, China is decades behind Japan, to say nothing of the United States. Its foreign investment and international trade lag behind those of major European countries. Its per capita income is below $1,000 per year, and inner China is likely to remain poor well into the next century. China's infrastructure, including roads, railways, ports, telecommunications, and electric power facilities, is at best several decades behind that of modern countries. Its institutions have not yet been restructured to accord with the needs of a modern state and a global market economy.

Within the next ten years the Chinese military is unlikely even to begin building a significant blue water navy. China lacks the capacity to invade nearby Taiwan, and it is decades behind the military technology and control systems used by the United States in the Gulf War, to say nothing of more recent breakthroughs in U.S. technology.

Yet the Chinese economy, as measured by purchasing power parity, is one of the three largest in the world, and in the 1990s China has grown more rapidly than any other country. Continued rapid growth over the next few decades is in the world's interest, but even if it were not, it is probably unstoppable by any feasible means the United States has at its disposal. China has a high savings and investment rate, and it has already acquired technology and management skills that will spread from its coast to the inner provinces. Its virtually unlimited supply of willing low-cost laborers, when combined with its new capital and technology, make high productivity increases almost inevitable. Most experts who have analyzed China's economy estimate that China is likely to sustain growth rates well above 5 percent per year for several decades. By then the Chinese economy, as measured by purchasing power parity, may be the largest in the world.

When Japan and the four little dragons (South Korea, Taiwan, Hong Kong, and Singapore) each grew at nearly 10 percent a year for over two decades, their exports, raw material imports, and accumulation of wealth had a tremendous impact on the world economy. China's population, 1.2 billion, is six times that of Japan and the four little dragons combined. Chinese growth may not have an impact six times as large as theirs, but it still will be enormous. China's willingness to use access to its markets to achieve political goals already leaves prominent foreign firms hostage to their nation's relations with China.

Some Westerners have assumed that China's Communist party, like that of the Soviet Union, will soon collapse and that regionalism will split China apart. Most China specialists believe the likelihood of this is very low. The Chinese Communist regime, unlike its Soviet counterpart, still has a strong nationalist appeal that originated with the expulsion of foreign colonialists. The Soviet Union was unified in the last century; China was unified 2,200 years ago. Minority members constituted over half of the Soviet Union's population, but make up just 8 percent of China's; only in Tibet and Taiwan are the forces of separatism strong.

China's Communist party is far along in its transformation; already its policy goals are determined less by Marxism-Leninism than by global markets. The party in China, unlike that of the Soviet Union, has earned support based on its success in guiding economic reform and rapid growth. Even many Chinese who seek more freedom and democracy and are by no means enthralled with the party are ready to accept its leadership; they see no other force able to guide China's progress and avoid the chaos that devastated the country in the century before 1949.

If China continues to grow stronger, as expected, how can the United States best encourage it to link its systems to those of the rest of the world and to be cooperative rather than confrontational in relation to other powers trying to maintain global order? In 2025, will a strong China threaten the security of other countries or be a force for peace and prosperity? In the meantime, how will Chinese leaders, still hypersensitive after a century of humiliation at the hands of Western powers and with little direct contact with the outside world, guide their country as it gains in power? Will China behave like Japan and Germany in the fifty years from 1895 to 1945, demolishing its neighbors, or will it, like Japan and Germany in the fifty years from 1945 to 1995, contribute to global peace and prosperity?

Can the United States, as the world's dominant power, adjust to the rise of a major new power as England did when the United States spurted ahead at the end of the nineteenth century? Or will it, like the Western powers dealing with Japan and Germany during the first half of this century, mishandle a rising power, alienating but not deterring China and contributing to a cataclysmic result?

To the extent that the United States can help shape China's behavior, what should be its goals and what methods should it use to achieve them? How can America provide consistent expectations that encourage China to join in constructive international activities but deter it from behavior that endangers the international order?

Relations between the United States and China have deteriorated badly since 1989. In March 1996, when China fired missiles off the coast of Taiwan and the United States moved two carrier forces into the vicinity, U.S.–China relations reached their lowest point since the Taiwan Straits crisis of 1958 and possibly since the Korean War.

Anti-Americanism, reflecting increasing irritation at American criticism and pressures, is now running high in China. Since the summer of 1996 tensions have been temporarily suspended, but the underlying problems remain. Until they are dealt with, the resolution of important international issues may be impossible. We cannot, as U.S. officials mistakenly did just before the Chinese entered the Korean War, rule out the possibility that resentments could spiral forward to direct conflict. How have U.S. relations with China, which had been improving so rapidly since 1971, fallen to such a low ebb?

The Origins of U.S.–China Tensions

The origin of certain problems dates back to World War II, when the United States, despite efforts at neutrality, was actually closer to the Kuomintang (KMT) than to the Communists. In 1937, when Japan invaded, the Communists chose to suspend the civil war against the KMT and cooperate with its adversary to pursue the war against Japan. The United States accepted the Chinese Communists as partners in the war effort and tried to encourage the KMT and Mao's Communists to continue to work together. But while they were allegedly cooperating, they began positioning themselves for the battles that broke out shortly after the end of World War II. Because the United States was allied to the government of China, led by Chiang Kai-shek, it had closer relations with the KMT than with the Communists. During World War II the KMT had blockaded the Communist base areas, and the United States did not break the blockade. At the end of the war, the United States helped bring in Chinese government troops to take over from the Japanese, and this helped give the KMT forces a better position from which to fight against the Communists. When the civil war broke out again in 1946, the Communists were desperate. They believed that the United States had favored the KMT, and their belief had at least some validity.

By 1949, when the Chinese Communists established their rule in Beijing, they were firmly allied with the Soviet Union against the United States and the KMT. In 1950 the Communists began preparing to invade Taiwan to complete their conquest of the KMT forces and allies who had fled there, but with the outbreak of the Korean War, the U.S. fleet moved into the Taiwan Straits, thus blocking the Communists' plans. In the Communists' view, were it not for U.S. assistance to Chiang Kai-shek and his successors, Taiwan would have been unified with the mainland and the civil war ended long ago. China and the United States regarded each other as enemies from 1949 to 1971. Fundamental changes, however, both domestic and international, reshaped relations between the two nations in 1969, 1979, and 1989.

In 1969 the crack in relations between China and the Soviet Union that had begun in the late 1950s broke open, first with a minor border skirmish and then with a substantial Soviet invasion of China that caused serious damage. China, aware that the Soviets were far stronger militarily, then made a strategic decision to open to the West. The initiation of relations between China and Canada, France, Belgium, and other European countries was a significant part of the process. President Richard Nixon and National Security Advisor Henry Kissinger could see the strategic advantage of seeking China's help to resolve the Vietnam issue and to work against the Soviet Union, the main adversary. Kissinger visited Beijing secretly in 1971, and President Nixon's public visit followed in 1972.

In their broad "tour of the horizon" talks over several years, Kissinger and Premier Zhou Enlai refrained from attacking each other ideologically and dealt with national interests in a pragmatic manner. China and the United States did not become allies, but relations continued to improve. The Shanghai Communiqué issued during President Nixon's visit set out the U.S. position on the delicate Taiwan issue:

The United States acknowledges that all Chinese on either side of the Taiwan Strait maintain there is but one China and that Taiwan is a part of China. The United States Government does not challenge that position. It reaffirms its interest in a peaceful settlement of the Taiwan question by the Chinese themselves. With this prospect in mind, it affirms the ultimate objective of the withdrawal of all U.S. forces and military installations from Taiwan. In the meantime, it will progressively reduce its forces and military installations on Taiwan as the tension in the area diminishes.

Relations between China and the United States took a dramatic step forward at the beginning of 1979 with the establishment of formal recognition between the two nations and the implementation of China's new program for reform and further opening to the West. These developments followed Deng Xiaoping's consolidation of power, some two years after Mao's death and the end of the Cultural Revolution in 1976.

Reforms unfolded rapidly after 1979. To experiment with new systems and to encourage foreign investment, Deng immediately set up four special economic zones. Private enterprises (initially with up to seven employees) were permitted. In 1982 communes were abolished and responsibility for rural production was shifted from the team to the household. Prices were decontrolled over the next decade; private enterprises were allowed to grow; the physical mobility of labor was permitted; and rationing was gradually abolished. People's fear of expressing divergent opinions subsided, and the range of ideas that could be publicly expressed increased. At the same time relations between the United States and China grew warmer and closer, until the Tiananmen Square incident of 1989.

In 1989, as the Soviet Union collapsed and the cold war ended, the strategic basis for the alliance between China and the United States against their mutual enemy also ceased to exist. In the same year, the bloody crackdown on demonstrators near Tiananmen Square in June 1989 led the United States to call off high-level visits, to withhold aid programs, and to distance itself from association with China's leaders. The crackdown has continued to have a negative impact on U.S.–China relations despite some resumption of activities after 1991.

The American public saw the crackdown as a brutal suppression of freedom and democracy. A few weeks earlier, when U.S. television anchors went to Beijing to cover the Gorbachev visit, they found demonstrators for freedom who became the focus of their programs. The U.S. public immediately identified with the protestors, and when the Chinese clamped down and shot at least several hundred of those involved, Americans were outraged.

Chinese leaders saw Tiananmen as a painful and badly handled incident that was perhaps unavoidable to restore order and clear the square of those who had paralyzed the nation's capital and the work of government. Authorities were divided on how to deal with the demonstrators. General Secretary Zhao Ziyang tried to work with them to persuade them to disband, but in late May he was removed from his position, and hardliners took over. To this day, many knowledgeable Chinese citizens and foreign specialists wonder whether the square could have been cleared peacefully. The Chinese Army was inexperienced in crowd control, young soldiers were frightened for their own safety, and some fired on crowds not because of orders but because of their own fear. Other observers, however, believe that Chinese leaders, worried about the rising tide of protests, concluded that simply dispersing the masses was not enough, that intimidation was needed to discourage others from threatening public order.

Immediately after the incident, President George Bush, a friend of several Chinese leaders since his tenure as head of the U.S. Liaison Office in Beijing and aware of the strategic issues on which he needed China's cooperation, hesitated to castigate its leadership. Although he soon banned high-level visits, reduced technology transfers, and restricted aid programs, Bush secretly sent National Security Advisor Brent Scowcroft to talk with Chinese officials. Yet Bush remained vulnerable to Democratic criticisms that by coddling Beijing's "dictators," he showed no respect for human rights. Since 1989 the negative attitude of the American public has made most U.S. politicians more receptive to criticizing China.

In 1992, while campaigning in Texas, President Bush announced that he would sell F-16 planes, produced in Texas, to Taiwan. China interpreted this as a violation of the Three Communiqués between the United States and the People's Republic, given that the new commitment upgraded equipment sold to Taiwan. The Chinese muted their response because Bush made it clear to them that he would not change the one-China policy, but the issue continued to rankle the Chinese military. Then presidential candidate Bill Clinton, taking advantage of Bush's mild response to Tiananmen, made it clear that he would be tougher on Chinese leaders if they did not improve their handling of human rights. After the election, President Clinton announced that he would continue most-favored-nation treatment of China only if it made progress in the human rights arena. In May 1994, however, he delinked the two issues. But the U.S. public knew little about the changes since 1979 that improved the livelihood and increased the freedom of expression and movement of the average Chinese. The image of Tiananmen suppression remained strong, and administration officials kept up the pressure on China. Republican critics agreed with the president's decision to delink but argued that by announcing a tough line and then yielding, he lessened his credibility.

Even after May 1994, the administration remained cool toward China, and U.S. cabinet members visiting China invariably pushed China on human rights. As of the fall of 1996, Secretary of State Warren Christopher had visited China only once; President Clinton had had brief formal meetings with President Jiang Zemin at two Asia Pacific Economic Cooperation (APEC) organization meetings and at a U.N. meeting in 1995. The U.S. president and vice president, however, chose not to visit Beijing, President Jiang was not invited to Washington for a high-level visit, and broad-ranging discussions between top officials of the two sides did not take place during Clinton's first three years.

China, too, has become more openly critical of the United States. From the perspective of some American officials, the Chinese had domestic disagreements and needed the unity that came from criticizing the United States. In China's view several actions by the United States upset the two countries' relationship. China saw U.S. demands that it grant more freedoms to and provide more information about its dissidents as interference in its domestic affairs. In 1993 the United States stopped a Chinese ship, the *Yinhe*, and searched it for forbidden chemicals that President Jiang had denied were on board; in the end the United States found no chemicals but did not apologize or compensate the Chinese for the commercial costs of delaying the ship for some days. Furthermore, American politicians campaigned to block the Chinese from hosting the Olympics in 2000, arguing that with such a human rights record, China did not deserve the honor. China lost its Olympic bid by a narrow margin, convincing many there that they would have been chosen had it not been for U.S. opposition. The Chinese, including many youth and intellectuals who had previously demonstrated for human rights, were furious at the United States. These incidents began to have a cumulative impact

Just as the West no longer has the cold war to provide clear policy guidelines, so China, after the collapse of the Soviet Union and the opening of the market economy, no longer has Communist or Maoist ideology to unify the country. Some Chinese leaders have in propaganda encouraged nationalism, including continued criticism of Japan's past imperialism and U.S. prejudice against China, as a way of uniting the country. U.S. pressure in the area of human rights, the *Yinhe* ship incident, U.S. congressional lobbying to prevent China from holding the Olympics, the annual review of most-favored-nation status, and especially the triumphal Lee Teng-hui visit to the United States have been well publicized in China, setting off the strong wave of anti-Americanism among young intellectuals mentioned earlier.

In 1995 tensions escalated when President Clinton, despite warnings from China, allowed Taiwan's President Lee Teng-hui to visit the United States. Since 1971 there had been an informal understanding that the United States, to show commitment to a one-China policy, would not welcome a top Taiwan leader. But American attitudes about Taiwan had begun to change as the island not only became more democratic, especially compared with Beijing, but mobilized its representatives with advanced U.S. degrees to lobby on its behalf. Chinese officials became more worried that with support from the United States, especially from the newly elected 1994 Republican Congress, Taiwan might move more boldly toward independence. When a buoyant President Lee Teng-hui returned from the United States amid growing popularity, China's leaders believed that they could no longer count on the United States to maintain a one-China policy. Chinese explained to Western visitors that they believed strong action was required to counter Taiwanese momentum toward independence, and China fired missiles off Taiwan's shores.

Many members of Congress and administration officials who had criticized mainland China's human rights actions and praised Taiwan were nonetheless sobered by the prospect that the United States might easily become involved in a war with a resolute China prepared to risk millions of lives to ensure that Taiwan and Tibet remained part of China. Beijing was sobered by the negative reactions it evoked with the use of force near Taiwan, not only from the United States but from its Asian neighbors. Hence both China and the United States recognized the desirability of avoiding conflict, thus creating a window of opportunity for meaningful dialogue about long-range interests.

Although tensions have already reached a dangerous level, many leaders in China and the United States are willing to make efforts to reestablish a more constructive relationship. As one Chinese official told the American Assembly delegation in June 1996, the largest established economy and the largest growing economy, working together, could have a major positive impact on world affairs.

Chinese Analyses of U.S. Strategy

In the negative climate of U.S.–China relations, the Chinese suspect U.S. motives. Because Chinese leaders are less responsive to democratic processes and more concerned with coherent long-range strategies, they tend to believe that other countries' policies also have a similar cohesiveness. Despite some U.S. administration efforts to reduce tensions, the Chinese often focus on various congressional statements that they tend to assume represent official U.S. government views. In 1995 many Chinese think-tank researchers and political leaders concluded that U.S. policies did have a coherent purpose: as an established power, the United States had become fearful of China's rapid growth and was trying to slow down the rise of a new rival power.

In China's view, why was America pressing so hard on human rights in the early 1990s just when China's human rights situation was vastly better than it had been twenty-five years earlier? Why was the United States now so tough on China and so soft on Russia, so vocal in complaining about China's treatment of Tibet and so understanding about Russian treatment of Chechnya? To many Chinese the answer was obvious: China had Communist leaders and Russia did not, and Russia was now a weak country, not to be feared, while China was a rising power, a potential threat. New U.S.

criticism of human rights, which focused on supporting dissidents who opposed the Chinese government, and new U.S. support for the independence movement in Tibet and Taiwan were seen as efforts to destabilize China, as the United States had done in Tibet in the 1950s.

Why were the U.S. president and vice president unwilling to visit Beijing during their several trips to neighboring Asian countries or to properly welcome President Jiang Zemin and Premier Li Peng in Washington? Why did the United States block China from holding the Olympics? Why was the United States so critical of China in multilateral meetings such as those of the Geneva Human Rights Commission? The answer seemed clear: to weaken China's influence in international affairs.

Why was the United States so tough on China on intellectual property rights, so reluctant to see China quickly admitted into the World Trade Organization, and why did it not fully restore the technology transfers that it had removed after 1989? The answer: to slow down China's economic rise.

Why was the United States suddenly recognizing Vietnam after failing to do so for two decades? Why did the United States, which had earlier stated in its East Asian Security Initiative that it was reducing troops in Asia, announce in its February 1995 East Asian Strategic Review that it was retaining its present troop level? Why was it now strengthening its alliance with Japan, encouraging Japan and South Korea to develop theater missile defense systems, and advocating multilateral alliances in Asia? What potential enemy did the United States have in mind? China seemed the obvious target.

And how to explain U.S. "engagement policy"? Through a selective limited engagement policy, it was thought, the United States hoped to gain Chinese allies who could help split China internally. Why did Clinton allow China to continue to receive most-favored-nation treatment, though he delinked it from human rights? Not out of strategic concerns, but because of pressure from American business people who wanted access to China's huge domestic market.

Actual Sources of U.S. Strategy

In fact the United States had no such overall strategy or strategic vision. Rather, the collapse of the Soviet Union with the concomitant loss of the cold war strategic vision had rendered unnecessary the alliance with China against the Soviets.

Some Americans, looking at Chinese gross national product figures as measured by purchasing power parity, do worry about the possible implications. A defense planner, asked to think of potential threats a decade ahead, noting that the increase in Chinese military expenditures and the lack of Chinese openness or "transparency," would naturally put China high on the list of nations to worry about. This does not, of course, mean that overall the United States regards China as a threat.

The Chinese, not having a democratic country, have difficulty understanding the power of American public opinion. The vivid and frequently replayed television coverage of the Tiananmen Square incident led the U.S. public to see Chinese leaders as despots cracking down on citizens demanding liberty. The enormous political and social progress that is taking place in China has had little impact on American opinion because only a small number of observers are aware of it. U.S. reporters in China who are harassed by the authorities, who did not see the horrors of the Cultural Revolution, and who do not read the Chinese papers where many new views are expressed tend to stress the problems, not the progress. In this climate Congress and the White House are unwilling to appear friendly to a leadership that so abuses the human rights of its citizens.

Americans still deeply identify with their forebears who escaped from oppression in other countries and gained liberty in the United States. Most in America believe that democratic countries do not invade other countries, but that totalitarian countries like Nazi Germany and the Soviet Union do. Many U.S. citizens believe that Chinese leaders who crack down on their own people are likely to become aggressive in international affairs.

Common Interests of the
United States and China

China today shares a number of common interests with the United States and other major powers.

- *Stability of the International Order.* The stability of the international order is clearly important. Like the United States, China has a stake in limiting the proliferation of weapons of mass destruction and in reducing arms levels.
- *Expanding Trade and Preserving Open International Markets.* Expanding trade and preserving open international markets are also significant interests. China benefits from open access to global markets, and the United States benefits from access to the Chinese market. Although China is not yet a member of the World Trade Organization (WTO), it already benefits from it and would benefit more if it became a member.
- *Strengthening International Organizations.* Strengthening international organizations is deemed important as well. Again like the United States, China has a vested interest in the success of the United Nations, the World Bank, the International Monetary Fund (IMF), and other groups to which it belongs. Since its opening in 1979, China has accepted the basic framework of international organizations and advocates gradual reforms, not revolutionary changes. Because China even now is a sizable power whose influence beyond its borders is growing, no international organizations can be strong without China's active and positive participation. It is in the interests of the United States to assist China in preparing to take part in these institutions at an early date.

In addition to these general common global interests, the United States also has a positive stake in issues central to China.

- *A Prosperous and Stable China.* A prosperous and stable China is a continuing priority. If China, with its 1.2 billion people, were to become unstable, the potentially huge numbers of refugees and massive requirements for assistance could cause hardship for neighboring countries and all major world powers. Domestic conflicts might spill across borders. But if the Chinese economy

continues to grow, this will promote regional stability and provide a positive stimulus for every trading country.
- *A Peaceful Resolution in Taiwan and Tibet.* A peaceful resolution of
Taiwan, Tibet, and other sovereignty claims is also a goal. If
these issues are not settled peacefully, they could lead to massive
commitments of military forces and possibly to international
conflicts.

Issues on which China and the United States Have Different Perspectives

At the same time, China's perspectives differ from those of the
United States on a number of issues.

- *Taiwan and Tibet.* Taiwan and Tibet are perhaps the most obvious areas of disagreement. As many officials told the American Assembly delegation, China, after a century of foreign encroachment
on its territory, is particularly sensitive about territorial integrity and
national sovereignty, and the Chinese instinctively feel that Taiwan
and Tibet are part of China. Because China regards Taiwan as the
last part of the country not yet conquered during its civil war and
believes that possession of the island is geostrategically essential, it
is prepared to fight to prevent it from becoming independent. China
is also firmly committed to keeping Tibet part of China and, being
confident that no other major power will fight to preserve Tibet's
autonomy, is prepared to put down any resistance. The United
States has, however, been willing to give military aid to Taiwan to
help it resist attack. China believes that U.S. support makes it less
likely that Taiwan will agree to unification, and the Chinese military in particular views U.S. military aid to Taiwan as constituting
interference in China's internal affairs. Although the United States
is formally committed to one China, many Americans have sympathy for Taiwan's desires for independence and for the Dalai Lama.
- *South China Seas.* The South China Seas, in contrast, though under
dispute, are not an area where China is as committed to claims of
sovereignty as it is in Taiwan and Tibet. The Spratley and Paracel
Islands themselves have little strategic significance, because they are
vulnerable to attack and too small on which to build meaningful

bases. Little oil has been discovered. Chinese claims do not affect U.S. interests in the security of sea lanes of communication, but the United States has an interest in ensuring that China does not resolve the issues by force and in reassuring the Association of Southeast Asian Nations (ASEAN) countries of U.S. commitments to the region.

• *Domestic Economic Development.* Domestic economic development is an issue on which perspectives differ to a greater degree. Since 1979 China has embarked on a massive project of rapid economic growth; it wants peaceful relations with other countries, and it wants access to world markets, capital, and technology as cheaply as possible. With over 100 million people who have migrated from rural areas to towns and cities since reforms began and with potentially several hundred million more redundant laborers as agricultural and industrial productivity improves, China needs to continue rapid growth to avoid social turmoil. Foreign businesses, however, want increased opening of markets, transparency, and predictability without arbitrary influence of Chinese officials. U.S. firms also want to keep control over their intellectual property and technology as much as they can. They also want a predictable environment with as few impediments as possible.

• *Multilateral Organizations.* Multilateral organizations are also viewed differently by the two powers. China sees multilateral organizations as tools used by dominant powers to extend their influence. Though wanting to take part in order to represent its interests, China endeavors to maintain multilateral organizations as forums for discussion rather than as strong organizations that can be used by the dominant power, the United States, to pursue its priorities. The United States wants to strengthen multilateral organizations but also to pursue its interests in them.

• *International Organizations.* In international organizations, China is not yet a global power and has less interest in maintaining the status quo than does the United States. Moreover, China has a far smaller stake in international organizations and regimes to which it does not belong.

• *Potential Threats in Asia.* The question of potential threats in Asia represents another area of disagreement. China believes that Japan constitutes the greatest threat in Asia over the next few decades. It is the dominant economy of Asia. It has superior technology, including rocketry, airplanes, and electronics that have military applications, and it could produce nuclear weapons possibly within weeks. Furthermore, China thinks that the U.S.–Japan security relationship may be aimed at China and that adding new missions and Japan's acquisition of new technology from the United States could pose dangers to China. The United States, in contrast, believes that the alliance with Japan eases U.S. burdens and promotes stability in Asia.

• *Korea.* In Korea, both China and the United States want to prevent the proliferation of nuclear weapons. If Korea were to be united, however, and the United States were to dominate the peninsula with U.S. troops remaining in place, China would lose its buffer zone. China prefers a buffer zone, but depending on its relations with the United States, it may or may not be willing to accept the presence of U.S. forces.

• *Strategic Alliances.* With regard to strategic alliances, there are many regions to consider. China believes that in addition to Japan, the greatest long-run threat in Asia could come from India. Therefore China would like to ally with Pakistan and assist it in countering India. The United States fears that aid to Pakistan could strengthen an arms race between India and Pakistan and is especially concerned that both might become nuclear powers. In the Middle East, China, which will need massive amounts of petroleum as it grows, wants to maintain good relations with oil producers to ensure access to supplies. The United States is concerned that China's relations with Iran, Iraq, and other Middle Eastern countries could complicate the region's balance of power and the peace process. In another area of the world, the former Soviet Union, some Chinese believe they can acquire a great deal of technology, including military technology. Some in the United States worry that this could create problems for the stability of Asia, especially if Russia takes a turn to the right or upgrades its weapons sales.

• *Weapons Proliferation.* Weapons proliferation is another important concern. Both the United States and China want to avoid widespread proliferation of weapons, but both are ready to bend international rules and understandings to help their allies. The United States has allowed Israel to develop nuclear weapons to defend itself against Arab countries. China has given military aid to Pakistan. China has been willing to restrain arms sales and nuclear proliferation to Iran and Syria, where the United States has signaled that it has vital interests and would retaliate. The United States has not been willing to give similar assurances to China regarding Taiwan, where China has signaled that it has vital interests.

• *Human Rights.* If we turn to the issue of human rights, we find further differences, as already noted. The U.S. public has great sympathy for Chinese dissidents, and some U.S. citizens take a particular interest in human rights violations in China. Chinese officials argue that antigovernment dissidents have the potential to destabilize the political and social order. Because the United States did not express concern over human rights violations during the Cultural Revolution, when perhaps a million Chinese were killed and tens of millions were sent to labor camps, Chinese intellectuals wonder why the United States, which was pragmatic in dealing with China after 1971, is now becoming more ideological. They complain that the U.S. media do not report on the many positive changes, such as the growth of elections for local officials, the expanding range of publications, and the greatly improved quality of life. As we have seen, they are suspicious that the United States is supporting the dissidents in order to weaken China's unity and slow down its rise as a global power. China has released a few dissidents after international appeals, but in response to foreign pressure it has generally become belligerent and more resistant to cooperation with the United States. Even Chinese intellectuals and other Asians who hope China becomes more democratic are overwhelmingly opposed to additional U.S. pressure on this issue.

• *Environment.* On the environment, the picture is mixed. Chinese officials in Beijing and many local leaders, especially in richer coastal areas and in localities with special pollution problems, are ready to work to maintain the environment. Many are willing to cooperate with U.S. specialists in introducing new technology and practices. But because China is poor, wants quick economic progress, and is short of clean fuel, many Chinese are prepared to delay efforts to control the environment until the economy takes off. Before introducing pollution controls, they seek assistance from foreign countries that have already made economic progress.

China and the United States thus have significant areas of both agreement and disagreement. Once the areas of disagreement are clearly identified, the challenge is to work out a way to manage them. Much is possible, but this requires not only a consistent policy but mutual confidence. Both must be rebuilt before progress can be made.

Chapter Summaries

In the chapters that follow, the authors' works can be summarized as follows.

Chapter 1. "Taiwan, Tibet, and Hong Kong in Sino-American Relations"

Taiwan, Tibet, and Hong Kong have been issues in Sino-American relations since the establishment of the People's Republic of China. Chinese leaders are dedicated to overcoming China's past humiliation, fulfilling their responsibility of uniting China, and providing national security. The U.S. government officially acknowledges the Chinese view that Taiwan and Tibet are part of China and that Hong Kong will be after July 1, 1997. But many Americans, believing in democracy, self-determination, and freedom of religion, are outspoken in their sympathy with local people who seek more autonomy. Chinese leaders, fearful that this may lead to U.S. policy change, consider this interference in China's internal affairs.

China's resumption of sovereignty over Hong Kong in 1997 and over Macao in 1999 will mark the end of European colonialism in Asia. From the perspective of Chinese leaders, this will solve the key Hong Kong question, sovereignty. For Hong Kong's residents and trading partners a key question will now be: will Hong Kong continue to thrive under Chinese jurisdiction? Will China's leaders be able to respond judiciously to Hong Kong's economic needs and to local residents' desire for autonomy? The 1984 Joint Sino-British Declaration and China's Basic Law on the Hong Kong Special Administrative Region provide a framework for rule, and business people and local stock markets reflect continued confidence. But many questions remain. How much autonomy will the Beijing appointed chief executive have? What role will the Chinese Communist party and the People's Liberation Army forces in Hong Kong play? How will dissidents be handled? Will freedoms be constrained and the rules of law curtailed? The United States has deep interest in Hong Kong, but paradoxically its ability to influence the course of events is limited. The United States lacks the leverage to become a protector of Hong Kong although access to U.S. markets provides leverage on trade issues. Carefully monitoring Hong Kong's performance and remaining involved in its activities are perhaps the best ways to pursue U.S. interests.

Problems over Taiwan reflect its complex history. Taiwan "locals," mostly descendents of seventeenth-century settlers from Fujian Province who brought Taiwan under Chinese control, have tense relations with the "mainlanders," the 15 percent of the population who fled to Taiwan from the advancing Communists and subdued the locals and their descendents. The United States has been allied to the Kuomintang since World War II, but the link was solidified in 1950 during the Korean War when the United States placed naval forces in the Taiwan Straits to prevent the Communists from completing the civil war. The United States remained allied with Taiwan against Beijing until the early 1970s when Kissinger and Nixon visited China. In 1979 the United States recognized Beijing and derecognized Taiwan as the legitimate government of China. Taiwan has maintained deep informal ties to the United States and other countries. Since 1987 when Taiwan began permitting opposition parties and 1989 when China cracked down on opposition leaders, the American public has again grown more sympathetic with Taiwan. The growth of Taiwan democracy since 1987 creates local pressures for independence, and the presence of U.S. voices supporting Taiwan frightens mainland leaders who are prepared to risk war to maintain sovereignty over Taiwan. Mutual suspicions between Taiwan and mainland China will make it difficult for the two sides to reach agreement in the next few years, but there is in the statements of the two sides the basis of a potential agreement: Taiwan would make a credible commitment never to seek independence; China would make a credible commitment not to threaten or use force against Taiwan; Taiwan's status as part of China would be less than a separate country but more than a province; Beijing would sponsor Taiwan's membership in international bodies. Such a solution must arise from within and cannot be imposed from outside, although the United States can encourage the two sides to move toward an agreement.

Although China became deeply immersed in Tibetan politics and established a small garrison in the 1600s and appointed a permanent representative in Lhasa in 1720, its actual control in Tibet has waxed and waned, giving some basis for Tibetan claims to independence. Although foreign countries have formally recognized Tibet as part of China in the twentieth century, foreign respect for the Dalai Lama and sympathy for Tibetan independence have given encouragement to Tibetans aspiring to autonomy. Han Chinese have misruled Tibet since 1950, sending in many Han settlers, weakening Tibetan culture and Tibetan monasteries, provoking Tibetan opposition. It would be irresponsible for the U.S. to nourish hopes for an independent Tibet that it is not prepared to fulfill; nourishing such hopes can only lead to tighter Chinese control and, if resistance increases, to massive cruelty. It is appropriate for the United States to honor the Dalai Lama as a spiritual leader, to publicize what it knows about Tibet, and quietly encourage a dialogue between the Dalai Lama and the Chinese government that could help preserve Tibetan culture.

New developments will make it difficult to keep the three issues off the U.S.–China agenda as in the 1970s and 1980s. Frank discussion between U.S. and China over these issues is essential to achieve the overriding U.S. and Chinese common interest: that as China inevitably increases its influence in all three areas, the process should be peaceful, evolutionary, and responsive to the desires of the local population.

Chapter 2. "China and the East Asian Security Environment: Complementarity and Competition"

The scale of Asia's economic achievement and the end of the cold war are feeding the pride of Asian peoples and prompting a search for new regional organizing principles. China, at the center of the Asian landscape, with an imperial tradition, the largest population and armed forces, and cultural and ethnic links with most of its neighbors, stirs ambivalent feelings throughout the region. Asian leaders expect that China's growing economic and military influence will one day be felt strongly throughout the region. Asia's other nations singly and collectively are not weighty enough to off-set China but are uncertain of U.S. staying power; Asian leaders are hopeful that China will not become a menace but they would like an insurance policy. They seek signs of U.S. commitment but they want to avoid steps that might inadvertently signal hostile intent to China. Being a distant power with no territorial ambitions, the United States is not seen as threatening.

The region's leaders thus seek from the United States signs of commitment, but they do not want to take sides against China and are frightened by U.S. mood swings, lack of coherent policy, and the inability to maintain a stable relationship with China. After the cold war the region is now uncertain as to whether the United States can maintain a steady course that does not provoke China.

Many key elements needed for a coherent U.S. Asian policy have survived six presidencies: a strong network of U.S. bilateral alliances in the region; forward deployed forces adequate to meet most contingencies and reserves capable of meeting the rest; international diplomatic and financial institutions; new subregional forums for security cooperation; and strong mutual interests in trade, investment, nonproliferation, the environment, and other transnational issues.

What the United States most needs therefore is an overall coherent strategy and effective management of the issues. Effective management requires consistent high-level dialogue between the United States and China. The United States should maintain its interest in values, but the first human right is not to be incinerated in war. The United States should remain firm in its commitment to maintain forces in Asia.

As for relations with other Asian countries, Beijing has been nervous about an enhanced military role for Japan in the region but is aware that a U.S.–Japan alliance can help preserve stability in the region. The United States also has long-term interests in maintaining an alliance with Korea, but there is a full agenda of issues such as securing a "soft landing" for North Korea's troubled economy, resolving North-South tensions, and encouraging a long-range stable Korean Peninsula. Though Russia has reduced influence in its Far East, its military remains formidable. In recent years the United States has been imbalanced in its treatment of Russia and China. Russia is accorded greater respect despite the horrors of Chechnya and its economic failings. As small powers desirous of freedom to maneuver, Southeast Asian countries are prepared to accept American involvement. After U.S. bases in the Philippines were closed in 1992 the new plan of "places, not bases" provides security for the region. China maintains a special relationship with Pakistan, which it sees as an ally against a potentially strong India, while the United States is now cultivating a better relationship with India since India weakened its links with Moscow.

To some extent tensions with China are inevitable, and China can be truculent and display a weak nation's fear of victimization combined with a potentially great nation's pride and ambition. China can be a difficult partner, but when the United States confronts Chinese bluster and manipulative hurt feelings, it needs to take a breath before reacting and remember that China will likely at most be a source of "problems" for America, not a "threat." With a coordinated policy to integrate China into the region and the globe, the United States may be able to keep deterrence as a latent aspect of its policy.

Chapter 3. "A Growing China in a Shrinking World: Beijing and the Global Order"

America's principal objectives with China should be the avoidance of a second cold war, the maintenance of regional stability, and the maximization of benefits from economic and other cooperation. These priorities can best be achieved by building and maintaining a productive bilateral relationship with Beijing and by China's early and full involvement in the principal institutions and global norms of world governance. America cannot achieve these objectives alone or without Chinese cooperation, but these should be the objectives of U.S. policy.

China's rise as a global power and its desire for global prestige mean that if world organizations and global norms are to be effective they will need Chinese participation. What is China's record of participation thus far, and how can China and current international organizations mutually adapt to each other in order to bring about productive cooperation with the least cost and disruption to the global system?

Since 1978 when it began its policy of reform and opening, China has rapidly expanded its participation in international organizations. In 1977, on the eve of its reforms, China was part of twenty-one international government organizations and seventy-one international nongovernmental organizations. By 1994 the figures were respectively 50 and 955. Between 1977 and 1988 China signed 125 multilateral treaties, whereas in the preceding twenty-seven years it had signed only twenty-three. In 1980 it joined the World Bank and the International Monetary Fund; in 1984 it was granted observer status in the General Agreement on Tariffs and Trade (GATT) and joined the International Atomic Energy Agency. In 1992 it ratified the Non-Proliferation Treaty and agreed in writing to observe the guidelines and parameters of the Missile Technology Control Regime (MTCR). In 1996 it agreed to the Comprehensive Test Ban Treaty and announced the suspension of further nuclear tests. China has signed eight international conventions on human rights, and in 1992 Premier Li Peng agreed that questions concerning human rights should be the subject of normal international discussion.

In the United Nations, China has played a relatively cooperative role. It has cast only two vetoes in open session in the Security Council since 1972 although it has blocked votes in closed sessions. Beijing has displayed reluctance in supporting the imposition of economic sanctions, believing that such acts violate sovereignty. China has sent peacekeepers to the Middle East, Namibia, and Cambodia. In the World Bank, where China has become the largest borrower, China has an unblemished record of repayment and an exemplary record of preparing appropriate reports. In the IMF, Beijing has been responsive to advice and repaid its first credit tranche in 1994. There is widespread agreement in the World Bank and IMF that China's participation has strengthened the organizations.

China's record of compliance with multilateral agreements and promises concerning human rights and arms sales/technology transfer has been less satisfactory. Chinese adherence to the Convention against Torture and Other Cruel, Inhuman, or Degrading Treatment or Punishment has been regularly breached, and Beijing's alleged and actual transfers of nuclear and missile technology (e.g., to Pakistan and Iran) have stretched or exceeded the bounds of Non-Proliferation Treaty and MTCR requirements. These violations appear to stem from Beijing's desire to woo countries it deems strategically important and also from the clout of military and other officials not fully coordinated with China's foreign policy apparatus and the absence of an effective export control mechanism. The most serious problems have come in areas where China is expected to comply with rules it played no role in writing. China is not one of the twenty-five members of the MTCR and complains that it is asked to comply with decisions that are made without China's participation. Chinese proliferation behavior is also affected by its belief that U.S. sales of F-16s to Taiwan violate the 1982 U.S. communiqué pledging not to upgrade military capacity and gradually reduce military assistance to Taiwan.

Chinese behavior in international institutions is fully consistent with realist axioms: derive maximum benefit from global institutions, minimize resulting obligations, use China's capacity to withhold compliance on agreements of high value to Washington to secure American compliance on agreements of high value to Beijing, and vigorously seek to safeguard the concept of sovereignty. China's record thus far seems to show that China's acceptance of membership in current global institutions represents a general willingness to acknowledge their legitimacy and play by the rules. Beijing has indicated that it expects to work within global institutions to promote its own perceived interests.

In deciding whether to support China's desire for participation in other organizations like the World Trade Organization, MTCR, and the New Forum technology control regime (successor to COCOM), and the Australia Group for the Control of Biological and Chemical Weapons, the United States faces trade-offs involving its own interests and the maintenance of international norms. For international institutions to be effective they must sooner or later welcome Chinese participation. It is in U.S. interest to be supportive of China's entry into international organizations of which it is not a member while maintaining the viability of the international organizations and regimes.

Chapter 4. "How China's Economic Transformation Shapes Its Future"

Economic growth has been the primary force transforming East and Southeast Asia in the second half of the twentieth century. It has built an industrial machine that provides the world with products. Domestically it created an urban society, where an urban middle class has replaced the uneducated peasant class as the dominant political force. Social and political transformation has not been matched by military buildup; since World War II none of these nations has yet tried to convert economic to military might capable of being projected beyond its borders.

China started this transformation beginning in 1979. Since then it has averaged GNP growth rates of 8 to 9 percent a year; since 1990 China has enjoyed double-digit growth. Exports rose from $10 billion in 1978 to $149 billion in 1995. The social and political transformation is already far along. In 1978, 70.5 percent of people of working age were in agriculture; in 1994 it was down to 54 percent. By the 1990s most urban households had not only television sets but washing machines and refrigerators.

Economic reforms have proceeded rapidly. Rural communes were dismantled and private enterprise was allowed to expand. The monopolies of state trading corporations were abolished. Central control over foreign exchange has yielded to a decentralized system of allocation based on markets. China is far along in moving to full convertibility of its currency. Township and village enterprises have blossomed and gained market share compared to the state enterprises, which are still influenced by central ministries and the State Planning Commission. State enterprise reform has been less successful because these firms provide welfare functions for millions of employees and are tied to the interests of local governments. Corruption is serious and, despite efforts to control it, is likely to continue on a large scale until government discretionary authority is vastly reduced. Debates continue over the role of the government in providing welfare and guiding industrial policy. New laws have been created but are not widely enforced by officials who use their discretionary decision-making powers to pursue local interests.

Over the next several decades the fundamentals for continued economic growth—capital, labor, and technology—are sound. Greatly expanded education, especially advanced training, will enable China to absorb and manage inputs of technology. China is therefore likely to continue rapid growth for several decades.

A China that is part of the international economic system has a large stake in maintaining it. A wealthy China dominated by an increasingly well-educated middle class is likely to be more democratic. It is in U.S. interests to promote these trends. Because cutting off most-favored-nation (MFN) status for China is tantamount to throwing China out of the international economic system, it follows that it is in U.S. interest to continue it to help integrate a prosperous China into the international economic system. On issues like intellectual property rights, if the Chinese enjoy widespread access to the U.S. market, the U.S. deserves access to areas where it has a comparative advantage, and it is appropriate to retaliate when this is not the case.

The considerations that should guide U.S. policy on the more complex issue of China's admission to the World Trade Organization are: it is in U.S. interest to have China in the WTO fully abiding by its rules; given China's economic structure, China cannot realistically be admitted to the WTO without granting it some modified form of developing country status; China can be expected to conform, within a realistic time frame, to international standards for dealing with issues like abolishing nontariff barriers, reducing tariffs, and eventually liberalizing trade in grain; and advice and technical aid for China to make these adjustments should be offered. China's entrance to WTO will not end all trade friction, but China is likely to grow rapidly whether it is in WTO or not, and it is in U.S. interest to encourage a timely decision on admission to increase China's incentives to play by the rules of the international trading system.

Chapter 5. "Breaking the
Impasse over Human Rights"

Since the Tiananmen crisis of 1989, human rights has been one of the most prominent and contentious issues in U.S.–China relations. Although America did not emphasize China's human rights violations in the early 1970s when millions of Chinese were being killed and sent to labor camps during the Cultural Revolution, paradoxically, as China became more open, the issue has attained new prominence. The geostrategic alliance with China against the Soviet Union that subordinated these issues had ended in 1989, and the televised images of Tiananmen convinced many Americans that Chinese leaders were brutal authoritarians suppressing yearnings for democracy. Beginning in 1993 the United States employed a variety of measures to increase respect for human rights in China, but none of these measures has achieved significant or lasting results.

Many Chinese would argue the last two decades have seen marked progress in their promotion of human rights. The massive killings and use of labor camps during the Cultural Revolution have come to an end. The standard of living has risen. Ordinary people have greater freedom from government or party intervention. The rule of law has been enhanced, and competitive local elections have been popularized. Yet many Americans continue to view China through the prism of 1989, not acknowledging Chinese progress and convinced that the brutal suppression of dissent in 1989 still symbolizes China's present-day human rights record. Many Chinese believe that the American approach to human rights, concentrated heavily on treatment of dissidents, is proof that the U.S. is a hegemonic power trying to weaken and destabilize China's government and party authority as it did in the 1950s and 1960s so that China would follow the same path of economic and political decay as Eastern Europe and the Soviet Union. The impasse over human rights is thus highly emotional.

How can the United States and China resolve this conundrum? China is unlikely to make dramatic changes in the near future. Some observers, Chinese and American, therefore argue that the only way out is for the United States to abandon its attempt to promote human rights in China. However, given the strong strain of idealism in American thinking, it is not possible to set aside the issue, but it could be made into an area of cooperation rather than confrontation. The question is: how can the issue be better managed? For more successful management, the United States should adopt:

- A more comprehensive definition of human rights, one that includes social and economic rights as well as political and civil freedoms.
- A longer-term perspective toward the issue of democratization.

China should:

- Acknowledge that the international community is governed by an international regime on human rights, in much of which China already participates.
- Undertake a gradual program of political reform, one that is based upon the realization that genuine stability in advanced societies is rooted in responsive political institutions.

The United States and China should:

- Identify areas of common ground on human rights and work together to promote human rights in their two countries.

Although some may consider such an approach as either excessively cautious or hopelessly naive, it is the only feasible way to manage the issue effectively. If the United States and China can adopt such a strategy, they can take a giant step toward intercivilizational dialogue and consensus and away from a "clash of civilizations."

Chapter 6. "Commercial Diplomacy"

In the 1990s China has been the world's fastest growing economy and, using purchasing power parity measures, already one of the three largest. Inflation, which peaked at 24 percent in 1994 following a two-year stimulus policy, had been reduced to single-digit figures in 1996. Per capita income is expected to rise to $6000 by the year 2000. By any measure China is likely to be the largest market in the world in the twenty-first century.

China is already the fifth largest trading partner of the United States. Excluding Hong Kong, the U.S. is China's largest export market. U.S. companies have made investment commitments in about 20,000 projects worth $26 billion in China. These firms, responding in 1994 to a survey questionnaire by the U.S.–China Business Council, reported that they were either profitable or at least meeting long-term profit goals.

Despite obvious benefits to both countries, many problems in U.S.–China commercial relations have arisen. Americans worry about the possible loss of jobs to China. Imports from China have grown faster than exports, but exports have doubled from $5 billion in 1988 to $10 billion in 1994 and are continuing to grow rapidly. For some months of 1996, the U.S. trade imbalance with China exceeded that with Japan, and this deficit with China is likely to continue to grow. This could escalate as a political issue in the United States, especially if the Chinese market is judged to be insufficiently open and if China does not make greater progress in protecting intellectual property rights.

Like other developing countries, China has been eager to acquire Western technology, and its companies have copied Western products, infringed trademarks, and exploited access to trade secrets without paying the companies that own them. Representatives of U.S. movie, recording, software, and book producers estimate that in 1995 piracy cost them $1.1 billion, and colleagues in the entertainment software industry estimate losses at $1.2 billion. While Beijing has taken steps to destroy products and punish selected firms that have violated intellectual property rights, more vigorous enforcement is needed. A potentially more serious problem in the long term is China's mastery of extracting foreign technology as the price of market access, playing off one multinational against another. The danger is that the technology is then often stolen.

Another source of great frustration for U.S.–China commercial relations is the annual review of the most-favored-nation status for China. According to the Jackson-Vanik amendment to the Trade Act of 1974, MFN status for "non-market economies" became conditional on freedom of emigration. Although Chinese emigration to the United States is limited more by U.S. law than by Chinese government action, China as a "non-market economy" is subject to the annual process of presidential certification. Most-favored-nation status is actually a basis of normal trade relations, not an award of special favor. Over 160 countries automatically receive this status, including Iran, Iraq, and Libya, whose human rights records are hardly laudable.

If as expected China becomes the largest consumer market in the world, U.S. businesses have a great stake in accessing that market. Recognizing this, China uses pressure on large American companies with substantial sales or potentially large projects in China, like Boeing, AT&T, Motorola, Westinghouse, and General Motors, to achieve its political objectives. In effect, U.S. firms are held hostage by China to the U.S.–China political relationship. Large firms with substantial investments in China not only require long-term predictability, but access to high-level officials and cooperation at lower levels, which may be withheld by the Chinese to achieve political goals. Since in most cases China has the option of turning to European, Japanese, or other businesses, this can be a serious problem for American investors and exporters to China. And increasingly, Chinese businesses are looking to American competitors where "political risk" is less intense and the supply lines more secure.

China's infrastructure demands, estimated by the World Bank at $750 billion in the next decade, provide another not to be missed opportunity for U.S. businesses. In certain sectors such as aviation, power, and telecommunication China is already the largest market in the world, and U.S. firms, facing "political risk," will have difficulty getting the economies of scales to retain their position in global markets. Like firms in other countries, U.S. businesses confront many problems in China, including corruption, lack of transparency, excessive bureaucracy, and obtuse regulations, but U.S. companies and U.S. jobs could be substantially disadvantaged if they do not have ready access to the substantial market opportunities presented by China.

U.S. businesses and workers would benefit if the U.S. would:

• Reassess and rationalize the U.S. export control system, eliminating most unilateral export controls.
• Extend eligibility for Overseas Private Investment Corporation insurance and financing from Export-Import Bank and Trade

and Development Agency financing to all countries in the Asia Pacific region, including China.

- Eliminate or rationalize country-specific policies, including those that single out China for less favorable treatment.
- Normalize U.S.–China commercial relations so that U.S. business is not held hostage by politics and adversely affected.

Chapter 7. "Energy, Agriculture, and the Environment: Prospects for Sino-American Cooperation"

As it moves from an inward-looking planned economy to one that is a major competitor in global markets, China has an opportunity to learn from mistakes made earlier in Western energy development and environmental protection. It may squander this opportunity. Energy strapped and capital constrained, most Chinese leaders and economic actors feel compelled to opt for energy choices that have the lowest initial investment, despite burdensome environmental consequences and higher long-run monetary costs.

China's energy resource endowment is dominated by coal, making it the backbone of its energy supply for the foreseeable future. Almost two-thirds of total commercial and non-market energy consumption is met through combustion of coal, and coal fuels a much larger percentage of China's swiftly developing electric power demand. Oil consumption from transportation is growing at a faster rate, but is starting from a much smaller base. While growth in energy use has been notably lower than that of the economy since the late 1970s, reducing China's energy intensity, expansion of fossil fuel consumption is still so swift that most air pollution hazards are intensifying. With few effective air pollution controls in place, much of the ambient air of Chinese cities and the indoor air of both urban and rural households has far higher concentrations of key air pollutants than deemed acceptable by the World Health Organization. This causes widespread respiratory and other health damages. Fossil fuel use is also creating severe acid rain problems in large parts of the country, with significant impacts on human structures, forests, fisheries, and agriculture.

Future global climate change may be an environmental time-bomb for the international community, especially developing countries, including China, whose agricultural economies and dense coastal settlements are vulnerable to changed climatic conditions and their effects. The leading international panel for scientific assessment of climate change has recently concluded with considerable confidence that a human role in such changes is already occurring. China's per capita emissions of carbon dioxide, the chief greenhouse gas, are much lower than those of the United States, but it has become second to the United States in aggregate emissions. Aggressive technological and other response measures can slow but not stop the rate of growth of emissions accompanying China's development. Absent an unlikely economic stagnation, China will surpass the carbon dioxide emissions of the United States within a couple of decades. These two leading contributors to the greenhouse threat will face increasing international pressure to lead the global strategy to reduce the hazards of climate change and to adapt to its impacts. Equitable Sino-American greenhouse cooperation that is cognizant of development disparities and comparative advantages may be critical to the success of such a strategy.

A number of so-called no regrets opportunities for cooperation already exist, which could yield mutual benefits that outweigh costs even without consideration of global environmental factors. China could draw on the know-how, experience, and investment capital of Western countries to develop its energy sector in a way that is more efficient and less polluting, addressing the local and regional environmental hazards that are China's greater immediate priorities while also reducing greenhouse gas emissions. To Western countries, the long-term market in China for more efficient and cleaner energy technologies and other environment related sectors is immense, and American companies are well posed to take advantage of trade and investment opportunities in these areas. In addition, exchange and collaboration in economic, energy, and environmental fields of scholarship could be a key element of a cooperative relationship. Especially valuable for the long run would be strengthening underdeveloped Chinese research capacities in climate related natural and social sciences and in the impact assessments that drive popular and political concern about the greenhouse effect.

Some have worried that China's continued population growth and its stagnation in agricultural productivity are likely to cause serious shortages in the global supply of grain. China within several decades may need to import 30 or 40 million tons of grain, but this would not be a serious drain on global supply. The projections for drastic shortages may overestimate China's future demand and underestimate the capacities of China to expand its own production and of world grain exporters, including the United States, to meet the demand. The effects of climate change on Chinese and world agricultural production, however, remain a key uncertainty.

A Sino-American initiative targeting specific areas of energy and environmental cooperation could help China build comprehensive long-term solutions into its development, with political and economic benefits to both countries. China will largely make its own decisions about energy use, environmental protection, and agricultural development. But respectful American engagement with China to address its domestic energy challenges, air pollution hazards, and food needs would be of great interest to both countries. Cooperation in these areas need not be contentious and could contribute to increasing trust in resolving more difficult political issues.

Chapter 8. "Domestic Forces and Sino–U.S. Relations"

Bilateral relations among major nations are generally analyzed as if a nation were a unified actor, whereas in fact not only nations like the United States but also those like China have complex and different constituencies that often do not act within a single coherent framework. The lack of coherence is most striking when there is no national crisis, as after the end of the cold war. National leaders, despite their sensitivity to their own domestic factors, generally have inadequate understanding of internal factors that shape the actions of their counterparts, and this lack of understanding often increases mutual distrust.

U.S. policy toward China during the years 1989–1996 was affected by:

- The Tiananmen incident, which has created powerful images of Chinese oppression that affect the images that shape the views of the U.S. public, its media, and politicians, often to the neglect of realistic appraisals of international events, leading to government decisions inconsistent with long-term U.S. interests. Once these images became powerful they begat further media reports consistent with those of the dominant images.
- Pressure groups that sought to use the China symbol to serve their own political ends. This includes labor unions concerned with job security, big business eager to take advantage of opportunities in China, human rights advocate organizations to increase their base of support, right-to-life advocates, Chinese students in the United States, and issue groups concerned with nonproliferation.
- Concern of U.S. political officials with the process of getting elected, sometimes to the sacrifice of concerns about broad long-range U.S. interests.
- The increased status within the U.S. bureaucracy of people and branches dealing with functional and global issues (like nonproliferation, human rights, affirmative action, economic issues) and a reduced role for those with regional expertise.

China's policy toward the United States has been affected by a different system. China lacks the formal separation of power and vote-getting and fundraising pressures, but leaders still cannot act independently of the people they govern and the system in which they operate. They are affected by:

- Massive changes as a result of reform, rapid economic development, population mobility, and especially decentralization of power to local officials who are granted great leeway as long as they have helped push forward economic growth.
- Close links between enterprises and their government sponsor, whether it be central ministries, the People's Liberation Army, or local government. This results in protectionism and assistance to local firms rather than balanced judicious efforts to allow an open market and makes it difficult for top officials in Beijing to

control activities of local officials. This may make it difficult for Beijing to control, for example, local violations of intellectual property rights.

• The fragmentation of decision making and competing jurisdictions because of reforms.

• A growing feeling of confidence from rapid growth that makes Chinese leaders less willing to appear to bend to foreign pressures.

• A growing sense of malaise from loss of discipline and the consequences of all-out pursuit of profit that causes leaders to find issues like Chinese dignity and national sovereignty to rally their supporters and reduce public malaise.

• The growth of sensitivity to public opinion, to views expressed in People's Congresses and other bodies.

• Pressure from state enterprises and agricultural regions to reduce the impact of foreign imports that may affect local profitability, the size of bad loans, and employment.

These factors reduce the flexibility of maneuver for leaders in their respective countries. The inability of leaders to understand the problems faced by their counterparts increases the chance of imputing mean-spirited motivation to the other side, creating a cycle of increasing mistrust. Domestic issues will continue to affect Sino–U.S. relations in the coming century, and China is likely to become increasingly pluralistic. It is therefore important to find ways to enable leaders of each country to deepen their understanding of the domestic factors that shape the behavior of their counterparts.

1

Taiwan, Tibet, and Hong Kong in Sino-American Relations

MICHEL OKSENBERG

Taiwan, Tibet, and Hong Kong have been issues in Sino-American relations since the establishment of the People's Republic of China (PRC). The leaders of China believe that all three places are integral parts of the country that they are still in the process of reuniting. All Chinese know that Hong Kong and Taiwan are territories lost to the British and Japanese during the imperialist wars of the nineteenth century; they involve matters of national honor and international justice.

MICHEL OKSENBERG is a senior fellow at the Asia/Pacific Research Center and professor of political science at Stanford University. He is the co-author of *An Emerging China in a World Interdependence* (1994), *China's Participation in the IMF, the World Bank, and GATT* (1990), and *Policy Making in China* (1988), as well as numerous other books and articles concerning Chinese domestic affairs, Chinese foreign policy, and Sino-American relations. He is a member of the Trilateral Commission, the National Committee on U.S.–China Relations Board of Directors, the Council on Foreign Relations, and the Forum for International Policy. He was a National Security Council staff member (1977–80) and president of the East-West Center (1993–96).

The United States government and private Americans have sought to assert their influence in all three areas without first consulting Beijing. In all three places, a considerable portion of the populace dislikes the Beijing government and opposes Beijing's assertion of the right to rule them. The Beijing government attributes this resistance in part to the machinations of the United States. Most Americans, unaware of the complexities involved, probably believe that the residents of these areas in an ideal world should have the opportunity to determine their own future. Americans tend to sympathize with the yearnings of those in Taiwan, Tibet, and Hong Kong to enjoy genuine political and economic autonomy. Despite this widespread American sentiment, however, the United States government officially acknowledges the Chinese view that there is but one China and that Taiwan is part of it, recognizes that Tibet is part of China, and accepts that Hong Kong became a legitimate part of China when it passed from British rule, and that the People's Republic is the sole legitimate government of China.

Significant differences obviously exist among the three locales. Indeed, many residents and observers of the three would undoubtedly object to an analysis that places them in the same category. With some justification, they would assert that such an analysis implicitly accepts Beijing's claim that the three areas fundamentally involve the same issues or that the United States does or should approach the three from the same vantage. Consider their differences.

• *Taiwan's* 21 million residents live on an island apart from the mainland. During the last hundred years, Taiwan has been ruled by the mainland for only three years. It now has its own democratically elected government, its own military force, and extensive representation abroad albeit largely through unofficial offices. Eighty percent of Taiwan's population traces its ancestry to subethnic groups of the Han people (the overwhelming majority ethnic group in China) in Fujian Province; they speak Taiwanese, a derivative of the Fukienese dialects.

• *Tibet* politically is an "autonomous region" of the People's Republic, although it is in fact tightly controlled by the Chinese Communist party (CCP) and the People's Liberation Army (PLA). Ethnically, the Tibetans are non-Han. They are adherents of Tibetan Buddhism, a religion with rich and distinctive traditions; they look upon the Dalai Lama as their spiritual leader. Two million of the 6 million Tibetans reside in the territory that the Beijing government has delineated as Tibet. The remaining 4 million Tibetans are scattered in regions within other provinces—Sichuan, Gansu, Yunnan, Qinghai, and Xinjiang—where they constitute a minority of the population.

• *Hong Kong's* 6 million people live in a territory that reverted to Chinese rule at 12:01 A.M. on July 1, 1997. Although over 90 percent of Hong Kong's Cantonese speaking population consists of subethnic Han groups from Guangdong Province, a majority of this population was born and reared in Hong Kong.

The differences in the political status, size, ethnicity, language, culture, and religion of Taiwan, Tibet, and Hong Kong, as well as differences in the American involvement with each, mean that the three pose distinctive problems in Sino-American relations that need to be analyzed separately. Yet as already suggested, common threads link the three. They all embody fundamental but sharply contrasting dimensions of Chinese and American values and aspirations.

Divergent Perceptions

Chinese Perceptions

To China's leaders, Taiwan, Tibet, and Hong Kong involve issues of sovereignty, national unity, and national security.[1] The revolutionaries who created the Chinese Communist party and founded the People's Republic of China had as one of their central objectives the reunification of China: the termination of China's internal divisions and the return to Chinese rule of those territories that foreign powers took away during the era of Western and Japanese military superiority. Indeed, the CCP's rival for power, the Kuomintang (KMT) or Nationalist party led by Chiang Kai-shek, was no less committed to the attainment of China's unity and hence to the inclusion of the three under its rule, although its strategy for attaining the reintegration of China and its definition of the precise regions to be returned to China differed somewhat. For example, the Kuomintang long considered Mongolia to be rightfully Chinese territory, while the Communists recognized its independence. At one point, Mao Zedong excluded Taiwan from a listing of territory he included within China's legitimate domain. But for most of their histories, both the Chinese Communist party and the Kuomintang have considered Taiwan, Hong Kong, and Tibet to be a part of China. (They also agree that Chinese territory extends deep into the East and South China Seas, including the Spratley Islands, and Beijing and Taipei are cooperating to extend their joint influence in the South China Sea, for example, in the exploration and development of petroleum.)

Thus, for Beijing's current, deeply nationalistic rulers, Taiwan, Hong Kong, and Tibet are connected. All three involve their lifelong commitment to reestablish a unified China. Nor is this sentiment simply a nationalistic one. China's rulers believe the unity of their country is tenuous; fissiparous tendencies, they think, threaten to pull the country apart and must be countered. To yield on Taiwan, Hong Kong, or Tibet might encourage separatist inclinations among other locales with large ethnic minorities, such as Xinjiang, or in places with strong Han subethnic and linguistic traditions, as along the southern China coast stretching from Zhejiang through Fujian to Guangdong and Guangxi.

Moreover, given their views of modern Chinese history, China's leaders are naturally suspicious of foreign powers. They believe that foreign leaders tend to be reluctant to welcome China's rise in world affairs and would prefer to delay or obstruct its progress. They fear that many in the outside world would prefer to divide China if given the opportunity, and Taiwan, Hong Kong, and Tibet are their entering wedges. Nor is this simply a paranoiac fear. All three places have been used both before and since 1949 as places to foment unrest and separatist movements elsewhere on the mainland.

China's leaders retain in their minds a strategic map of the points on their periphery that make them vulnerable to foreign influence. Foreigners have used these access points over the centuries to penetrate and divide their land: for example, the Ili River valley and the string of oases stretching across Xinjiang; the Gansu corridor; the mountain passes northwest of Beijing separating Hebei from

Inner Mongolia; the area to the west of Harbin offering Russia access to Manchuria. Tibet is the route of entry to the core of China from the Indian subcontinent. And Taiwan and Hong Kong, along with the southeast coast of China more generally, are the native places of commercially oriented Chinese, long resistant to the bureaucratic, imperial rule of Beijing. Since the Song dynasty, the maritime Chinese, including their kin who migrated to Southeast Asia, have served as intermediaries in the transmission of foreign influences into China. Hence Taiwan, Tibet, and Hong Kong are strategically significant regions that, in the hands of hostile powers, would threaten Chinese security. In the next century these locales could offer a militarily strong China desirable bases from which to project its own power into South Asia, Southeast Asia, and the Western Pacific.

Roles in history are also at stake. Chinese history is written for didactic purposes. The past is populated by moral exemplars: the virtuous though often cruel rulers and ministers who pacified and ordered the realm, and the evil and weak emperors and their advisors who brought famine and chaos to the land. Engraved in the minds of most Chinese is the notion that the moments of the nation's greatness coincided with the eras of strong and effective imperial rule, while the eras of despair occurred when dynasties collapsed. The heroes in Chinese history achieved its unity; its villains contributed to its division and defeat by foreigners. To the extent that China's leaders are fighting for their place in their nation's ongoing saga—how future historians will record their deeds—they are impelled to assert control over Taiwan, Tibet, and Hong Kong.

Finally, there are succession politics. In the complex and poorly understood struggles through which preeminent Chinese leaders achieve dominance, the rising ruler must evidence a sufficient ruthlessness and lust for power to discipline his faction-prone inner court and hold the vast and heterogeneous country together. Succession politics in China through the centuries has not been a game for gentlemen. There is little reason to believe this enduring feature of Chinese politics has suddenly disappeared. In light of this, an aspiring leader can show little flexibility on Taiwan, Tibet, and Hong Kong. They offer litmus tests of a leader's resolve to defend his power and the integrity of his country.

For all these reasons, Taiwan, Tibet, and Hong Kong are deeply felt issues for the leaders of China, or at least they must feign emotion over them. And yet, in all three locales, although they have not wavered from their eventual goal, China's leaders have demonstrated some constraint, patience, and pragmatism. After all, they could have seized Hong Kong at any point since 1949, as India did with Goa. They could have launched an intense effort to destabilize and subvert Taiwan, but rather, since 1978, they have dramatically expanded their commercial and cultural contacts with the island. They have acquiesced to American arms sales to Taiwan and permitted Taiwan to join several international organizations, albeit at a lower status than the Beijing government. In the early 1950s China pursued a less oppressive and somewhat accommodating approach toward Tibet. The revolt of the Khamba tribesmen, stimulated in part by covert American and Kuomintang support, tragically ended this effort of limited cooperation with the prior order. Briefly in the early 1980s Hu Yaobang, Deng's designated successor at the time, seemed interested in reviving these policies, though his alleged softness toward Tibet may have contributed to his subsequent fall. And China has not been harshly critical of India's providing haven and assistance to the Dalai Lama and his large community of supporters in Dharamsala. The behavior of China's leaders has thus not always matched their strident rhetoric.

American Perceptions

The average American and even many officials and opinion leaders understand little of this, and approach the three locales from a very different perspective. They feel no remorse for having helped to keep Taiwan apart from the mainland since 1949. To the contrary, they take pride in having assisted the people on Taiwan attain their present level of prosperity, security, and political development. And although the United States has not been responsible for Hong Kong's governance, clearly its economic dynamism has been largely due to the access to American markets its entrepreneurs have enjoyed. In Tibet, to the extent Americans are aware of their government's earlier intervention, they may very well believe that China's subsequent harsh rule shows that U.S. assistance was warranted. Such Americans might assert that their nation's shame is in the abandonment of the Tibetan rebels who in the late 1950s acted on the assumption of American support, a scene repeated in Hungary in 1956 and in the Bay of Pigs in 1961. The American support for the people of Hong Kong, Taiwan, and Tibet goes beyond their natural sympathy for a David against Goliath. Fundamental to U.S. foreign policy throughout most of this century is the Wilsonian notion of the right of nationalities to self-determination. (We will not probe the inconsistency between this belief and the predictable American reaction were there to be extensive foreign support for independence of the Eskimos or native Hawaiians.) Americans look askance upon multiethnic empires that have been brutally pieced together, particularly if the empire is dominated by a single ethnic group that rides roughshod over others. (We will not probe the inconsistency between this view and the extolling of Daniel Boone, Kit Carson, and other heroes who seized the land of America's first settlers as the pioneers spread across the continent.) Americans tend to see Beijing's behavior toward Taiwan, Tibet, and Hong Kong not as the reunification of a country but as the creation of empire, especially since the Beijing government does not offer democracy and local self-rule to those who fall under its domain.

The Chinese government response to this view is that the fate of these three locales ultimately is none of America's business. American values and beliefs are irrelevant; Chinese values and beliefs must govern. Chinese sovereignty is at stake. But as with the human rights issue, the American national essence precludes acceptance of this argument. In contrast to Chinese, Americans lack a sense of a common past. Their forefathers come from throughout the world. They are bound together by a sense of a common destiny and the common ceaseless pursuit of the values enunciated in the Declaration of Independence and the Gettysburg address.[2] Moreover, Americans believe that their values are universally applicable. Stripped of confidence that their values transcend the cultural differences of their diverse origins, Americans would remain divided by their separate pasts. Moreover, values that apply to culturally diverse Americans and that have attracted immigrants from around the globe logically have international appeal. If the Declaration of

Independence pertains to Italian Americans, it should be germane
to Italians still in Italy. If the Gettysburg address speaks to the aspirations of Chinese Americans, it should be valid for Chinese still
in China. So the United States cannot limit the pursuit of its values to its own shores. To do so would call into question their universal validity and jeopardize their pursuit at home.

Particularly in recent years, international developments have reinforced the American self-perception. For a good deal of the twentieth century, the American commitment to democracy, liberty, and
human rights was challenged by other doctrines that claimed universal validity, such as Leninism, Stalinism, or Cultural Revolution
Maoism. But today, the values championed by Americans no longer
have a global competitor, while countries around the world—including many in Asia—have become democratic. Naturally, at this
juncture in history, Americans are confident and perhaps overcon-
fident that their political ideology appeals to all humanity and coincides with the historical trends of the era.

Summary

American and Chinese leaders and publics view the Taiwan,
Tibet, and Hong Kong issues through dramatically different perceptual lenses. To China's leaders and many among their populace
(including nationalistic intellectuals), all three places engender
thoughts about national security, unity, and the carving up of China
in the past century; to Americans the same localities evoke notions
of democracy, self-determination, and freedom of religion. Americans and Chinese therefore tend to approach the same events and
policy choices concerning the three areas from different vantages.
Nonetheless, these differences do not preclude accommodation,
cooperation, and pragmatism. The past record reveals that agreement is possible. After all, the policies of Washington and Beijing
toward the three locales are governed largely by economic and security concerns and by the aspirations, attitudes, and behavior of
the people who inhabit and lead the three regions.

Thus a focus on the perceptual and conceptual issues does not
imply that differences over Taiwan, Tibet, and Hong Kong will inevitably drive China and the United States apart and thereby

threaten the entire fabric of the relationship. Rather, the point is more limited: advocates of accommodation over these issues risk condemnation within their own society for betraying core values of their country. Yet, to the extent that the leaders of the United States and the People's Republic attach importance to their bilateral ties, each side must manage its involvement in the three places with considerable sensitivity to the other's concerns. Increasingly since 1989, this has not been the case, to the detriment not only of Sino-American relations but of the welfare of the peoples in Taiwan, Tibet, and Hong Kong as well.

Taiwan

History

Through much of Chinese history, Taiwan was sparsely inhabited.[3] Its first settlers, who made up a significant portion of the total population until the eighteenth century, were ethnically and culturally distinct from the Han people. They apparently came originally from either Oceania or Southeast Asia. From an early date, however, and especially from Song times (960–1127), seafaring Chinese used the island as a base for carrying out expeditions and commerce both northward to the Ryukyus, southern Korea, and the Japanese island of Kyushu and southward to islands and harbors of today's Philippines, Indonesia, Malaysia, and Thailand. This trade grew in Ming times (1368–1644). Much of this commerce fell outside the officially sanctioned trade that the central government permitted, though it was often tolerated or even accepted by Chinese provincial or local officials who profited from it. In official history, the people who engaged in this illegal trade were frequently labeled as "pirates" and "brigands," and indeed they often did seize and smuggle goods. But their main crime was that they did not fit within the restrictive commercial practices allowed by the far-off imperial government, and as long as their activities did not come directly to Beijing's attention, local government officials went unpunished for the unlawful actions within their regions. As a result, local officials had little incentive to report on the extent of unofficial commerce. The official view of commerce along the coast and of Taiwan's role in it differed from the reality. Although precise data are lacking, Taiwan probably played a more important role in the history of maritime China—a history that was poorly recorded in the official imperial records—than is currently understood. But these activities were beyond the control of the emperor and his court.

Taiwan first became a base in the sixteenth and seventeenth centuries for the Portuguese and Dutch who used its harbors as they traded from Southeast Asia to China, Korea, and Japan. Remnant Ming officials, including one of the last claimants to the throne, found refuge there at the end of the Ming, as a result of which the Dutch became involved in the last stage of the struggle between the Ming and the new Qing dynasty. With the assertion of Qing control over Taiwan in the seventeenth century, the central government placed the island within the jurisdiction of the Fujian provincial government. It lacked the population, economic significance, or transportation routes to warrant full provincial status. Unlike the smaller Ryukyu Islands to the north (such as Okinawa), it was clearly a part of China. These links with the mainland strengthened throughout the Qing, as the migration from Fujian Province intensified. This migration of thousands of Han Chinese in the eighteenth and nineteenth centuries gradually transformed the island into productive agricultural land, though it also continued to be a haven of seafarers. The Qing formal bureaucratic presence was weak, and order on the island was maintained through the influence of several very large and strong lineages that managed vast tracts of land. (Descendants of these lineages remain wealthy and influential today.) By the mid-1800s, the official Qing presence began to be strengthened.

The transformation of Japan in the 1870s and 1880s from an isolationist to an expansionist country set the stage for a struggle between Japan and China over control of Taiwan. By the early 1880s, some Japanese had begun to cast a covetous eye upon the island. In their own turn outward, their tradespeople were annoyed by the Chinese who interfered with their commerce and who continued to find refuge in Taiwan harbors. The Japanese saw Western powers secure treaty ports on the China mainland, and some began to dream of building their own empire in emulation of the West. They began to think Taiwan would serve Japanese interests as a colony and base for commerce on the Chinese mainland. Aware of Japanese designs, the Qing government converted Taiwan into a directly ruled province in 1885, but as a result of its defeat in the Sino-Japanese War of 1894–95, the Qing was forced to cede Taiwan to Japan.

From 1895 until Japan's defeat in World War II, Taiwan was a Japanese colony. Though harsh, Japan's rule of the island was not as severe as the Japanese occupation of Korea, nor did it engender the same enmity among the populace. The Japanese turned the island into a source of agricultural produce for Japan: pineapples, rice, and especially sugar. They developed a transportation infrastructure and, while maintaining a strict and oppressive rule, sponsored an extensive educational system in the Japanese language. Thousands of Taiwanese received higher education in universities in Japan.

Various political currents developed among the people of Taiwan. Some left Taiwan to join nationalistic movements on the mainland; others participated in resistance activities on the island. Such Taiwanese—and they were relatively few in number—sought a restoration of Chinese rule over the island. Others planned for the independence of Taiwan, while still others thought of themselves as part of the Japanese empire and willingly donned the uniform of the Japanese imperial army. Most simply sought to endure a difficult situation.

At the Cairo Conference in November 1943, Roosevelt and Churchill met their wartime ally, Chiang Kai-shek, for the first time. They declared that Taiwan and Manchuria would be returned to China as part of the postwar settlement. This decision was reaffirmed at the important Potsdam Conference, a decision to which the People's Republic still refers in documenting its claim to the island. Then, in 1945–46, the United States assisted the Republic of China to establish its authority over Taiwan's populace. Having no role in determining their fate, Taiwan's populace at first welcomed their Chinese kin to be their rulers, but Chiang's Kuomintang rule proved rapacious. The mainland officers and troops that Chiang had dispatched to the island were ill behaved, and Chiang sought to extract resources from the island to help sustain his fight against the Communists on the mainland. By February 1947 the Kuomintang had squandered the good will that existed upon its arrival only sixteen to eighteen months before, and sentiment for an independent Taiwan was growing rapidly. Violence erupted between the local populace and KMT forces, and the Kuomintang then cracked down brutally, incarcerating and killing thousands whom it suspected of being dissidents. With the collapse of its rule on the mainland, the KMT government enacted tough legislation on May 10, 1948, ostensibly to deter infiltration and aggression from the mainland. But the law, which was not rescinded until July 1987, established the basis for authoritarian rule. From 1945 to 1950, nearly 2 million mainland Kuomintang soldiers, officials, camp followers, and their relatives fled to the island. Most of the Taiwanese looked upon these mainlanders as an invading army, and in subsequent decades significant tensions existed between the mainlanders and the Taiwanese.

Until June 1950 the United States remained aloof from the Taiwan imbroglio. Deep differences existed within the U.S. government: some officials were prepared to allow Taiwan to fall to the Communists; others viewed Taiwan as a strategically valuable base and felt personal obligations to Chiang and the Kuomintang as a former ally against Japan. The outbreak of the Korean War terminated the debate on American policy toward Taiwan. Fearing that the North Korean invasion of the South was a prelude to a worldwide Communist offensive, the Truman administration dispatched the Seventh Fleet to the Taiwan Strait to prevent a mainland takeover of the island, and thereafter Taiwan became in effect a ward or protectorate of the United States.

More than that, Generalissimo and Madame Chiang Kai-shek and their entourage learned the art of American politics during their wartime alliance with the United States. They formed a powerful pro-Taiwan lobby that deeply influenced American China policy. They cultivated strong supporters in the American government, the media, and educational, business, and religious circles. They helped to provoke a debilitating national debate in the United States over "who lost China." They helped to stimulate a purge of China specialists in the State Department who in the 1940s had aroused their wrath by reporting accurately on the likely KMT loss to the Communists.

The Korean War, China's entry into it, the cold war, the political clout of the Taiwan lobby, and growing tension in the Taiwan Strait prompted the conclusion of a formal defense treaty between Taiwan and the United States in 1954. This alliance and Sino-American hostility led Taipei and Washington to cooperate in covert activities on the mainland that were intended to foment unrest and instability. Taiwan's intervention in the conduct of American foreign policy was extensive, locking the United States into a hostile relationship with the People's Republic for over two decades that adversely affected the American posture elsewhere in Asia as well. For example, John Foster Dulles refused to shake Zhou Enlai's hand when the two met at the Geneva Conference on Indochina in 1954. He feared the reaction from pro-Taiwan Republicans if a photograph of a handshake appeared in American newspapers. In another instance, the Kennedy administration was on the verge of establishing diplomatic relations with Mongolia. But upon learning of Washington's intent, Taipei complained that since it considered Mongolia to be part of China, the United States should not recognize Mongolia as an independent country. Rather than risk arousing the pro-Taiwan lobby, the initiative was quietly shelved. And diplomatic historians wonder whether the United States would have stumbled into the Vietnam War had it pursued opportunities to normalize relations with China in the mid-1950s and the early 1960s.

During these years, however, the United States did limit its support of Taiwan. American military forces not only deterred a PRC attack on Taiwan but prevented overt Taiwan military action against the mainland. The United States refused to sell some of its most advanced weaponry that Taiwan sought for its arsenal. To Taiwan's displeasure, the United States carried out ambassadorial talks with China, first in Geneva and then in Warsaw, which helped stabilize the situation in the Taiwan Strait on several occasions. And Chiang Kai-shek proved to be a proud and stubborn ally who frequently resisted American pressure. In particular, the United States encouraged him to remove his forces from the vulnerable offshore islands of Quemoy and Matsu, located very close to the Fujian city of Xiamen, and the United States probably would have welcomed his acceptance of a "two-China" policy. But throughout his life, Chiang adhered rigorously to his claim that his government was the legitimate government of all of China. His resolve on this matter prompted Mao Zedong and Zhou Enlai to acknowledge that in the final analysis, Chiang did not allow the United States to control him. Despite the rhetoric, by the mid- to late 1950s, Chiang apparently had concluded that his government would not regain the mainland in his lifetime. While retaining a dictatorial political system, he turned to sophisticated economic development specialists to pursue a strategy of rapid growth. Earlier, the government had implemented a major land reform that simultaneously tried to weaken the political base of the Taiwanese landlord class and placed capital in the hands of these Taiwanese. In effect, Chiang forged a compact with the Taiwanese: the Kuomintang and the mainlanders would retain a monopoly over political power and formulate a development strategy; the Taiwanese could own property, enter the commercial and manufacturing realms, and become prosperous. The Kuomintang pursued an export led development strategy, based on access to American markets. Through the 1960s and 1970s, Taiwan's economy was propelled by the sequential rise of a number of industries: textiles, plastics, electronics. Chiang initiated elections of village and township officials as early as 1950, as long as KMT authority went unchallenged. The roots of Taiwan's eventual democratization are to be traced to these exercises in local self-government.

Throughout these years, tension in the Taiwan Strait remained high. Each side tested the resolve of the other. The nationalists maintained a large garrison force on Quemoy and Matsu on a state of alert, and Beijing looked upon Fujian Province as a frontier defense zone. The U.S. Seventh Fleet regularly patrolled the Strait to deter provocative behavior by either side, while U.S. planes periodically approached Chinese air space to test its radar systems.

Change in American Policy

U.S. policy toward Taiwan was transformed in three steps.[4] First, in 1971–72, the Nixon administration established direct, high-level contact with the Beijing government, culminating in President

Nixon's February 1972 trip to Beijing and the issuance of the Shanghai Communiqué. China and the United States opened liaison offices in each other's capitals in 1973, and both Presidents Nixon and Ford pledged to establish diplomatic relations with the Beijing government within the formula that Japan had used when it established relations in 1972. President Carter undertook this second step in December 1978. Since Beijing claimed sovereignty over Taiwan while Taipei claimed to be the government of all China, Beijing insisted the United States sever diplomatic relations with Taipei when establishing relations with the Beijing government. In response to another Beijing demand (and since the United States could not have a defense treaty with a government it does not recognize), the United States also terminated its defense treaty with Taiwan. The third step came in 1982, when the Reagan administration agreed with Beijing on the rules governing U.S. arms sales to Taiwan.

These steps were obviously the product of considerable diplomacy and internal debate. Many factors produced the change in U.S. policy toward China and Taiwan in the 1970s, some tactical, some strategic. The timing of the initial step was unquestionably related to the Vietnam War and the Sino-Soviet dispute. The second and third steps were facilitated by and partly a response to Soviet expansionism. But these were transitory considerations. From a longer-term perspective, America's China policy of the 1950s and 1960s could not be sustained. It was based on American acknowledgment of an absurd claim. Taiwan was not, as it asserted, the government of mainland China. At the same time, China's position was unrealistic. The People's Republic was not the government of Taiwan. In fact, the two governments ruled different parts of Chinese territory, each asserting that it was the rightful authority for all of China, each denying the legitimacy of the other.

The diplomacy of the 1970s and early 1980s created a framework enabling the United States to bridge the differences. It had four components.

• First, the United States acknowledged the position held by Chinese on both sides of the Taiwan Strait that there was but one China and that Taiwan was part of it. The United States recognized the government of the People's Republic as the sole legitimate gov-

ernment of China. The United States also pledged that it would
not encourage Japan to replace it as Taiwan's protector. The American position signaled that the United States did not intend permanently to detach Taiwan from the mainland.

• Second, the United States continued to have a full range of unofficial economic and cultural relations with the people of Taiwan.
The governments of the United States and Taiwan established private agencies, staffed by personnel on temporary leave from their
governments, to carry out the business between the two countries.

• Third, the special legislation—the Taiwan Relations Act of
1979—that enabled the unofficial relationship with Taiwan also
mandated that the executive branch provide Taiwan with the capacity to provide for its self-defense and consult with Congress in
the event that Taiwan's security was endangered. This portion of
the act specified an American intent that had been conveyed to the
Beijing government during prior negotiations, namely, that the
United States would continue to sell weapons to Taiwan that were
defensive in nature. In 1982 the United States pledged to reduce the
quantity and quality of weapons it would sell to Taiwan as tension
in the area diminished, a policy to which Beijing reluctantly but explicitly acquiesced in a joint declaration with the United States.

• Fourth, the United States would accept any solution that the
People's Republic and Taiwan could negotiate without duress on
the issues that divided them. The U.S. interest was in a peaceful
process of mainland-Taiwan interaction, not in the outcome. Implicit in this posture was an American expectation that neither Beijing nor Taipei would unilaterally seek to alter the situation or
pursue its objectives through the threat or use of force.

These four components governing U.S. policy stemmed from
pragmatic calculations that the continued, deep U.S. involvement
in the lingering Chinese civil war not only harmed America's global
and regional interests but also did not serve Taiwan well. The
change in America's China policy in the 1970s and early 1980s improved Taiwan's prospects. The new strategic setting enhanced Taiwan's chances for a peaceful and prosperous future. Taiwan's
security would best be attained within the context of simultaneously
constructive relations among the United States, Japan, and the People's Republic; this context would dramatically reduce the PRC's

incentives to pursue an aggressive policy toward Taiwan and would encourage Taiwan to develop its own direct links with the mainland. America's gradual disengagement from the Chinese civil war, accompanied by a reduction in tension between Taiwan and the mainland and by improvements in Sino-Japanese relations, was thus intended to promote a more stable Asia Pacific region.

This calculation yielded far greater success than the most optimistic observers expected. Military tension in the Taiwan Strait subsided. Not only did China alter its development strategy to take advantage of its new-found access to foreign markets, technology, and capital, but it welcomed Taiwan's participation in the PRC's economic growth. By 1995 Taiwan entrepreneurs had invested $25 billion in the People's Republic, and were earning billions in profits from trade with the mainland. The mainland had become a favorite destination of Taiwan tourists and the largest customer of its exports. Taiwan's economic prosperity and growth increasingly depended upon the PRC's economic dynamism.

Even more dramatic, the new context encouraged and permitted Taiwan's evolution into a democracy. After an initial, cautious reaction to the severance of diplomatic and alliance relations with the United States, Taiwan's leader Chiang Ching-kuo (the son of Chiang Kai-shek) initiated the process of democratization that his successor Lee Teng-hui completed. Competitive elections, the organization of political parties to compete with the Kuomintang, cessation of martial law, cessation of press censorship, major reforms of the legislative *yuan*, stronger civilian control over the military, greater independence of the judiciary, and the direct election of the president were the major steps that brought democracy to Taiwan in a relatively short period of time. The Kuomintang is the world's only authoritarian party organized along Leninist lines that engineered a democratic transformation and remained the ruling party through the ballot box.

Erosion of the Framework of the 1970s

Ironically, the success of the policy framework of the 1970s brought into question its applicability in the 1990s. The democratization of Taiwan ended the government on Taiwan's claim to be the government of all China, a claim that the 1972 Shanghai Communiqué and the normalization agreement of 1978 explicitly took into account.

The Democratic Progressive Party (DPP) that emerged in a democratic Taiwan as the major opposition party to the Kuomintang traces its origins to the Taiwan independence movement of the late 1940s. Supporters of independence continued activities abroad in the United States and Japan, or in subterranean fashion in Taiwan. They resurfaced with democratization and formed a core base of support for the DPP. The DPP also initially drew its support from those Taiwanese who resented the continued political dominance of mainlanders—that is, those who had fled to Taiwan in the late 1940s and early 1950s and their descendants—in the KMT.

Mainlanders continued to control the Kuomintang and the military officer corps until the ascent of Lee Teng-hui to the presidency. Lee, a native Taiwanese, sought to broaden the appeal of the KMT and accelerated the promotion of Taiwanese to leadership ranks, a move that many mainlanders in the KMT welcomed. To broaden KMT appeal and compete with the DPP for support among voters of native Taiwanese background, Lee Teng-hui and the Kuomintang altered their stance on a number of key foreign policy issues. In effect, they embarked upon a policy of "indigenization" or "Taiwanization." The changes included: (1) ceasing to claim that the "Republic of China" was the government of all China—instead, it considered itself to be the "Republic of China on Taiwan"; (2) recognizing the government on the mainland as a legitimate authority of equal status; (3) hence, asserting that the territory of China had two governments with equal claim for international recognition and participation in international organizations; and (4) expressing the hope that the two would be reunified when the mainland had become democratic and prosperous. The government on Taiwan became less content to accept a subordinate status to the mainland or to accept the confines Beijing had established for it. Taipei's Ministry of Foreign Affairs intensified its competition with the People's Republic for diplomatic recognition, winning the nod from a few small states that had previously established formal relations with Beijing. The ministry sought greater status and dignity in its unofficial relations with major powers. President Lee Teng-hui began to travel abroad, first on an unofficial visit to Southeast Asia, then to several countries with which Taiwan has diplomatic relations, and finally an unofficial visit to the United States in June 1995 to accept an honorary degree from his alma mater, Cornell University.

By the mid-1990s democratization and the free circulation of ideas were also transforming the sense of identity among many Taiwanese residents. The social survey data do not yet permit the identification of long-term trends, but scholars in Taiwan who measured and analyzed popular opinion noted that by late 1995, most Taiwanese identified themselves either as both Taiwanese and Chinese or simply as Taiwanese. People were less inclined than in the past to perceive themselves as just Chinese. The cultural affiliation with "Chineseness" was weakening. This was reflected in language choice. Taiwanese increasingly preferred to speak the local Taiwanese dialect, a derivative of the dialects of their Fujianese ancestors, rather than the Mandarin Chinese that the mainlanders had imposed upon the populace since 1945. The teaching of history in elementary and secondary schools was also changing, so that the history curriculum designed by the Ministry of Education began to dwell on the continuous history of Taiwan as a distinct entity rather than focusing on Chinese history with Taiwan as a side current. Some observers sensed the possible early stages of the emergence of a separate Taiwanese identity and a drift away from the national culture. The rise of localist identity and community separation, after all, is occurring in many places around the world and is beyond the control of central governments. Few lessons exist on how to respond effectively to separatist tendencies, other than that repression and force do not always halt them and frequently intensify them.

As Taiwan shed its authoritarian system in favor of democracy, the United States naturally began to feel greater affinity for its government. And since the United States, especially many in Congress and among human rights lobbies, had long prodded Taiwan to move in this direction, many Americans felt an obligation to offer greater support to the island. Particularly after the brutal suppression of the 1989 demonstrations in Beijing and China's continued oppression of political dissidents, the contrast between Taiwan and the mainland sharpened.

As a result of these developments, all four aspects of the 1970s framework came under stress. No longer was it clear that the people on both sides of the Taiwan Strait accepted the idea that there was one China. In acknowledgment of Taiwan's economic and political progress, the United States infused its relations with Taiwan with a greater degree of "officiality." The unofficial Taiwan representatives in Washington received increased and more open access to the executive branch, and more and higher-level U.S. government officials visited Taiwan. The 1992 sale of F-16 aircraft to Taiwan, despite ebbing tensions between Taiwan and the mainland, certainly violated the spirit and possibly the letter of the U.S.–PRC 1982 agreement on arms sales to Taiwan. The executive branch of the U.S. government did not exert strenuous efforts to quash Taiwan's unilateral efforts to gain greater international recognition such as membership in United Nations organizations, while Congress openly supported Taiwan's moves. Following Beijing's harsh reaction to Lee Teng-hui's Cornell visit, for the first time in over twenty years, a U.S. aircraft carrier sailed through the Taiwan Strait in December 1995.

In this environment, Beijing feared that Taiwan's leaders, emboldened by American support, had embarked on a course leading toward independence. In February–March 1996, as Taiwan undertook its first presidential election, the mainland conducted military exercises near Taiwan that were clearly meant to intimidate the people on the island and to affect their votes. To reassure Taiwan and to remind Beijing of America's commitment to deter the use of force in the western Pacific, the United States dispatched two naval battle groups to the region. The United States was reengaging itself in the Chinese civil war. By mid-1996 the framework governing Sino-American-Taiwanese relations appeared badly tattered. Although cross-Strait tensions subsided in the second half of 1996, the questions of the moment were whether the framework was beyond repair or remained basically applicable, and if so, how to restore it.

Washington's Policy Choices

The history of Taiwan and of Beijing-Washington-Taipei relations has several implications for American policy. First, the American involvement in Taiwan's evolution since 1950 has been deep, extensive, and persistent. The United States will not lightly abandon this relationship. Deep friendships and moral obligations are entailed. At the same time, the record shows that U.S. policy toward Taiwan has been quite instrumental. In the final analysis, the American posture toward Taiwan has been continually adjusted to maintain peace and stability in the region.

Second, Taiwan's economic and political accomplishments are very impressive. A once destitute, authoritarian, and tension-ridden people who faced imminent external danger has become a wealthy, free, democratic, and secure populace. To be sure, a political cleavage still separates mainlanders and Taiwanese on the island. The People's Republic remains a threat. Some political challenges must be met domestically before democratic rule is fully consolidated. But Taiwan's gains could not be easily reversed. Its achievements are a tribute to the talents of its people and the foresight of its three rulers. Taiwan deserves a status and respect in international affairs commensurate with its attainments.

Third, Taiwan's accomplishments are also due to American support. Without U.S. military protection, economic aid, the openness of American markets, easy access to education in American universities and residential status (that is, "green card" immigration status) for the Taiwanese people, protracted tolerance of Taiwan's authoritarian regime, and then prodding to improve its human rights performance, Taiwan would not enjoy its current situation. Through the years, this has not been a reciprocal relationship. On balance, Taiwan has received far more from the United States politically and strategically than it has contributed to American interests; in some respects, for most of its history, it has been more of a burden than an asset to the United States. The United States need not be embarrassed, therefore, in expecting Taiwan to exhibit more respect for American interests and needs than its leaders have tended to show through the years. To realize this objective, Washington must have a clear sense of what it seeks from not only Beijing but Taipei, and it must communicate its expectations clearly, credibly, and effectively.

Fourth, although the basis for Taiwan's transformation was laid in earlier decades, the full modernization it experienced after the Sino-American rapprochement of the 1970s altered the strategic landscape of the Asia Pacific region. Taiwan has enjoyed peace and flourished economically in the context of the simultaneously constructive relations that have existed among China, Japan, and the United States and that have permitted Taiwan to develop its own direct ties with the mainland. The People's Republic, needless to say, has also benefited from this setting. Tampering with the existing security arrangement would jeopardize those gains. That is, the underlying strategic reality is that, at best, Taiwan is a middle power located a hundred miles away from a potentially hostile nuclear power. Its security depends upon relations among the major powers in the region: China, Japan, and the United States. Its future is derivative of the arrangements the major powers make on its behalf. This induces an understandable nervousness, a desire to improve its situation, and the pursuit of policies that are intended to make Taiwan more a master of its own destiny: enhancing its defense capabilities to deter a mainland attack; acquiring representation in international bodies; accumulating and using its massive foreign currency reserves to advance its foreign policy interests; and penetrating the American, Japanese, and Chinese systems in order to gain leverage over them. But these policies can only marginally alter the underlying strategic reality, and if they are pursued with excessive exuberance, they risk engendering a self-defeating reaction from others, especially Beijing.

These considerations prompt the fifth conclusion: despite the strains and Taiwan's evolution, the framework of the 1970s offers the best, indeed the only realistic alternative for managing Taiwan–PRC–United States relations. Some minor adjustments seem warranted so that Taiwan can enjoy an enhanced status in international affairs, but Taiwan is best advised to secure this objective in consultation with the People's Republic. Taiwan must recognize that its campaign for membership in United Nations organizations is quixotic. After all, as a permanent member of the Security Council, Beijing has the authority to veto Taiwan's entry into the United Nations. But in light of the size of Taiwan's economy, its entry into the World Trade Organization, the World Bank, and the International Monetary Fund is warranted. The United States should quietly encourage Taiwan to agree with Beijing on a formula to permit this to happen, as has occurred with the Asian Development Bank and the Asia Pacific Economic Cooperation (APEC) process. Discussions also are needed between Washington and Taipei, Taipei and Beijing, and Beijing and Washington on how best to prevent an arms race in the region. The introduction of F-16s into the Taiwan inventory and the addition of SU-27s and various advanced surface-to-surface missiles into the PRC inventory will significantly increase the capabilities of both sides. Is an informal agreement on a mutually satisfactory balance of strength beyond hope? Short of that, perhaps the time has come to discuss means of preventing accidental confrontations and reducing felt needs to acquire and deploy additional weaponry. The Association of Southeast Asian Nations (ASEAN) states have a keen interest in discouraging a Taiwan–PRC arms race that would spill over into their region, and Washington should encourage Southeast Asian nations to address this issue with Taipei and Beijing.

Regarding unofficial visits to the United States by Taiwan officials, Washington will have to make clear to Beijing that the United States cannot ban private organizations from issuing invitations to democratically elected leaders of other governments—whether national, provincial, or municipal—to visit the United States. The executive branch cannot halt Congress from doing so. Further, American values preclude denying visas to such visitors. The United States is an open country. Whether recipients of the invitations decide to accept is their decision, but the issuance of an invitation and the extension of a visa involve American sovereignty. Just as the United States must respect legitimate Chinese protection of its sovereignty, the United States must firmly defend against improper Chinese encroachment upon U.S. sovereignty.

Beyond such marginal modifications, it behooves all sides to return clearly to the path pursued until mid-1995: for Taiwan to temper its political provocations, for China to temper its military threats and actions, and for the United States to encourage the two sides to resume their dialogue. There is a danger that Beijing's assertive nationalism or Taiwan's changing sense of national identity could preclude a peaceful reconciliation between the two sides, but it is premature to come to that conclusion. On a more optimistic note, there is also a possibility that eventually the two sides can reconcile their differences. The basis is there, in President Jiang Zemin's eight-point proposal of January 1995 and the initial six-point response by President Lee Teng-hui. The Beijing government has indicated its willingness for Taiwan to retain a separate army with its own access to arms, its separate, unofficial representation to other countries, its own political system, and its own economy. Taiwan has indicated its willingness to enter into a union with the People's Republic when China has become a prosperous democracy. The challenge for each side is to convince the other that its offer is sincere, a process that will take years of patient, consistent, and non-provocative words and deeds.

Implicit in the stated positions is the basis for an agreement: Taiwan making a credible commitment never to seek independence; the PRC making a credible commitment, in that light, not to threaten or use force against Taiwan; a status for Taiwan as part of China that would be less than that of a separate country but much more than a province; and with Beijing's sponsorship, membership for the government of Taiwan in all international bodies including the U.N. General Assembly. To reach that agreement, however, would require strong leaders in both Taipei and Beijing and confidence of people in Taiwan that their way of life would not be put at risk, and the political conditions in both capitals currently preclude such bold statesmanship. Although both Lee Teng-hui and Jiang Zemin have publicly expressed a desire to meet, neither is strong enough to accommodate the political needs of the other in reaching a total, peaceful reconciliation.

Short of a comprehensive solution, which ultimately must arise from within the two sides and cannot be imposed or brokered from the outside, Beijing and Taipei have a keen interest in resuming their disrupted dialogue. Both have major incentives to do so. Many concrete issues should now be addressed, especially to negotiate agreements to establish direct shipping, air, and telecommunications.

The prospects for Taiwan's continued prosperity and the mainland's uninterrupted economic growth would be improved by such agreements. The United States should quietly encourage both sides to focus on this pragmatic task.

Tibet

The obvious point must be stated first: since 1950, Han Chinese have misruled Tibet. The central government and its agents in the region have greatly weakened the centerpiece of Tibetan culture: the elaborate system of religious monasteries that enabled Tibetan Buddhism to flourish. They have oppressed the population and denied Tibetan yearnings for a meaningful degree of self-rule. To be sure, Tibet was not an idyllic society before 1949. A large portion of the populace lived miserable lives as serfs in a feudal order, subject to the arbitrary rule of their masters. With some justification, Beijing claims that under its rule, the quality of life of the average Tibetan has improved substantially, particularly in the past fifteen years, with longer life expectancy, somewhat expanded educational opportunities, improved transportation facilities, and so on. But even in these areas, the Han inhabitants of Tibet have benefited far more than the ethnic Tibetans. What can and should the United States do about this situation? Should the United States assist the people of Tibet? Should Washington make Tibet an issue in Sino-American relations?

History of Tibet

Modern Tibet dates to the seventeenth century.[5] In 1642 the realm became unified under the religious and spiritual authority of the Dalai Lama situated in Lhasa. Although China's imperial rulers had extended their influence into Tibet in both the Tang and the Yuan dynasties, Beijing became deeply immersed in Tibetan politics only in the 1600s and 1700s, stationing a small garrison and appointing a permanent representative in Lhasa in 1720.

Politically, from the 1600s on, several Dalai Lamas entered into unambiguously tributary relations with the imperial court, and on several occasions, a Dalai Lama sought political and military in-

tervention by Qing authorities. The imperial court also involved itself in age-old rivalries among the Tibetan monasteries, cultivating
some and thereby alienating others. Beijing frequently had a closer
relationship with the Panchen Lama and monasteries near Shi-
gatse than it did with the Dalai Lama in Lhasa. During the Qing
dynasty, emissaries from Tibet joined leaders of other Inner Asian
kingdoms, tribes, and other types of political entities every summer
at Chengde, several hundred kilometers north of Beijing, to pay
obeisance to the emperor. The Qing court retreated to Chengde in
the summer and held court for those Inner Asian leaders who
looked upon the emperor as their protector and patron. To make
the Tibetans feel at home at Chengde, the Qing constructed a
replica of the Potala in Lhasa. All these dimensions of the imperial-
Tibet relationship might suggest Chinese suzerainty. In reality, however, Chinese political involvement in Tibet was superficial,
sporadic, and often by invitation, while the influence of Tibet upon
China was slight.

In the religious domain, although both Tibetan Buddhism and
Chinese Buddhism fall within the Mahayana school or sect of Buddhism, significant differences separate the two. Thus the Han and
Tibetans are not linked by common religious beliefs. According to
some accounts, Buddhism initially spread to Tibet from China, not
from India, though by the 700s the religious influence came from
both south and north. In the Qing dynasty, as in the Yuan, the imperial court patronized Tibetan Buddhism, such as at the Yong-he
gong, the ornate temple in the northeast quarter of Beijing, but this
may have been done less out of religious conviction than as a tech-
nique for asserting imperial influence over Tibet.

Qing influence in Tibet reached its apogee in the 1700s, and
then gradually declined in the 1800s. The ebbing Chinese influence
coincided with increased British activity in the Himalayan states of
Nepal, Bhutan, and Sikkim, which had paid obeisance to the Dalai
Lama, and as the nineteenth century wore on, the British became
more interested in Tibet itself, particularly the western region where
mountain passes granted access to India from Central Asia. The
British feared that Russia might seek to extend its influence from
Central Asia to Tibet and then to India itself. In response to the increasing British presence, the Dalai Lama sought to keep the Chi-

nese involved in Tibet, and he and his advisors inflated Chinese strength to deter British penetration.

Today, proponents of an independent Tibet assert that Tibet was never under the extensive control of the Chinese government, that the two periods of maximum imperial control occurred in the alien Yuan and Qing dynasties, when China was under Mongol and Manchu rule, and that the thirteenth Dalai Lama declared independence in 1913 when Tibetans expelled remnant Qing forces garrisoned in Tibet. However, Beijing claims that for centuries, Tibet has been a part of China except during those periods when China lacked a central government. Neither the Qing nor its successor governments ever acknowledged the Dalai Lama's claim of independence. And throughout the twentieth century all the major powers accepted Chinese claims of sovereignty over Tibet.

In fact, as a cursory reading of Tibetan history reveals, relations between the imperial government in Beijing and the leading Buddhist lamas of the Tibetan theocracy were sufficiently ambiguous and varied over time and place to make both claims credible. The situation was multilayered, leading Joseph Fletcher to conclude:

From the Qing point of view, the Dalai Lama was a mighty ecclesiastic and a holy being, but nonetheless the emperor's protégé. From the Tibetan point of view, the emperor was merely the Lama's secular patron. This meant that in Tibetans' eyes the Dalai Lama's position was superior to that of the Qing emperor, because in Tibet . . . the monastic community was the ruling body, and lay persons, no matter how rich or powerful, were thus in a subordinate position. The Tibetan government was well aware of the Qing view of the matter, but it was impolite for the Tibetans to question the Qing interpretation.[6]

Emblematic of the deliberately fostered ambiguity was the method of selecting the high-level incarnated lamas: the Dalai Lama, the Panchen Lama, and so on. Again to quote from Fletcher:

The traditional method had been based on a series of tests (administered by Buddhist clerics), such as the ability of the infant candidate to distinguish objects that had belonged to his previous incarnation. The winning candidate had customarily been a nobleman on whom the chief Tibetan officials agreed. In 1793 the Qing Emperor had sent a golden urn to Lhasa, ordering that thenceforth the names of the leading candidates should be written on slips of paper and placed in the urn, then drawn by lot. The Qing court decreed that the candidates should be commoners, and had sent the urn to prevent Tibetan officials from choosing the Dalai Lama in accordance with the interests of the dominant political group among the nobility. From the Qing point of view, it was also unthinkable that an important dignitary like the Dalai Lama should be chosen by any system that excluded the emperor's authority. . . . Upon the death of the Dalai Lama, therefore, the Lhasa government was obliged both to lead the Tibetan public to suppose that the traditional method of selection had been used and at the same time to reassure the Qing authorities that the Dalai Lama had in fact been selected by lot from the urn.[7]

Fletcher states that the extent to which the lottery-run urn was actually used remains a mystery, though it probably was used in 1841 and 1858. Fletcher concludes, "The Tibetans were willing to use the urn to keep up the semblance of Qing protection when the imperial power was weak, but when the Qing was strong, the Tibetans left some doubt about the urn's use so as to emphasize Tibetan autonomy." Today neither the rulers in Beijing nor the Dailai Lama and his supporters are prepared to tolerate the ambiguity that their predecessors embraced for nearly three centuries. In this sense, neither side upholds tradition.

Tibet since 1950

During the warlord and nationalist eras (1911–1949), Tibet for all practical purposes was independent of central government control, as were many other parts of China. But throughout this period, the central government continued to dabble in Tibetan politics, cultivating allies who were rivals of the authorities in Lhasa. With the ascent of the Communists, the PLA entered Tibet in 1950, and the new government in Beijing dispatched officials to Lhasa to establish a provincial government. In 1951 the new authorities negotiated a seventeen-point agreement in Beijing with representatives of the young Dalai Lama that granted the Buddhist religious order considerable autonomy. The agreement proved unworkable.

By Chinese standards, the regime adopted a moderate approach during the early 1950s, but tensions soon mounted. By 1956–57 Tibetan resistance had begun to flare, aided by covert American-

Taiwan operations. In 1959 a full-fledged rebellion broke out among the Khamba tribesmen in eastern Tibet, and additional PLA forces entered the province from Sichuan to quell the revolt. The tribesmen retreated westward to Lhasa, pursued by the PLA, who then entered the provincial capital and the religious center of the Dalai Lama. He and an entourage fled to northern India, where with United States and Indian assistance, he established the base that has been his home ever since. Many rebels met their fate at Chinese hands. The Chinese attributed the unrest to the Dalai Lama, whom they henceforth looked upon with animosity.

In the immediate aftermath of the 1959 debacle, Chinese rule became more harsh and oppressive. To ensure Han mastery, the government sponsored a migration from other provinces to Tibet's major urban areas. During the Cultural Revolution (1966–1976), especially in its early years, marauding Red Guards committed unspeakable crimes, killing many monks and destroying monasteries throughout Tibet. Deng Xiaoping himself, in meetings with Americans, acknowledged the extensive Chinese misrule during that era.

Under Deng and especially with the encouragement of Deng's anointed successor Hu Yaobang in the early and mid-1980s, the government sought to compensate for its previous errors, allowing monasteries to reopen and young monks to be recruited, permitting greater religious freedom, opening Tibet to tourism, and increasing central government subsidies for education, public health, transportation facilities, and so on. The increased benevolence, however, did not lead to an outpouring of Tibetan appreciation. Rather the religious freedom resulted in open displays of reverence for the Dalai Lama, and the arrival of foreigners meant that the outside world acquired a keener appreciation of the horrors of the previous twenty years.

Since 1950 three underlying issues have plagued relations between the Beijing government and Han Chinese on the one hand and the Buddhist hierarchy and Tibetans on the other. First, the two sides cannot agree on the boundary between the secular and the religious domains. On occasion, the Chinese government has granted increased autonomy to the monasteries, but the monks have used their greater religious freedom to intrude into areas that the authorities consider to be in the secular domain. The Dalai Lama personifies the issue. He is the spiritual leader of Tibetan Buddhism, although his precise authority is somewhat contested and limited by other leading lamas. Monks and the faithful alike consider him a holy being to whom they owe deference. To Buddhists, a major indication of increased religious freedom is their ability to express their reverence for the Dalai Lama and to acknowledge his spiritual authority over them. But to Chinese leaders who seek a monopoly of authority, the Dalai Lama offers an unacceptable alternative to state authority. They view as threatening any authority apart from that held by the state.

Traditional Chinese political thought does not easily accommodate the idea of a division of authority between church and state, among levels of government, or within the central state apparatus. In the well-ordered state, authority is unified, hierarchical, and converges on a single individual or institution to whom all owe their loyalty. China's current leaders adhere to this tradition.

The second issue is social and economic. Tibetans remain overwhelmingly an agricultural people; many are nomads. Their illiteracy rates are high. Han Chinese are the bearers of an industrial economy. In Tibet they tend to live in cities and dominate commercial life. Somewhat better educated, urban oriented, entrepreneurial, and Mandarin speaking, the Han are significantly better equipped to take advantage of the limited economic opportunities that Tibet offers. Tibetans are ill prepared to participate fully in the economic development of their region. The long-term prognosis for a possible renaissance of traditional Tibetan civilization is bleak. The Han-Tibetan encounter is part of the global confrontation between inhabitants of lowland industrial societies and upland agrarian and nomadic societies. The story everywhere has been brutal and tragic. Beijing's challenge in Tibet, as for central governments in their peripheral areas elsewhere in the world, is to make it less so.

Third is the ethnic and cultural tension between the Han and the Tibetans. Many Han look upon Tibetans as an inferior and primitive people, steeped in superstition and ignorance. The stereotypes are quite derogatory. Underlying Han-Tibetan relations are considerable racism and Han chauvinism. Intensifying the problem is a Tibetan historiography that glorifies the past and neglects many cruel and unjust aspects of the traditional social system.

The Han and the Tibetans are thus divided by political, religious, economic, social, ethnic, and cultural differences. A wide gulf separates them, although to be sure a portion of the Tibetan populace and even some of the monasteries have at least superficially cordial relations with the government. In particular, the previous Panchen Lama accommodated himself to Communist rule, though even he was attacked during the Cultural Revolution.

Recent developments have added to the complexity of the Tibetan situation. The loosening of controls over population movement in China has prompted an upsurge of voluntary Han migrants in addition to those on government assignment. Many newcomers have moved from impoverished adjacent areas in Yunnan, Guizhou, Sichuan, and Gansu. Although the total number of Han is still limited in core Tibet—the best estimates are that they total less than a fifth of the total population—the Han dominance of Tibet is increasing in urban areas. The influx of Han has generated resentment among Tibetans.

In addition, on the international scene, the Tibetan government-in-exile headquartered in India has acquired increased stature and private support in recent years. Tibetan Buddhism itself is acquiring adherents and establishing an increased institutional presence not only in the United States but in Western Europe as well. The interests of the government-in-exile and the monks abroad, concerned with securing financial support and sustaining themselves apart from China, do not fully coincide with the desires of the majority of Tibetans. Indeed, were the Dalai Lama and the Chinese government to reach an accommodation, the government-in-exile and its minions in the United States, India, and Western Europe would lose their raison d'être.

In 1995 the Chinese government intensified its problems through its clumsy handling of the selection of a successor to the Panchen Lama. Contrary to Beijing's instructions, the lamas in China surreptitiously sought to involve the Dalai Lama in the selection process. The Dalai Lama, perhaps unwisely and probably in a deliberate provocation of Beijing, publicly revealed his participation and approval of the final choice. Thus the Dalai Lama destroyed the ambiguity that had preserved peace over this crucial issue in traditional times. After some delay, indicating indecision in Beijing, the government chose to countervene the Dalai Lama's intervention. Beijing could have overlooked the consultations with the Dalai Lama by treating the matter as illegal but superfluous. Instead, Beijing placed the six-year-old boy and his family in protective custody, ostensibly to shield him from curiosity seekers, and secured the designation of another young boy as the real reincarnation of the Panchen Lama. The affair caused Beijing officials to conclude that many lamas whom they had considered politically reliable actually remained loyal to the Dalai Lama. Beijing has decided that its problems in Tibet are greater than it had earlier realized. Beijing's repressive response to the situation has created the potential for a schism among the Panchen Lama's followers, previously one of the sects more favorably inclined toward Beijing.

The present course is costly to both Tibetans and the Chinese government. Tibetan culture is endangered, and Tibetans are being overwhelmed by the outside world. The central government has the power in the short run to enforce its will through a policy of oppression, but brute force has an insidious effect on the Chinese state and damages China's image abroad. The moral authority that the Dalai Lama commands makes his Chinese tormentors appear to be callous and brutal despots. Both sides would benefit from an accommodation that would preserve Tibetan culture, yield Tibetan Buddhism a well-defined sphere of autonomy, and yet preserve Tibet as part of China.

U.S. Policy

The American interest in Tibet was rekindled in the 1980s. Following the opening to China in 1971, American financial support for the Dalai Lama had ceased, and the Dalai Lama's first trips to the United States in the late 1970s and early 1980s avoided political controversy. But in the 1980s Tibet joined the human rights concerns that private Americans were voicing with increasing stridency. The tragedy of Tiananmen brought these concerns to the forefront of the American agenda, and the Dalai Lama and Tibet found growing support in Congress. This trend culminated in congressional resolutions supporting Tibet, legislation mandating fellowship support for Tibetans, meetings between the Dalai Lama and Presidents Bush and Clinton in the White House, and by 1995, legislation demanding the appointment of an American ambassador to Tibet. Tibet has joined the Indonesian government's control of Timor as a cause on many college campuses. And a number of celebrities, movie stars, and wealthy Americans have become Tibetan activists, their commitment sometimes linked to an interest in Buddhism. The humanitarian impulse is understandable, and the expressions of personal respect for the Dalai Lama, a Nobel Peace Prize recipient, are appropriate. He is, in fact, a very impressive, gentle, spiritual individual.

The Dalai Lama has publicly stated that he does not seek Tibetan independence (his privately held aspirations are less certain), that he would return to Tibet if he could be assured of its genuine autonomy within China, and that he is prepared to enter into talks with Beijing without preconditions. China's leaders have rejected the offer, stipulating as a precondition that the Dalai Lama can only meet them after, in effect, accepting their authority over him. The Dalai Lama is concerned, however, that even a return to Tibet under terms satisfactory both to him and to Beijing could generate spontaneous demonstrations that would undercut any agreements. The Dalai Lama, who is a reasonable and politically sensitive individual, is clearly more moderate than many of the Tibetan exiles who surround him in India. They seek Tibetan independence and a vast extension of Tibet's boundaries from the current core of Tibet to the entire area inhabited by Tibetans. For Tibetans to become the majority in this territory would require "ethnic cleansing." Either knowingly or unknowingly, most American supporters of the Dalai Lama endorse the expansive objectives of his more extreme supporters rather than the circumscribed goals of the Dalai Lama himself.

What should the policy of the United States government be? It is certainly appropriate for the U.S. government to honor the Dalai Lama as a spiritual leader, to publicize what it knows about Chinese rule in Tibet, and quietly to encourage a dialogue between the Dalai Lama and the Chinese government. International, U.S. government, and private development assistance to Tibet, working through Chinese government channels, seems warranted, for example, in the education, public health, environmental, and agricultural spheres. A particularly constructive course the United States can undertake, primarily through international agencies and nongovernmental agencies, is to train Tibetans to participate in the development of their region. Meanwhile private Americans, acting on their values, serve a worthy purpose by vigorously disseminating accurate information about conditions in Tibet. But neither the public nor private sectors should encourage those who seek Tibetan independence. Americans should not arouse expectations that the United States is not prepared to fulfill. Nurturing hopes that somehow the United States will assist in the emergence of an independent Tibet is cruel and irresponsible. Tibetans who act on the basis of such promises will surely be disappointed. In the final analysis, the United States government is no more likely to defend the Tibetan cause than that of Chechnya. The Tibet issue involves profound humanitarian and human rights issues, but it does not involve matters of sovereignty.

Hong Kong

On September 26, 1984, Britain and China signed an agreement concerning the future of Hong Kong, thus terminating sixteen contentious months of continuous negotiations.[8] Unveiling the agreement the next day, Britain informed the over 6 million dwellers of Hong Kong that the territory would be returned to Chinese rule on July 1, 1997. Prime Minister Margaret Thatcher, in fact, had already secretly communicated in October 1983 her government's willingness to quit Hong Kong in 1997 under certain conditions, and even before that, in June 1983, the prime minister had notified Beijing that Britain did not challenge China's claim to sovereignty over Hong Kong. The die had been cast. After 155 years under the Union Jack, Chinese banners again wave supreme over Hong Kong.

Significance

Hong Kong's return to Chinese rule symbolizes the end of Western colonialism in Asia, an epoch that began in the 1500s. The significance of this historical moment should not be lost. With the exception of Macau, which will remain under Portuguese rule until

1999, and the Kurile Islands, which remain under Russian rule, nowhere in East Asia will a foreign flag fly supreme: neither the Portuguese nor the Dutch nor the British, French, American, German, or Australian. Asia's European colonial era has ended.

Moreover, the People's Republic will become directly and immediately responsible for one of the world's great cities. Hong Kong's economy and society are far more productive and prosperous than any metropolitan area now under Beijing's control. As Frank Ching has pointed out,[9] this enclave of 6.3 million people has a gross domestic product that is equal to roughly 20 percent of China's, a nation of 1.3 billion. Hong Kong is responsible for 65 percent of external investment in China. It has the world's busiest container port, the eighth-largest stock market in terms of capitalization, and major foreign currency reserves. Under British rule, Hong Kong became the most important metropolitan center in East Asia between Tokyo and Singapore. Will it continue to thrive under Chinese jurisdiction? Will the Chinese government effectively draw upon the talents of its people, with considerable benefit for the mainland itself? Or will Beijing squander this opportunity through misrule and thereby seriously damage its prospects both at home and abroad? No issue looming in the years immediately ahead is more likely to affect Sino-American relations than how Beijing answers these questions.

Furthermore, after July 1, 1997, strong, separate, and proud inheritors of two Chinese traditions were joined within one country. Some of the world's wealthiest and most internationally oriented people are Hong Kong Chinese. They bear the traditions of the trade and commercially oriented coastal Chinese who date back to the Song dynasty. Beijing continues to be ruled by the inheritors of China's imperial and bureaucratic traditions. These two traditions have long coexisted in uneasy tension, adversarial yet needing each other. Many families indeed straddled both worlds. The commercial Chinese provided financial support to officialdom, often through corruption and the purchase of scholarly degrees, and they provided access to rulers of foreign countries. But they were also a challenge to the values propagated by officialdom, and they threatened China's political unity. The absorption of Hong Kong under the "one country, two systems" formula means that each of the two

Chinese traditions will have its separate base, though the upper hand—the coercive force of the state—is still held by Beijing. Although in recent years the central government has sought to draw upon the talents of the coastal entrepreneurs, the underlying issue concerns who will dominate whom, or whether a synthesis of the two traditions will eventually emerge.

History

Britain acquired the entire territory of Hong Kong in three stages: the island itself was ceded in perpetuity after the Opium War (1839–1842); Kowloon Peninsula in perpetuity after Chinese defeat in the Arrow War (1860); and the New Territories secured in a ninety-year, rent-free lease obtained from the moribund Qing dynasty in 1898. The territory is the product of British gunboat diplomacy of the nineteenth century.

From the outset in the 1840s, Hong Kong served as a base for Western operations in China. It also provided a safe haven from the turmoil that periodically swept the mainland, as well as a political base for revolutionaries who sought to induce change on the mainland. It gradually attracted entrepreneurially talented people from throughout the world—mainly Cantonese and Shanghainese but also Europeans, Indians, Middle Eastern merchants, and in recent years, Americans, Australians, and Filipinos—who together provide the city its dynamism.

Hong Kong, in fact, did not achieve its current preeminence along the China coast until the establishment of the People's Republic. From the 1850s until 1949, Shanghai was China's premier commercial city, and Hong Kong's rise can be attributed largely to Shanghai's demise. Mao Zedong and his associates failed to sustain Shanghai's economic vitality, in part because the American imposed embargo deprived the city of its international markets, and in part because the new government's economic policies channeled its wealth to the Chinese interior.

Hong Kong did not suffer this fate. Although the Communists, claiming that the agreements upon which Britain based its right to rule Hong Kong had been forced upon a weak China, repudiated the treaties, they chose to leave the territory in British hands. Mao and his colleagues initially wished to avoid antagonizing Britain. Hong Kong soon turned into a valuable contact point between China and the outside world and a place to evade the American embargo. Assisted by Shanghai émigrés, its economy took off in the 1960s and 1970s; European and American markets welcomed its textiles, plastics, and electronic goods manufactured by low-wage workers, many of whom were recent mainland refugees. As a result of its growth and consumption of mainland products, Hong Kong became a major source of China's foreign exchange. Then, with the opening of China in the 1980s, it became a funnel for investment in the mainland. In short, Hong Kong thrived from the 1950s on because it served Chinese interests.

It also prospered for another reason: British rule. In the immediate aftermath of the civil war, only an external power could have kept the peace between the anti-Communist forces, the pro-Communist forces, and the apolitical majority. The British calculated that any move toward self-rule would bring latent political tensions to the surface and anger the Beijing government, on whom the British relied to supply the territory with food and water and to control the border to prevent a massive influx of refugees. British rule also exempted the territory from the corruption and abuse of power that has so often characterized Chinese governance through the decades. They enabled a market economy to flourish. In sum, the British provided the rule of law, but they did not cultivate a democracy.

The Transition

The delicate equilibrium could not be sustained indefinitely. Hong Kong's prosperity depends upon a cooperative Beijing and upon the inclusion of the New Territories in Hong Kong's domain. That is where the airport, several large industrial and residential areas, and the new universities are located. By the early 1980s the question could no longer be avoided: what would happen after 1997, when the treaty governing British rule of the New Territories would lapse? Would Beijing allow the British to remain in some capacity as the administrators of Hong Kong? Forcing the issue onto the agenda was the need to clarify the enforceability of contracts and financial commitments beyond 1997. If China were to reacquire the territory, would it recognize the legality of these agreements?

As late as 1981, Deng Xiaoping wished to focus on the recovery of Taiwan first and then address Hong Kong, but by mid-1982, these questions forced Deng to change his priorities. In subsequent months, perhaps somewhat angered by the angularity of Prime Minister Thatcher's initial approach, Deng made four major decisions: first, Britain should quit Hong Kong in 1997; second, the transition to Chinese rule should not disrupt Hong Kong's prosperity; third, after 1997 Hong Kong should retain a separate political and economic system and enjoy considerable autonomy for fifty years; and fourth, PLA units should be stationed in Hong Kong.

Deng's stipulations established the parameters for the 1983–84 Sino-British negotiations and for the subsequent planning for Hong Kong's transfer to Chinese rule, while the ambiguities of his formulations created sources of dispute between the British and Chinese. Two documents have established the legal framework for the future of Hong Kong: the September 1984 Joint Sino-British Declaration, and the PRC's Basic Law on the Hong Kong Special Administrative Region enacted by the National People's Congress in April 1990. The two documents contain many ambiguities that require additional interpretation. Ancillary letters and the negotiating record between British and Chinese officials give further meaning to these two documents, but questions arise as to whether this side commentary is binding.

The transition period since 1984 has involved both cooperation and acrimony. All the major parties involved—the British in London, the government in Beijing, the Hong Kong government, and the Hong Kong business community—have done a great deal to preserve confidence in the territory's future. At the same time, each of these parties has sought to exploit the ambiguities to advance its particular interests. Particularly contentious have been China's efforts to intervene in the governance of Hong Kong prior to the 1997 transfer, and British and Hong Kong government efforts to alter Hong Kong's institutional arrangements in the hope that these reforms would survive after 1997.

In particular, Christopher Patten, appointed governor of Hong Kong in 1992, vigorously sought to expand the representative character of the Legislative Council, the government's parliamentary body, by increasing the number of members who were democratically elected and by expanding the electorate. Patten hoped the council would survive 1997 and become a democratic check on Beijing's arbitrariness. Beijing rejected the initiative as a violation of previous understandings and an affront because the proposal had not been first vetted with PRC officials. In response, in July 1993, Beijing appointed its own preliminary Preparatory Committee and in 1996 named a formal committee that is to straddle the 1997 transition and represent public opinion. The membership of these committees, however, excluded prominent Hong Kong critics of Beijing and supporters of Governor Patten, thereby raising serious doubts about the degree of autonomy Hong Kong would actually enjoy after 1997.

Hong Kong's Prospects

Many reasons exist for guarded optimism about the territory's future, not the least of which are the gains the People's Republic would secure from handling the transition well. Beijing will emerge with greater credibility in its efforts to entice Taiwan if it adheres to its commitments to Hong Kong. Further, the leaders of China have made clear they are prepared to draw upon China's foreign currency reserves to defend the Hong Kong economy and currency in case of a panic. Beijing's key allies in Hong Kong—especially the very wealthy business people—also have a huge stake in making the agreement work. In addition, several factors that have contributed to Hong Kong's economic development will remain. Hong Kong offers an unrivaled harbor for trade with south China and a base of operations in China. The record of the past fifteen years prompts confidence at least in the economic future; mainlanders repeatedly have shown some willingness to invest in the territory.

Nonetheless, numerous uncertainties exist. Various fundamental issues concerning Hong Kong's governance after 1997 will take some time to settle, such as the autonomy of the chief executive of Hong Kong appointed by Beijing and his relations with two Beijing appointed representatives in Hong Kong, the first secretary of the underground Hong Kong branch of the Chinese Communist party and the commander of the PLA forces in Hong Kong. Indeed, will the party remain underground? How will civil unrest, demonstrations, and political dissent be handled? Will the Hong Kong populace restrain itself from assisting dissident activity on the mainland? Will political censorship or self-censorship constrain previous freedom and thereby erode one of the sources of the creativity of the populace? Will Hong Kong remain under the rule of law? How will the increasing corruption on the mainland affect rule in Hong Kong, especially since Hong Kong business people are one of the sources of that corruption? And will Shanghai emerge as a rival to Hong Kong, seeking to develop at Hong Kong's expense? These serious questions suggest some caution about Hong Kong's future.

Implications for the United States

This account reveals a paradox. The United States has had and will continue to have a major interest in the future of Hong Kong. This interest far transcends its economic interest in terms of its direct investment in the territory and the trade and investments that flow through it to other destinations, especially China. More important, U.S. strategic interests are well served by the region's stability and prosperity and by China's steady development, and any disruption of Hong Kong's economy will damage the prosperity of the entire region because of the pivotal role its financial market plays. And as we have seen, China's own evolution now depends heavily on what will transpire in Hong Kong after 1997.

Yet the ability of the United States directly to influence the course of events is quite limited. To be sure, continued access to the American market is crucial to Hong Kong's future, and the United States' Hong Kong Policy Act of 1992 makes this access conditional upon China's adherence to the Sino-British Declaration. The act does give the United States some leverage by mandating economic sanctions against the governments of Hong Kong and China should they violate or ignore the declaration.

The U.S. government and the private sector should also quietly express their concerns and hopes in meetings with both China's leaders and the new Hong Kong government, and identify some of the indicators they will be using to measure Hong Kong's success:

(1) the clear role of the government as the leading authority in the territory, ahead of the Hong Kong branch of the Chinese Communist party and the local PLA; (2) continued rule of law, maintenance of an independent judiciary and civil service, and avoidance of extensive corruption; (3) continued freedom of the press and a nonoppressive response to dissident activity and demonstrations concerning the situation in Hong Kong; (4) continued, effective management of Hong Kong currency, foreign currency reserves, and financial markets; (5) avoidance of pressure by mainland firms on profitable nonmainland companies to "sell" shares and to invite the mainland companies to become joint venture partners at bargain-basement prices; (6) maintenance of academic freedom and of international faculty and professional contacts in universities; (7) continued and routine access of United States naval ships to Hong Kong harbor for the rest and relaxation of its crews; and (8) restraint by Shanghai from using its political clout to accelerate its development through poaching of Hong Kong enterprise. These are some of the practices that will give real meaning to the slogan of "one country, two systems" and that will enable Hong Kong to flourish.

The United States cannot become a protector of Hong Kong. Its 6 million people became a part of China, and this must have implications for their culture, society, and polity. But the United States does have an interest and responsibility in facilitating successful implementation of the 1984 declaration, and carefully monitoring Hong Kong's performance and remaining involved in its activities are among the best ways to pursue its interests.

Conclusion

Taiwan, Tibet, and Hong Kong are all important issues in Sino-American relations. Each poses distinctive problems, but all are irritants. American and Chinese interests in all three locales currently diverge more than they converge. The U.S. government is concerned with the human rights of Tibetans. It is nervous that Chinese control over Hong Kong after 1997 may damage the pivotal financial and commercial role this thriving metropolis plays in the global economy. And it seeks to ensure that Taiwan has the capacity to deter the Chinese threat or use of force against it. The Chinese government rejects all these as unwarranted intrusions into its domain.

If the Sino-American relationship is to flourish, both sides must exhibit some sensitivity to and understanding of the views and interests of the other. The United States and China were able to concentrate on their common interests when the issues posed by Taiwan, Tibet, and Hong Kong were successfully kept off the agenda. The inhabitants of the three areas were major beneficiaries of the progress in Sino-American relations. However, as this chapter has stressed, developments in the coming decade may make it more difficult to keep attention off these three subjects: Taiwan's changing self-identity; increasing Han pressure on Tibetan civilization; and the dissatisfaction of Hong Kong dwellers with PRC rule. The residents of the three locales and their American supporters have the capacity to introduce these thorny issues onto the Sino-American agenda.

More extensive discussions between the Chinese and the Americans are needed to minimize the potential difficulties and confrontations that each area may pose. In these discussions, both governmental representatives and private Americans should speak frankly about their hopes and fears. China's rise in world affairs is one of the major developments of the era. But what kind of a powerful China will stride across the world stage a generation from now? Will its government be oppressive within and expansionist abroad? Or will its society flourish, its people reaching their creative potential, its civilization enriched by the diversity of its own population? The latter China would contribute greatly to the world; the former China would be a threat.

In June 1973 Zhou Enlai asked a young member of a visiting American delegation, "Do you think China could ever become a hegemonic power?" She replied, "I doubt it," to which the premier swiftly responded, "Do not count on it. China could embark upon a hegemonic path. But if it does, you should oppose it. And you must inform that generation of Chinese that Zhou Enlai told you to do so."

That exchange is germane to the issues at hand. Early in their ascent, rising powers establish habits and patterns of behavior that endure, in part because these practices become embedded in the elite political culture and domestic institutional arrangements. China's handling of Taiwan, Tibet, and Hong Kong provides an early harbinger of the Chinese future. Patient and flexible postures rooted in self-confidence in China's rise and sensitivity to the local residents' aspirations would suggest that a true renaissance of Chinese civilization is in the offing. Persistently aggressive and oppressive policies toward these locales foreshadow a possible militaristic trajectory. They increase the likelihood that as its military might expands, China will resort to the threat and use of force to press its claims elsewhere. Perceiving the danger, the major and middle powers in the Asia Pacific region will seek to balance China's increasing might, bringing tension to the region that will serve no one's interests.

Therefore, despite the divergent Chinese and American perceptions about Taiwan, Tibet, and Hong Kong and the conflicting short-term interests the two countries have in the three locales, both Beijing and Washington share an overriding interest: that the process through which China inevitably increases its influence in all three areas should be peaceful, evolutionary, and responsive to the desires of the local populace. Under those circumstances, the United States and China's immediate neighbors will have less fear about the implications of China's rise, and China is likely indeed to emerge as a respected and responsible power in world affairs. The challenge for both Washington and Beijing is to give vitality to this common long-term objective. But it also is somewhat doubtful that domestic politics in either capital, the political dynamics in the three places, and the broader strategic context will encourage the required accommodations. To use the metaphor Richard Solomon employed at the American Assembly program held in 1980 solely in reference to Taiwan, the three locales remain time bombs in Sino-American relations.

Notes

[1] The wellsprings of Chinese foreign policy are traced in Hunt (1996); see also Robinson and Shambaugh (1994).

[2] See in particular G. Wills (1993); see also Schlesinger (1992).

[3] This section draws on several authors: Clough (1978); Gold (1986); Tien (1996); Tucker (1994); Wackman (1994); J. Wills (1974).

4 See Brzezinski (1985); Kissinger (1979); Ross (1995).

5 On the history of Tibet, see Avendon (1984); Fletcher (1978); Goldstein (1989); Grunfield (1987); Richardson (1984); Stein (1972); Welch (1968). Avendon and Grunfield detail the longstanding ties of the Dalai Lama and his immediate family with the Kuomintang and the CIA in the 1950s and 1960s.

6 Fletcher (1978), p. 101.

7 Fletcher (1978), pp. 101–102.

8 On Hong Kong, see Ching (1984, 1996) and Segal (1993).

9 Ching (1996).

2

China and the East Asian Security Environment: Complementarity and Competition

DOUGLAS H. PAAL

S ince the precipitous decline of China's traditional imperial system in the early nineteenth century, Asia has lacked a political
and security system that is stabilizing, durable, indigenous, and regional. The huge shift in global financial and trade flows to Asia over
the past few decades has occurred in a largely stable environment
enforced by the patchwork cold war balance-of-power system managed by the United States.

Today the scale of Asia's economic achievement and the end of
the cold war are feeding the pride of Asian peoples and prompting
a reexamination of the world in which they find themselves. Prag-
matists, they are not eager to throw out the existing system in the

DOUGLAS H. PAAL is president of the Asia Pacific Policy Center, a newly
formed institution in Washington, D.C., promoting trade and investment
as well as defense and security ties across the Pacific. Prior to forming the
center, Mr. Paal was special assistant to President Bush for national security affairs and senior director for Asian affairs on the National Security
Council. Mr. Paal has served in the U.S. embassies in Singapore and Beijing as well as on the State Department Policy Planning Staff and as a senior analyst for the CIA.

hope that something better will turn up. Nevertheless, throughout Asia the search for new regional organizing principles is palpable.

China's reemergence is both a reflection of and an impetus for this regional reawakening. As the central feature of the Asian landscape, with the largest population and armed forces, cultural and ethnic links with most of its neighbors, and a turbulent modern history, China stirs ambivalent feelings throughout the region.

Asia Responds to China's Rise

Although China today is focused more on its internal concerns than on its external influence, little extrapolation of current trends is required to foresee a day soon when China's economic and military influence will be felt strongly throughout the region. Tensions with Taiwan periodically serve as reminders of the potential downside of a rising China, and thus Asian policy planners everywhere are increasingly seeking to position their national policies to account for greater Chinese power.

Adding to the uncertainties of the region's calculations about the future are lingering concerns about U.S. staying power. Having seen colonial powers come and go, the hasty U.S. departure from Indochina in the 1970s, and the continuing debate in the United States about its presence in Asia, the region's leaders are naturally reluctant to accept verbal assurances at face value. They are constantly looking for concrete signs of a commitment by the only outside major power trusted widely or, as some say, least disliked—the United States.

Simply put, singly and collectively, Asia's other nation states are not weighty enough to offset China; only the United States can bring about a balance of power that permits them vital freedom of maneuver among diplomatic, political, and economic options. The balance-of-power concept that permeates the region, however, is not one that assumes that China will necessarily become a menace. Rather it is intended to serve as a hedge or an insurance policy against the possibility that China might become confrontational. This perspective introduces subtleties in the region's calculations that Americans often need time to understand. Asians want to cultivate a strong U.S. stake in the region, but they prefer not to take precautionary steps that might inadvertently or prematurely signal hostile intent toward China. For this reason, for example, Thailand and the Philippines turned down Clinton administration proposals to pre-position war materials for regional contingencies. Yet they continue to welcome joint military exercises and other defense cooperation with the United States and others.

Given the swing position occupied by the United States in the region's calculations, the conduct of American policy toward China and the region is obviously a matter of vital interest to each of the region's states. Yet all too often, U.S. policy has moved in fits and starts, reducing the long-term effectiveness of the American role and denying the United States the commercial, political, and security advantages that a more coherent approach would deliver.

American "mood swings" with regard to China can be documented by a simple look at the covers of major news and business journals over the years. Somehow the United States tends to be either too warm or too cold, alternately predicting booms and busts. A major achievement on the path to an effective policy toward China would be a deliberate effort to narrow the range of these mood swings, being neither too optimistic nor too pessimistic, but realistic about the promise and problems of U.S. ties to Beijing.

Affecting China's Behavior

From the perspective of bilateral U.S.–China relations, the end of the cold war and the lag of China's political reform behind economic reform have brought into question the previous rationale for close Sino-American ties. It is the contention of this chapter, however, that while the challenges posed by China's potential are great, the opportunity to shape that potential is at least equally great. To position the United States for maximum effectiveness requires an integrated regional strategy.

The Clinton administration has variously characterized its policy toward China as "engagement," "constructive engagement," and "comprehensive engagement." The East Asian Strategy Review of 1994, produced by the Department of Defense under then Assistant Secretary Joseph Nye, amplified the Clinton administration's approach. The Nye report offered welcome assurances to the region concerning U.S. staying power and introduced the notion of hedging against the possibility that events in China could prove damaging for regional stability.

Unfortunately, however, conflicting rhetoric and shifting priorities marked the practice of U.S. diplomacy in the region in the early 1990s more notably than did the Nye report. This was also reflected in squabbling between the executive and legislative branches during previous administrations. The conclusion of the 1996 election year is an opportune moment to suggest how U.S. policy toward China and the region might be better articulated and integrated.

Complementarity and Competition

Americans understandably have a difficult time reconciling their nation's idealism with balance-of-power notions that they identify with the wasting European struggles their immigrant forefathers fled. After all, the United States achieved great power status without having to fight a cataclysmic war with its neighbors, something all other great powers have undergone. Lacking powerful neighbors to resist their rise, Americans have felt that their "exceptionalism" is something natural.

History, however, teaches that major conflicts are more the norm. The challenge thus becomes to learn from history and to temper American feelings of exceptionalism while managing the inevitable rise of China to great power status in a manner that avoids war. The explicit goal is to integrate China constructively and fully into the activities of the international community, thus deterring China from seeking to obtain its goals through the use of force. The means to do so can be summed up in a search for complementarity among Sino–U.S. interests and the development of mechanisms to contain the two nations' natural competition in constructive channels.

Elements of a Coherent Asia Strategy

Most of the elements that make up a coherent security strategy to integrate China while avoiding the necessity to deter have been present in the activities undertaken during the last six U.S. administrations. These include a strong network of U.S. bilateral alliances in the region; forward deployed forces adequate to meet most contingencies and reserves capable of meeting the rest; international diplomatic and financial institutions, such as the Asia Pacific Economic Cooperation (APEC) organization and the World Bank; new subregional forums for security cooperation, such as the Association of Southeast Asian Nations (ASEAN) Regional Forum (ARF); and strong mutual interests in trade, investment, nonproliferation, the environment, and other transnational issues. Moreover, trends toward globalization in finance, communications, manufacturing, and other fields constitute a major resource in a strategy of enhancing the complementarity of Chinese and American interests.

U.S. allies and friends in the region are an extraordinarily robust group of nations with, by and large, effective governance and reasonably complementary interests in stability, economic growth, and expanding political freedoms. They are also, however, extraordinarily diverse nations, very far from approaching the homogeneity of the European Union, for example. This diversity presents challenges to any effort at leadership, because any nation in that role must find ways to appeal to the wide range of interests involved.

The Future Can Be Bright

To scan the recent headlines of America's press, one would conclude that the record of U.S. interaction with China is essentially a failure. China's human rights situation is described as worse than at any time since the Tiananmen massacre of 1989. Beijing is accused of exporting the precursors of chemical weapons, the manufacturing components of nuclear weapons, and conventional weapons to dangerous parts of the globe.

Yet, though some of these charges may be more accurate than others, the media and U.S. officials often fail to point out that a great deal has also improved in China's outward and inward behavior in the nearly twenty-five years since the United States began to normalize relations with Beijing. From an Asian perspective, China has made rapid progress in modifying its behavior since the 1970s. It is now, for example, an active partner in trade and investment. China has long since ceased aiding pro-Beijing insurgencies in Southeast Asia. One is therefore led to ask: what is there to keep the United

States and its partners from making even further progress in its goals vis-à-vis China over the next twenty-five years, if it can sustain a steady policy?

Failed attempts by outsiders to bring about rapid and fundamental change in China are legion. From the seventeenth-century Jesuits to General George Marshall's mission to end the Chinese civil war, China has resisted outside demands for change. Yet China has changed. Today, for example, Beijing no longer exports revolution in Asia and Africa, as it did into the 1970s. The lives of individual Chinese are more relaxed. Career choices are up to individuals, not the state. Beijing has signed the Nuclear Non-Proliferation Treaty and joined other international regimes.

The list of the cooperative efforts the United States desires from China is not complete, but it is far more fulfilled than anyone dared predict twenty-five years ago. It is too early to despair. There is no current need to write the script for a new containment of China, and there will be no such need if U.S. strategy is effective.

The Key: Policy Management

U.S. policy most conspicuously needs effective management. The Tiananmen massacre shattered the bipartisan consensus on China, a consensus that was already frayed as the cold war ended and Americans grew more aware of China's shortcomings, often overlooked in the early years of euphoria after the opening to the Middle Kingdom. Today, unusual coalitions of left and right in the Congress have become the norm on issues related to China. Human rights advocacy and staunch anticommunism find comradeship in pressing China to reform.

Within the executive branch, for a time one had a sense of crisis *du jour* as U.S. demands on China flitted from weapons proliferation to human rights to trade abuses to Taiwan. Clearly, when all issues appear to share an equal priority, they in fact receive no priority at all. If one were asked to identify who is in charge of policy toward China, the answer would be difficult, and probably depends on the issue and the bureaucracy supervising the issue.

By mid-1996 this situation appeared to be changing, although the signs of more effective coordination were more often implied than made plain in policy. Unfortunately the previous few years of almost random U.S. demands on a broad range of fronts have made the challenge of convincing China of the United States' benign intentions more difficult. Many in China have construed the statements and actions of the U.S. government to constitute a new "containment strategy" designed to prevent China from achieving its potential, even though Washington has intended no such approach. This perception has made the task of righting the U.S. policy course that much more difficult.

Taiwan: The Need for Policy Management

On key sensitive issues, such as Taiwan in the context of U.S.–China relations, one is hard pressed to find a coherent thread in U.S. policy. The importance of careful, considered management of this issue cannot be overemphasized. The perception by China of mismanagement or, worse, active dismantlement of past, delicately negotiated U.S.–China agreements regarding Taiwan will fundamentally destabilize bilateral relations, and so upset regional and global cooperation.

The record shows that pursuit of a positive relationship between Washington and Beijing is the foundation for improving Washington's ties with Taipei. But tensions on any side of this triangle are quickly reflected in the others. The 1980s progress in cross-Strait trade and other interaction was built on a sound U.S. strategic approach to China through the 1970s and 1980s. Since then, the breakdown of the bipartisan consensus on China has rapidly helped to build distrust and suspicion in the Taiwan–U.S.–China triangle. The path to constructive adjustment to new democratic, economic, and other realities in Taiwan, as many now call for, begins with a comprehensive adjustment and improvement of U.S.–China ties.

Regional Leadership and High-Level Communication

Fifty years of post–World War II experience have accustomed Asia to American diplomatic leadership. The moral and economic leadership that Americans also assume is theirs is under question in Asian minds, however, as a consequence of what is regarded as human rights "preaching" and the region's own economic success. But in terms of regional security, the United States still looms large in Asia. After all, with the collapse of the Soviet empire, the United States has achieved a kind of benign global hegemony, one that must remain benign and not intrusive if it is to stand.

The key to managing the region and fostering greater cooperation, including with China, is Washington's coordination of its own internal policy making and its projection of a sense of priorities to the region. Asia is prepared to accept rational, consultative American leadership. It is not ready, however, to risk a future abutting a more powerful China aggravated by American policy whims and emotional reactions. Asians expect a coherent approach from their outside security partner. Barring that, they will be forced to assign greater priority to China's desires and concerns than they would otherwise prefer.

Priorities begin with high-level dialogue with China. Not since 1989 has an American president or vice president visited China. The meetings that have occurred elsewhere have been short, often ineffective, and too few. This is disappointing, especially because the diplomatic record reveals that early, high-level presentations to China of American policies have helped to mold Chinese behavior for the past twenty-five years. In effect, by presenting to China's leaders the United States' strategic view of the world, Washington helped to write the "first draft" of Chinese foreign policy. If Washington does not start the process, another player will. The Clinton administration's agreement in principle to exchange state visits during 1997–98 is an important step in the right direction; it should be carried out in fact, with a concerted effort to chart America's vision of cooperation with China.

Human rights also rank high in U.S. priorities. But it is time to ask: what is the first human right? One activist suggests that the first human right is the right not to be incinerated in war. If true, this argues for a strong security policy ahead of, say, the release of dissident political activists imprisoned in China, although that cause should not be abandoned. In effect, this idea came to be recognized in the aftermath of the Taiwan confrontation in March 1996, as National Security Advisor Anthony Lake embarked on a new "strategic dialogue" with Chinese officials. Signs emerged that the United

States, in order to arrest the downward slide in relations, was beginning to mute official public expressions of displeasure or threat concerning a variety of Chinese actions. Setbacks to human rights and other issues are now being compartmentalized, so that progress in other areas, such as nonproliferation, can still continue. The point here is not to determine what issues should occupy which rank among American priorities, but to say that some priorities must be established and adhered to if a coherent and effective policy is to be fashioned. There is an urgent need to identify responsible personnel for the overall conduct of policy toward China and Asia, and then to identify the priorities those personnel should pursue.

Long-Term Security in the Pacific

The prospects are not dim for a new security order in East Asia that accommodates an increasingly powerful China. The China of today is a nation that can develop a modern sense of equality and respect for its neighbors, rather than a traditional imperial Chinese relationship of superior and inferior or a traditional Western arrangement of hegemon and client states. The achievement of such an outcome, however, requires a steadiness of purpose and policy that would be unusual in U.S. dealings with Asia.

The Asia Pacific Region

The United States has enjoyed an enormous advantage over the years in East Asia and the Pacific in that, being a distant power, it has little or no stake in the bilateral disputes that still crisscross the region. Washington is thus in a position to enjoy better relations with each of the regional parties than they are likely to enjoy with one another. The United States briefly flirted with disaster by simultaneously picking fights over trade, human rights, and other issues with all the major states in the region. But since the Nye initiative and subsequent developments, America has returned to emphasizing improving ties, not straining them.

The economic anxiety of the American people, experienced during the long restructuring of the U.S. economy and the recession of the late 1980s and early 1990s, has declined with the current economic expansion. Americans are now less prone to seek scapegoats for their troubles in Japan, Korea, or other so-called unfair traders. Although this does not mean there are no trade and market access problems to wrestle with, it does mean that security planners are freer today to reconstruct relations in the region, improve bilateral ties, and make plans for strategic cooperation.

Japan

An essential element of a post–cold war Asian order is the continuation and evolution of the U.S. bilateral alliance structure. As Japan is encouraged—and finds the will and skill—to become a mature and normal power, bearing its share of regional responsibilities (in the political and security spheres as well as economic) commensurate with its enjoyment of the benefits of the international system, the U.S. presence may well take new and reduced forms. But the core alliance relationship, coupled with American power projection capability, is unlikely to change substantially, as seen in the joint U.S.–Japanese declaration of April 1996.

Many in China saw the signing of the declaration by President Clinton and Prime Minister Hashimoto as aimed at China, and coming as it did after tensions flared over Taiwan, there was some reason to think so. China's foreign minister flew to Tokyo to try to head off, unsuccessfully, agreement between Tokyo and Washington on language that could be interpreted to embrace concern about China. But the declaration had its origins well before the renewed tensions over Taiwan, and its essence is closer cooperation between Washington and Tokyo. This key regional security relationship, which also involves global partnership, sustains a power projection capability to deter any potential aggressor and is clearly not directed specifically at China.

China remains highly sensitive to Japan's potential to become a regional security power once again on its own. To the extent that Beijing can persuade itself that Japan's alliance with the United States forestalls what might become a "remilitarization" of Japan, the Chinese are likely to remain resigned to the alliance and America's regional presence. Japanese officials the American Assembly group spoke with in June 1996 appeared prepared for China to think along these lines, so long as this perspective is not the formal justification for the alliance.

Korea

The U.S. alliance with Korea, since its inception in 1953, has successfully deterred a new outbreak of war on the peninsula. The Republic of Korea is an enormous political and economic success story as well, even producing a bilateral U.S. trade surplus in recent years. The alliance, however, suffers from a variety of strains that will become more obvious once reunification of the peninsula is achieved. At the same time multiple factors—underlying regional tensions in Northeast Asia, America's interest in protecting its growing stake in the region and in Korea specifically, and the Korean people's undeniable desire to have the means and the alliances necessary to guarantee genuine Korean independence—argue that on balance Korea will increasingly become an active partner in regional security affairs, lifting its gaze from its longstanding preoccupation with the division of the peninsula.

The American Assembly group's visit to Korea revealed, in conversations with academics, officials, and military leaders, that there will undoubtedly be serious difficulties in adjusting the U.S.–Korean alliance in the aftermath of reunification, however and whenever that comes. But at the same time Korea—situated as it is among disparate major powers in the region—retains a strong interest in a healthy alliance with a benign, distant power as it confronts its future. The question of the presence of U.S. forces, the missions of the alliance, and sensitivity to China's concerns about a U.S. ally on its doorstep remain to be worked out in detail. Meanwhile Seoul and Washington have a full agenda in seeking to secure a "soft landing" for North Korea's troubled economy and state and, failing that, in reducing the collateral damage, including that done to ties with China, that will result from a hard landing.

Certainly, from the U.S. point of view, two active, cooperative, bilateral alliances in Northeast Asia will provide Japan, Korea, and the rest of the region with a stabilizing counterforce to the rise of any hostile regional hegemonic power, a U.S. foreign policy priority since the nineteenth century. Moreover, two alliances are stronger than one; like sticks bundled together, they give the partners greater strength to resist domestic pressures not to cooperate and greater voice in the region's affairs.

The modest, relatively low-level trilateral and multilateral dialogues that have so far addressed Japan's, China's, and Russia's interests in a changing Korea need to be increased in pace and level of official involvement. The "two plus two" formula for Beijing and Pyongyang to talk with Seoul and Washington could be a start, but should be pushed harder on Pyongyang. If the talks get started, Russia and Japan should be closely involved, and formally included at the earliest possible time.

U.S.–South Korea consultations on the human, economic, and security consequences of Korean reunification should be increased, in the process reassuring China of U.S. intentions and containing the impact of problems such as hunger and refugee flows following the possible collapse of the North. China's tendency not to want to talk about North Korea's internal situation should be addressed. Senior American officials should press Beijing to open up, noting that China's calculations about the North appear to be changing, given recent substantially increased Chinese aid to Pyongyang.

The president ought to consider appointing a special emissary to oversee the many aspects of U.S. interests in the evolving Korean situation. A principal function of such an emissary would be to engage the Chinese constructively in managing the humanitarian and arms control issues that will follow a collapse of the North, in addition to facilitating an international conference to guarantee reunified Korea's security.

Russia

The weakness of Russia today and its return to strength tomorrow affect regional calculations of security. Moscow's military capabilities in the Far East, though substantially depleted from cold war levels, are still formidable. Effective governance cannot be said to have been fully restored to Russia, but it seems likely that the period of greatest weakness in control over the Far East has passed, removing for now the danger of a regional rush to fill a power vacuum there.

It is to be hoped that the successful development of democracy in Russia will temper Moscow's relations with its Eastern neighbors. But even that cannot be assured. Serious territorial issues are unresolved, and those that are being resolved now, during Russia's weakest moment, may be a source of resentment later on.

It was in this context of relative weakness, during President Boris Yeltsin's state visit to China in May 1996, that he elicited from his Chinese hosts an assertion of their "strategic partnership." Both China and Russia eyed the U.S.–Japan Joint Declaration in April as potentially aimed at them, or perhaps more accurately as a sign that Washington and Tokyo were not taking them as seriously as they would like. The hint of "strategic" cooperation that they gave should, therefore, be viewed more as a tactical wake-up call than as the harbinger of a new alliance.

China and Russia at present have certain complementary interests. China has an interest in extracting as many concessions and as much weaponry and technology as Russia will sell it during this down period for Moscow. So, too, Russia wants to keep customers for its ailing arms industries and a market for other products, so long as Russian national security is not sacrificed. In the final analysis, however, there appear to be firm limits on how far these former adversaries will go to cement their relationship.

It is unlikely that the United States will enter into arms sales to China in competition with Russia, and probably inadvisable in any case. But the apparent need of Russia and China to show their dissatisfaction with their treatment by Washington indicates an opportunity for U.S. policy. The watchword should be to pursue relations with each that are better than they are likely to have with each other.

U.S. policy toward China and Russia currently shows a significant imbalance. Russia is accorded greater respect, such as quasi membership in the G-7 grouping and exchanges of state visits, notwithstanding the horrors in Chechnya and economic failings. China feels slighted, despite its perception of its economic success, its relaxation of certain social controls, and its repeated cooperation with the West, because of Tiananmen and subsequent human rights abuses. The "strategic dialogue" initiated by Anthony Lake offers a path out of this contradiction.

Southeast Asia

The states of Southeast Asia are a diverse lot, with great differences in per capita gross national product and political systems. They diverge less, however, when it comes to policy toward China. Most of these countries would seem large indeed if they could somehow be dropped into the middle of Europe. Indonesia, Thailand, and Malaysia all have sizable populations and rapidly growing GNPs. But set against the profile of China, they seem quite small, and often feel that way. Each state has its own tradition of compliance or defiance or a mixture of the two in its policy toward China. All, at some point, were viewed by China as subordinate in its traditional view of the region.

China has also had ties with Communist and other insurgent groups in the area. But one of China's great success stories is the way it has ended its support of Southeast Asian insurgencies and forged effective, mutually profitable ties in the region instead. Overseas Chinese citizens of these countries often served as a vanguard in those efforts.

Yet China's relations with the region have recently seesawed. On the one hand, the discovery in early 1995 of Chinese occupation of a reef in the Spratley Islands claimed by the Philippines triggered regionwide concern that China was not prepared to honor its previous commitment to settle disputed claims by dialogue rather than by preemptive action. On the other hand, U.S. mismanagement of its relations with Taiwan put the same states in an awkward position, because they could not support U.S. actions with respect to Taiwan that they viewed as clumsy and counterproductive. For example, the Southeast Asian leaders had successively hosted visits by Taiwan's leaders on an informal basis, demonstrating good substantive, if not formal, relations. But unlike Washington, which said it was following their example in bringing Taiwan's president to the United States, they had previously cultivated their ties with Beijing in order to moderate its reaction to their improving ties with Taiwan.

As relatively small powers concerned to preserve their freedom to maneuver vis-à-vis China, the nations of Southeast Asia are prepared to accept American involvement and leadership. When the Philippine bases closed down in 1992, a new plan known as "places, not bases" was quietly put into effect in Indonesia, Singapore, and Malaysia. This approach permitted American forces to procure local services to maintain fleet and aircraft mobility and training.

A special word about Myanmar (Burma) is in order here. Owing to the 1988–89 crackdown on democracy by the military, Myanmar has been sanctioned and isolated. Unsurprisingly, this has created an opening for China, whose own record of sanction busting must have an appeal for Rangoon's rulers. China's influence has grown dramatically since then, underpinned by a huge and growing economic connection.

In years past, it was customary to say that Chinese influence could grow in Myanmar, only to be reduced eventually by an exercise of strong Burmese nationalism. Today, however, for the first time since China's vibrant eighteenth century and the era of the Qian Long emperor, China is strong enough to strike back in its own interest if Myanmar resists. In the absence of other sources of influence on the government of Myanmar, China appears headed toward a special sphere there that even nationalist passions among the Burmese may not be powerful enough to dislodge.

India and Pakistan

Frictions between the United States and China have erupted regularly since the 1980s over Beijing's sensitive dealings with Pakistan, whether involving missile transfers, unauthorized access to Western technology, or nuclear weapons. Yet at the onset of U.S.–China relations in the 1970s, cooperation in the defense of Pakistan was a strategic hallmark of the relationship.

The change since then reflects more a shift in U.S. priorities than in those of the Chinese. Beijing, despite India's loss of a strong ally in Moscow, still regards New Delhi as a potential strategic rival, a nuclear power, and a disputant over significant boundaries. To maintain a check on Indian ambitions, China has shown that it is prepared to go to great lengths to support Pakistan.

By contrast, the United States sees the decline of the Soviet Union as an opportunity to cultivate India, to wean it from a reliance on a nuclear deterrent and from the missiles to deliver it. As a consequence, the United States has repeatedly found itself in disputes with China over the latter's continuing support for Pakistan's efforts to counter India's nuclear and missile capabilities.

This region's disputes may prove to be the most vexatious to resolve in U.S.–China relations, partly because its physical remoteness from the United States makes it more susceptible to larger doses of American ideology than realpolitik. Moreover, the two major parties to the dispute are extremely unwilling to climb down from uncompromising positions.

From a U.S. policy perspective, here as elsewhere it may be wiser to start from a basis of better bilateral relations with China than to address this regional issue early on. If China discovers that it has a higher stake in sustaining good U.S.–China relations, it may then be more interested in finding solutions to the disagreements in South Asia that trouble those bilateral ties. After all, China's recent forays into sensitive transfers of technology and equipment to the region (as well as to Iran) often seem to be intended at least in part as reminders to Washington that Beijing needs to be taken seriously, and that there are consequences to not doing so.

Nonproliferation

One of the key challenges of the post–cold war era is reining in the proliferation of weapons of mass destruction. Repeatedly the U.S. and China have fallen afoul of one another over proliferation issues. Yet the record shows China slowly growing increasingly cooperative, progressing from a rejectionist stance some twenty years ago to following the U.S. as the second signatory to the Comprehensive Test Ban Treaty in 1996.

On May 11, 1996, moreover, China announced its adherence to a policy of not transferring technology and equipment to unsafeguarded nuclear facilities, ending an impasse with Washington over a sale of ring-magnets to an unsafeguarded reactor in Pakistan. What then are areas of further cooperation? First, the United States already is urging China to join a cap or ban on the production of fissile materials that goes beyond the requirements of the Nuclear Non-Proliferation Treaty (NPT). As a power with an increasing stake in stability and appetite for imported energy, not only in its immediate neighborhood but also in places like the Persian Gulf, Beijing should come to realize the benefits of restraining the rise of new nuclear weapons states that may destabilize those regions.

China's close ties to Pakistan have often constrained its willingness to cooperate in nonproliferation, as it intends to counterbalance India over the decades to come. Some Chinese have said to Americans that Pakistan is China's Israel, when it comes to nonproliferation. Yet judging from media reports, it would appear that as of now, Pakistan has enough of what it needs for China comfortably to agree to greater limits on sensitive transfers.

A second area of U.S.–China cooperation is a bilateral nuclear cooperation agreement. The American nuclear power generation industry wishes to compete for the nuclear plants that are to be built in China, but the U.S. government requires that Beijing first reach an agreement guarding against the transfer of the plants' equipment and technology. Such an agreement will in any event have difficulty receiving necessary congressional approval if continued clandestine or sensitive transfers to Pakistan, or possibly to Iran, can be demonstrated.

Since the bilateral agreement was first drafted in 1985, China has hedged about past and future cooperation with candidate nuclear weapons states. To conclude the agreement successfully, the U.S. may have to compromise by "grandfathering" China's past transfers to suspect states in exchange for a firm guarantee against new transfers. Even then, it is highly possible that China will decide the price is too high, especially in terms of its interests in Pakistan and Iran.

A third agenda item for cooperation is in the detargeting of nuclear armed intercontinental missiles, on the model of the U.S.–Russia detargeting accord. During the presidential debates in 1996, President Clinton stated that for the first time nuclear missiles are not targeted on the United States' people. But there is substantial evidence to indicate the president was only partly correct. China has a small force targeted on the U.S.

Beijing resisted, according to various Chinese informants, an early end to its underground nuclear tests in order to complete a series aimed at miniaturizing its weapons so that they could reach the U.S. on Chinese current missiles. That Beijing would do this is a reflection of its perception of comprehensive power and its great power ambitions. Now that it apparently has achieved this aspect of its ambitions and signed the Test Ban Treaty, an agreement to detarget should be possible on the basis of reciprocity. The cost of agreement by Beijing would appear to be fairly low, given that targets could be readily reassigned if a crisis subsequently developed warranting the action.

Another agenda item, less promising than those above, is encouraging China to adopt full-scope safeguards that go well beyond the constraints imposed by the safeguards of the NPT. Here again, China's interests in cooperation—under existing safeguards—with Pakistan and Iran are the problem. Beijing sees its cooperation there as serving several purposes: reminding the U.S. of China's importance and its need to be taken seriously, guaranteeing future energy flows, and restraining radical Islam on Chinese territory. An effort to move to full-scope safeguards will have to recognize these motivations.

Also worthy but not yet promising is an effort to put China's chemical weapons technologies under safeguards like those of the full-scope version of the NPT. The U.S. Senate recently rejected the Chemical Weapons Convention over its intrusiveness; all the more China sees the expanded pervasive requirements of an expanded full-scope approach as too much. This goal should not be abandoned, however, in view of the agreements China has reached, like the Comprehensive Test Ban Treaty, which previously seemed impossible.

Finally, one new area of cooperation with China deserves to be pushed forward on the agenda as overall relations improve. Given China's complex and enduring relationship with Pakistan, it has enormous leverage with Islamabad, something the U.S. has diminished in recent years. A shrewd approach would be to encourage

China to use its leverage to press Pakistan to subscribe to full-scope safeguards. Conceivably, this could be linked to the U.S.–China bilateral Nuclear Cooperation Agreement, but the current state of U.S.–China relations may not be strong enough to bear the burden of Pakistan's full-scope safeguards at the same time.

Persistence has paid dividends in the nonproliferation arena with China, even though the struggle seems constant. If negotiators show due regard for China's interests and respect the principle of reciprocity, workable agreements are possible. Realism dictates, however, that the United States probably will not be able to forestall China from acquiring capabilities before it agrees to limit them. The goal, therefore, should be tailored to helping China realize the costs to itself of not limiting the spread of weapons of mass destruction.

Peace in the Pacific

This outline for peace in the Pacific suggests a continuation of, not a departure from, the successful but incomplete process of integration of China into the region's and globe's affairs pursued since the 1970s. It offers an opportunity for the Chinese people to rise from the humiliations they experienced at the hands of foreigners when China was weak, without the devastating costs of confronting them directly now that China is stronger.

The U.S. alliance structure, "places, not bases" in Southeast Asia, and U.S. unofficial security guarantees that Taiwan's status not be resolved by force, all create the preconditions for increased interaction with China. With this system providing the region's fundamental security, and with continued rapid economic growth, the prospects are bright for acknowledging China's right to speak on an increasing number of issues. In exchange, the United States and the region will continue to expect China to acknowledge its neighbors' and global interests.

In becoming stronger, China will continue to build a leaner and more capable military force. It has acquired and appears ready to acquire more SU-27 fighters from Russia. With some foreign assistance, Beijing is completing an indigenous fighter bomber. In the aftermath of the Taiwan tensions and disputes over the South

China Sea and Senkaku/Diaoyu islands, experts expect an increase in China's naval budget and force structure.

Throughout the Asia Pacific region, old weapons systems are being replaced, and in doing so, planners must ask themselves what threats they will face during the lifetime of the systems they are to acquire—twenty years or more. Thus China's intentions and capabilities over the next two decades are very practical considerations in current decision making.

Nothing would turn the present situation of deliberate military modernization into one of an all-out arms race faster than U.S. abdication of its security role in the Pacific. Perceptions of American staying power are constantly being exchanged throughout the region.

The regional security structure will evolve. The United States will make adjustments in the U.S. presence even as the "revolution in military affairs" through information technology renders the U.S. more powerful globally. U.S. allies will be expected gradually to increase their regional roles, at a pace acceptable to the region generally. And China can contribute to regional stability by increasing the transparency of its capabilities, something that tradition and current convenience resist.

New Multilateral Dialogues

To achieve a balance between needed military modernization and increasing regional missions on the one hand, and reduction of post–cold war tensions and continued regional prosperity on the other, greater multilateral security arrangements are required. These must be built on the only foundation available: America's bilateral alliances and access arrangements in the region. Taken together, they form an implicit counter force to any major threat to the region's stability and peace. Their readiness to cooperate reflects an intention to deny the option of force to those who would be willing to use it.

This loose coalition, whose principal member in the region is Japan, however, is not capable of sustaining an aggressive posture or maintaining a strategy of containment in the absence of a clear threat, which is not now perceived. Nonetheless, questions about

China's intentions with respect to the region have been raised over the past two years, after Chinese actions in the Spratley Islands, tensions with Taiwan and over the Senkaku/Diaoyu islands. Public attitudes toward China in Japan, for example, have become significantly more skeptical than before.

This is precisely why new multilateral institutions need to be built on the foundation of American alliances and access arrangements, so that China will have additional opportunities to demonstrate the benign and cooperative behavior it says is its policy. The Asia Pacific Economic Cooperation forum allows China and the seventeen other members to demonstrate progress toward freer markets in the region over the coming decades, and in the process for the leaders to meet and get to know each other.

The ASEAN Regional Forum includes all the major powers in the Pacific specifically to discuss security issues. It offers an opportunity for China to familiarize itself with the benefits of transparency (or openness about military capabilities). Because the members of the ARF are ministers of foreign affairs, and not defense officials, there is room for an additional forum for military-to-military regional dialogue. This appears too sensitive and official for now for China, but perhaps a private group could first invite military in their individual capacity from throughout the region to a dialogue on regional security issues, on the model of the *Wehrkunde* conferences held annually in Germany to discuss European security.

Finally, Northeast Asia cries out for a six-party forum that can address the very significant security issues there. The U.S., China, Japan, Russia, and the two Koreas dispose enormous power in the subregion, notably with more than a million troops under arms along Korea's demilitarized zone. The ARF has too many non-players to speak with authority on Northeast Asian issues. Building on policy toward the security of the Korean Peninsula, such a six-party forum could move on to address other matters such as conflicting territorial claims, seabed resources, and arms control.

The prospects for bilateral U.S.–China cooperation will brighten as the two sides work at disentangling themselves from thorny issues such as weapons proliferation, trade disputes, and human rights controversies. Given the different levels of development of the two societies in so many dimensions, resolution of these issues will require patient and persistent efforts. Short-term solutions—the stuff of headlines and congressional resolutions as well as of Chinese demands and "hurt feelings"—are particularly unwise and inappropriate. This is a long-term transition requiring long-term methods.

Success in this process of China's emergence may also require a reevaluation of the skills and experience of the Americans selected to manage relations with Asia. The modern tradition that emphasizes a strong record in arms control and European and Soviet affairs for advancement in foreign policy circles is clearly not enough for responsibility in the region that is the fastest growing—both economically and in terms of population—in the world. In an arena where personal relationships are key, extensive familiarity and experience are required.

America's best days are ahead. The revolution in military affairs underway in the U.S. armed forces, the restructuring of the American economy, painfully endured during the Bush administration and bearing fruit under President Clinton, and the risk/reward structure of the American system all militate toward a continuation of U.S. global dominance. Technological leaps presage greater American power with each passing year at ever lower cost to the taxpayer. The information revolution is an American hallmark.

If the United States can sustain its focus on key objectives in dealing with China and Asia, it possesses the other attributes of power to produce results that will buoy U.S. might and influence. From time to time, tensions will emerge. Voices will warn ominously that China should not be "provoked." Yet to some degree, tensions and perceived provocation will be necessary and inevitable components of a policy intended to dissuade China and others from counterproductive paths, even as the United States emphasizes cooperative integration and complementarity over competition.

China, moreover, has an established record of often truculent entry into bilateral and multilateral arrangements. Jealous of its sovereignty and possessed of a weak nation's fear of victimization combined with a great nation's pride and ambition, China can be a difficult partner. Beijing, for example, agreed to abide by the rules of the Missile Technology Control Regime only after repeated confrontations and sanctions, arguing (correctly) that it had been excluded from the regime's creation. In the ASEAN Regional Forum, too, China's behavior appears intended to minimize cooperation multilaterally, favoring bilateral approaches that take advantage of its relative size, or postponing issues such as territorial disputes to a later time when Beijing presumably expects to be in a much stronger position to assert its claims. When the United States confronts bluster, efforts to trade today on tomorrow's greatness, and manipulative hurt feelings, it needs to take a breath before reacting and remember that China will likely be at most a source of "problems" for America, not a "threat." And problems can be fixed.

With a coordinated will to seek the integration of China into the region and the globe, deterrence should prove to be—more often than not—only a latent aspect of U.S. and regional policy toward China. If integration fails, however, deterrence will be required to preserve the enormous regional successes of the post–World War II period. Again, the past is prologue; twenty-five years of more success than failure argues for another twenty-five years of effort.

3

A Growing China in a Shrinking World: Beijing and the Global Order

DAVID M. LAMPTON

The United States will not have the basis for a sound China policy if it does not develop a historical, global, and developmentally grounded perspective on China that geographically embraces the People's Republic of China, Taiwan, and Hong Kong and looks ahead to the next quarter century.

DAVID M. LAMPTON has been president of the National Committee on United States–China Relations since 1988. Prior to assuming that position, he was associate professor of political science at Ohio State University and director of China Policy Studies at the American Enterprise Institute. Dr. Lampton has lived and conducted research in the People's Republic of China, Hong Kong, and Taiwan. His research addresses bureaucratic and elite politics in China, U.S.–China relations, and Chinese foreign policy. His articles have appeared widely, including *Foreign Affairs*, *Foreign Policy*, *The American Political Science Review*, and *The China Quarterly*. Among his recent books and edited volumes are *Paths to Power: Elite Mobility in Contemporary China* (with Yeung Sai-cheung), *Bureaucracy, Politics, and Decision Making in Post-Mao China* (with Kenneth Lieberthal), and *United States and China Relations at a Crossroads* (with Alfred Wilhelm). He has testified before House and Senate committees on U.S.–China relations. The views expressed in this chapter are Dr. Lampton's own.

America's principal objectives in its relationship with the People's Republic should be the avoidance of a second cold war, the maintenance of regional stability, and the maximization of benefits from economic and other cooperation. These priorities can best be achieved by building and maintaining a productive bilateral relationship with Beijing and by China's early and full involvement in the principal institutions and global norms of world governance—the latter being the principal subject of this chapter. These goals cannot be realized by Washington alone or without Beijing's cooperation, but they should be the object of U.S. policy.

To feel comfortable with such comprehensive involvement on China's part, Americans must gain confidence that the People's Republic will play a constructive role and seek only gradual change through its participation in international institutions and their norms. Similarly, China will need to feel confident that the United States will treat it fairly, make room for its participation, and also take account of its special circumstances. China's involvement (on an equitable and nondisruptive basis) in the global order is a key, perhaps the key, issue confronting the international community today, and will remain so for some time. China could gain international support by articulating its view of the world that is emerging at the close of the twentieth century and describing in compelling and reassuring fashion the role it foresees for itself.

It is not yet fully clear that China accepts this vision or that the United States and others will make the accommodations and exercise the patience necessary to move along this path. Indeed, China has a latent fear that "integration" means "Westernization," the erosion of Chinese identity and acceptance of U.S. dominance. As one Chinese interlocutor put it to us in the June 1996 American Assembly trip to the region: "China is most concerned with its own internal development and the United States is most concerned with trying to maintain international order. Therefore, our agendas are different." The Chinese and American agendas are somewhat different, in part, because China is not yet a truly global power with comprehensive global interests. Consequently, Beijing currently has less of a perceived stake in the full range of institutions and global norms that the United States supports. But this situation is changing and will continue to do so.

When Westerners, particularly Americans, speak of China's rise and the need for its participation in global institutions and the accepted rules of the game, they tend to use two formulations, neither of which is very congenial to Chinese ears or likely to be very successful. The first formulation is that China "must play by international rules and norms" if it is to be a full partner in international organizations. For the Chinese, this statement immediately provokes concern. Who wrote the rules? What is the difference between legitimate international norms and international law, on the one hand, and the policy preferences of the currently dominant powers, on the other? Will those rules be adapted in order to take account of Chinese characteristics? The second formulation says that China must be "integrated" into the international order. Here China again fears that it will be acted upon and changed, with the burdens of conforming to developed country standards falling upon it alone.

Although it is essential that international bodies and the global norms they include not have their mandates and purposes subverted in the process of negotiating China's entry or compliance, a more productive approach nonetheless would be to ask: how can China and current international organizations mutually adapt to each other in order to bring about productive cooperation with the least cost and disruption to the global system?

China's rise as a global power, the increasing impact of its activities on the world beyond its borders, and Beijing's own desire for global status and prestige all mean that if world organizations and global norms are to be effective, they will need Chinese participation, and that China itself will be desirous of playing an ever greater role in them. China's entry into these institutions of global governance, however, raises four generic questions for China and the rest of the world community. First, what are the rules by which China is to abide, who writes them, and who interprets the strictures? Given its history, China frequently has not been instrumental in writing the rules it is now asked to observe. Second, is China a unique case (because of its size, if nothing else) and should preexistent organizations adapt to take account of this? If so, what degree of flexibility is desirable and sustainable, given that many other countries will seek entrance after China, each of which will demand terms of entry that take its predecessors' arrangements as the place from which negotiations begin? Third, what are the appropriate means or incentives by which international organizations enforce their rules? Are some methods, such as sanctions and military/peacekeeping operations, appropriate and consistent with state sovereignty? Fourth, what debt (if any) do the early industrialized countries owe late modernizers like China? For instance, should China bear all the costs of meeting current environmental standards when the early industrializers produced the situation whereby the earth's capacity to absorb pollution is so diminished? On what terms should environmental technology be transferred to later modernizers, and what intellectual property rights should govern the use of such technologies?

Global Interdependence, Sovereignty, and Responsibility

Adapting to the demands placed on sovereign states by transnational regimes, international governmental and nongovernmental organizations, and global markets is painful, takes time, and is not unique to China. One Chinese foreign policy advisor commented to the American Assembly group in June 1996 that China is still a "learner" in international organizations, not yet a "full partner," and it is therefore difficult to reconcile the demands of institutions of global governance with "China's national interests" in all cases.

The United States too is going through difficult adaptations to the demands of global institutions, international law, multinational companies, and transnational financial networks and the loss of exclusive national decision-making power associated with them. That this is painful is seen in attacks by some Americans against the World Trade Organization (WTO), the North American Free Trade Agreement (NAFTA), and the United Nations. The American attraction to the notion of world peace through world law is offset by a strong coexisting sentiment in favor of unilateralism. Washington has chosen not to sign several important international human rights, environmental, and weapons conventions, including the 1982 U.N. Convention on the Law of the Sea, a measure that would be helpful in Washington's disputes with Beijing over international shipping lanes in the South and East China Seas. In February 1996 then-presidential candidate Patrick Buchanan tapped into these sentiments by blasting multinational organizations, saying, "These institutions of the new world order . . . [make] the world's greatest superpower the equal of Cuba, Bangladesh and Burundi."

Interdependence calls for mutual adjustments. From 1970 to 1990 American jobs in manufacturing fell by about 300,000, the first such decline in U.S. history. This drop was the result of several developments, including the massive relocation of manufacturing investment abroad, reduced global transportation costs, the diffusion of technology and manufacturing processes, and lower trade barriers resulting from the General Agreement on Tariffs and Trade (GATT) and the WTO. In 1995 Jeffrey Madrick observed in *The End of Affluence* that "economic insecurity has spread across working America, no matter one's ethnic origin or education." The same forces of economic globalization that are giving rise to increasing insecurity and a sense of sovereignty lost in America are fueling growing nationalist and populist sentiment worldwide—Russia being a prime example. These insecurities and the accompanying potential for populist appeals and rising nationalism have great force in today's People's Republic.

China's Participation in International Institutions and Regimes

In light of the problems of adaptation and global trends, compounded by the historical experience of the Chinese people with diminutions of their sovereignty as a result of foreign penetration in the second half of the nineteenth century and the first half of the twentieth, what is most surprising is how far China has come in joining worldwide institutions and in taking part in agreed-upon rules. In 1977, the year before adopting the reform and open policy, China was part of twenty-one international governmental organizations (IGOs) and seventy-one international nongovernmental organizations (INGOs); by 1994 China had joined fifty IGOs (two more than Russia) and 955 INGOs. Between 1977 and 1988 China signed 125 multilateral treaties, whereas in the preceding twenty-seven years it had signed only twenty-three.

After joining the Bretton Woods institutions of the World Bank and International Monetary Fund (IMF) in 1980, for example, Beijing became an active participant in the governance of these organizations and was the largest recipient of multilateral assistance in the world by the end of the decade. In addition, in November 1984 China was granted permanent observer status in the GATT and applied to join the organization (now the WTO) in July 1986, though its accession negotiations continue with no end in sight (only Bulgaria has been waiting for accession longer). Key points of contention are China's desire for longer transition times in order to protect its economy than the G-7 countries seem willing to provide and for permanent most-favored-nation (MFN) treatment from the United States. Other issues include China's partial or noncompliance with previous commercial agreements and the development of new nontariff barriers as old obstacles are removed, the need for a unitary trade regime, safeguards against Chinese export surges, Beijing's industrial policies, forced technology transfer, rights to engage in trade, access to China's market in services, and agricultural exports to the PRC. In addition, there are roughly twenty-six other nations and areas that have also applied to join WTO, and the terms of Beijing's entry will set a pattern for many of the applicants that follow.

China joined the International Atomic Energy Agency in 1984. It ratified the Non-Proliferation Treaty (NPT) in March 1992 (in the process overturning its long-held opposition to the pact as discriminatory), and Beijing supported the treaty's permanent extension in 1995. Indeed, during the 1982–1992 period, China ratified or acceded to seven of the then-eleven multilateral arms control agreements, though its participation was usually reluctant and calculated to least constrain Chinese military development. In March 1992 Beijing agreed in writing (and reaffirmed its agreement in October 1994) to observe the guidelines and parameters of the Missile Technology Control Regime (MTCR). Earlier, in 1986, China had pledged to observe the Limited Test Ban Treaty, and Beijing agreed to the Comprehensive Test Ban Treaty (CTB) in late 1996. Beijing announced the suspension of further nuclear tests in July 1996.

Beijing was one of the first to sign the Biodiversity Treaty (which the United States has not ratified). With respect to the Montreal

Protocol on Ozone-Depleting Substances (founded 1987), as Jessica Poppele reports, China ratified its participation in June 1991 and since that time has "championed the ODS phase-out campaign."[1]

In the area of human rights, China has signed eight international conventions. In 1992 Premier Li Peng said that "China agrees that questions concerning human rights should be the subject of normal international discussion."[2]

But Chinese citizenship in these institutions and its adherence to various treaties and agreements had been uneven. In general, China's compliance and "citizenship" have been best in organizations where it has been deeply involved in writing the rules and where the international community has made tangible economic inputs to assist China in whatever transition is required. Beijing's citizenship has been less praiseworthy in areas where it has not been a member or has not had a role in drafting the rules or interpreting them, where the international community has not made economic inputs to assist it, and where compliance would harm powerful domestic political or economic interests.

With respect to the United Nations, however, China has cast only three vetoes in open session in the Security Council since 1972, though it has blocked votes in closed sessions; the United States cast sixteen vetoes from 1987 to 1990 alone. China has adopted the method of articulating its position on controversial items and then abstaining if its views cannot prevail. Beijing is especially reluctant to support affirmatively the imposition of economic sanctions, believing that such acts violate sovereignty and that its support for such actions would legitimate measures that have from time to time been imposed on it by others, principally Washington. Despite misgivings about prosecuting the war in the Gulf in 1991 and the Somalian operation thereafter, China either supported or abstained on votes on key Security Council resolutions with respect to these undertakings. These votes, however, were not without their price: a White House meeting and an agreement by the United States not to oppose expanded World Bank loans to Beijing.

In the area of peacekeeping operations, China has sent peacekeepers to the Middle East, Namibia, and Cambodia, where it lost two soldiers. Given the stated reluctance of the Chinese to intervene in the internal affairs of other nations, such participation has been a significant departure from Beijing's past preferences.

In the World Bank, China has been a very good citizen, being the largest borrower, possessing an unblemished record of repayment, and acting as a buffer between the bank's developing nation clients and its developed nation funders. In their 1990 work, *China's Participation in the IMF, the World Bank, and GATT,* Harold Jacobson and Michel Oksenberg comment that China has "played an important role in resolving a North-South confrontation." Generally China has completed planned projects in accordance with agreements, provided extensive statistical data, and shown remarkable receptivity to bank advice. Jacobson and Oksenberg conclude that "the Chinese posture has been to facilitate the work of the World Bank and International Monetary Fund by espousing and adhering to their norms." Similarly, China has proved a good citizen of the Asian Development Bank (ADB), becoming the ADB's largest borrower and working out a formula for Taipei's participation. With respect to the IMF, China has benefited greatly from advice and standby credits during periods of economic retrenchment, high inflation, and foreign exchange difficulty, repaying its first credit tranche early in 1994.

China's record of compliance with international multilateral agreements and promises in the areas of human rights and arms sales/technology transfer, however, has been less pristine. Chinese adherence to the Convention against Torture and Other Cruel, Inhuman, or Degrading Treatment or Punishment has been regularly breached, and Beijing's (frequently secret) alleged and actual transfers of nuclear and missile technology to Pakistan, Iran, and others have pushed NPT and MTCR requirements to the limit, if not beyond. Aside from the money to be made and Beijing's desire to woo countries it deems strategically important, two other factors appear to underlie some military weapons and technology sales— first, the domestic clout of the military and others who are not fully coordinated with China's foreign policy apparatus, and second, the absence of an effective export control mechanism. It is understood that a high-level central coordinating group has been established in Beijing to bring some order to this aspect of Chinese policy and behavior. More broadly, China's agreement to join the NPT represents a major shift in thinking about security, moving toward the recognition that security cannot be achieved solely through unilateral action. China's agreement to the CTB in late 1996 signals an even larger step in this direction. Winston Lord, assistant secretary of state in the Clinton administration, in 1996 put Chinese arms control and nonproliferation behavior in historical perspective: "Even in an area like nonproliferation, where we have great difficulties, if you look at China's position now versus 10 or 15 years ago when they were saying nuclear weapons were good for you, in effect, they have come a long way."[3]

With respect to the Missile Technology Control Regime, it is important to understand what it is, and is not, and the Chinese perspective on this combustible issue in U.S.–China relations. The MTCR is not a treaty; it is an agreement among twenty-five member supplier states, of which China is not one. The MTCR pertains only to missiles, not to other categories of weapons capable of delivering the means of mass destruction. The states that are party to the agreement use their own domestic legal systems to determine how to respond to missile exports in contravention of the regime. The essence of the Chinese critique of the MTCR is that the member countries decide what the parameters governing exports are, interpret what the parameters mean in specific cases, change standards at will, decide what weapons are of most concern, and maintain the right to transfer missile technology among themselves; China, meanwhile, is not party to any of these decisions but is expected to comply. From the perspective of the People's Republic, the United States seems free to violate its bilateral August 1982 agreement concerning weapons sales to Taiwan with impunity. The Chinese analyst Liu Huaqiu, senior fellow at the Program on Arms Control and Disarmament at the China Defense Science and Technology Center in Beijing, commented in 1995:

We believe that missile technology control regulations should be built on fair, reasonable, and [a] complete foundation. Therefore, we recommend that the "regulations" be expanded into a treaty whose limitations extend to aircraft, all participating countries having equal rights and obligations. Clearly translating the above recommendation into reality will be no easy matter. Nevertheless, we believe that as a first step, the United States should halt the sale of F-16s to Taiwan. This will help China and the United States cooperate in halting missile proliferation.[4]

Also of concern to Beijing is the possibility that Washington will build a missile defense system for itself and agree to transfer advanced theater missile defense (TMD) systems to Japan and/or Taiwan. The Chinese see this as threatening their own painstakingly constructed ballistic and cruise missiles and strategic deterrent system and strategy. They believe that such actions would feed a regional arms race, forcing China to increase spending on defense modernization, and could provide Taiwan with a shield behind which Taipei might feel more able to pursue independence activities. With respect to such possible American transfers to Japan, Beijing fears that they could further reinforce the chance of "militarism" in Tokyo. China's mid-1995 and March 1996 missile exercises near Taiwan, however, and the poorly substantiated (but nonetheless alarming) spring 1996 rumors that China had alluded to the strategic vulnerability of Los Angeles and New York, breathed new life into the drive in the U.S. Congress and elsewhere in the American body politic, as well as in Japan and Taiwan, for theater missile defenses in Asia and a missile shield in the United States. Those developments may turn out to have been among the more counterproductive and destabilizing results of Beijing's 1995-96 military exercises.

China's Pattern of Behavior

In China's expanded participation in the institutions of global governance, its good citizenship in some, and deficient performance in others, there is a clear pattern to its behavior. The axioms governing China's behavior in these organizations and global norms are perfectly understandable to "realists": derive maximum benefit from global institutions in terms of resource flow to China; minimize resulting obligations (the "free-rider" approach); use China's capacity to withhold compliance on agreements of high value to Washington to secure American compliance on agreements of high value to Beijing; and vigorously seek to safeguard the concept of largely unfettered national sovereignty. These principles of Chinese international organization behavior, what Samuel Kim, in a 1996 paper for the Council on Foreign Relations on China and the United Nations, calls "state enhancing functionalism," give rise to several questions. Does China basically accept the legitimacy of current organizations and regimes? How much change will it seek in them once it has joined? Will China assume greater burdens? Will it play a leadership role (and does the United States really want it to)? Will its behavior in key areas where American vital interests are at stake be acceptable to Washington? And will the concept of unfettered sovereignty fade and ideas of cooperative security and interdependence gain greater currency over time?

China's patterns of behavior are visible in a number of areas. In 1978, for example, China for the first time sought aid from the United Nations Development Program (UNDP), becoming by the late 1980s the largest recipient of UNDP funds, and the following year successfully sought to have its annual assessment for U.N. support reduced from 5.5 percent of the organization's budget to 0.79 percent. As of 1996 its support was down to 0.72 percent according to Kim. Similarly, in 1974 China covered 5.5 percent of the U.N. peacekeeping budget, but by 1994 this percentage had dropped to 0.978. In contrast, Russia covered 8.5 percent of the peacekeeping budget in 1994, even though its economy was in steep decline and China's was undergoing dramatic expansion, albeit from a lower absolute base. Put crudely, by the mid-1990s, China had 20 percent of the U.N.'s veto power and was responsible for less than 1 percent of the budget. As its economy and national power increase, Beijing will be expected to accept burdens of financial and policy responsibility commensurate with its organizational power.

In the future, the problem will, of course, be that the outside world's assessments of China's capability to support international undertakings are likely to exceed China's own evaluation. This is one reason China consistently rejects the accuracy (or fairness) of purchasing power parity (PPP) methods of assessing China's gross domestic product because that methodology leads to what Beijing feels is an "overestimation" of China's strength. Chinese leaders and advisors with whom I have met assert that "China should contribute [to international organizations] according to national strength," a reasonable principle. But there is likely to be disagreement in the future over how to measure that strength and over outsiders' perception of a disproportion between China's rights, privileges, and power in organizations and its level of financial contribution.

Another concern is reform of the U.N. Security Council, especially the question of expanding its permanent membership. On this issue, China behaves according to the principle that it will rhetorically assuage Third World desires for a greater role in the Security Council, that it will not oppose outright permanent German and Japanese Security Council membership, but that it will call for Charter review, a procedure that makes the realization of such objectives improbable. At all costs, Beijing will not support any change that gives the veto power to others (for example, Germany and Japan) beyond the current Permanent Five. The Chinese note, fairly enough, that "not only will China not support it [permanent Security Council membership, with veto, for others], also others do not support it."

In short, what one sees in Beijing's behavior vis-à-vis international organizations and agreements is an active and constructive participation in those organizations that bring a net positive benefit to China; the attempt to preserve advantages where they exist and gain new ones when possible; noncompliance with some bilateral and multilateral agreements to obtain the compliance of other states with other commitments; and marginal or noncompliant behavior when such agreements constrain Chinese economic advantage or are inconsistent with sovereignty, particularly those that might limit the regime's ability to maintain internal political control. For example, in order to obtain extension of MFN tariff treatment from Washington in mid-1994, Beijing indicated to American officials and to the International Committee of the Red Cross a willingness to arrange for regular international visits to Chinese prisons; once MFN was extended, these discussions ground to a halt. In another area, the lucrative trade in endangered species, Chinese compliance with the Convention on International Trade in Endangered Species (CITES) requirements has been weak, at best. In this case, part of the compliance problem reflects the behavior of undisciplined local leaders and entrepreneurial citizens not subject to effective control.

Behind all of these matters is the nagging question of whether China accepts the basic legitimacy of the current rules of international organizations and norms and whether it will seek to drastically alter them once admitted. Thus far, the answer seems to be that China's mere act of seeking admission to current global institutions represents a willingness to acknowledge their legitimacy, generally play by the rules, and seek to be a member of the "club." As long as China has basically constructive relations with the other big powers, we can expect that this will remain the case. It was reassuring to be told by one Chinese policy analyst in 1996, "China is realistic about regimes. China doesn't want to change them unilaterally. In the long term China will ask for change in unfair rules, but it won't seek to change them unilaterally." Another said about the same time,

Regarding the issue of China playing by the international rules, my own view is that China will uphold our own decision making, but the world is interdependent, China wants to enter the world, and we will observe international norms. The Chinese leadership must act responsibly. The main question is what is China's attitude [regarding rules] it did not help write? Our basic position is that if there are international laws and practices that are universally accepted, China will observe them. But if the United States takes its norms and tries to enforce them, we will reject it.

Issues for the United States and the West

China's increasing involvement in global institutions not only raises the questions of burden sharing, responsibility, and compliance on Beijing's part, but also presents major questions for the United States and the West. Are the United States and its allies willing to include China in the writing of rules Beijing is asked to observe? For example, Beijing is asked to observe the MTCR's guidelines and parameters and observe strictures governing the export of other potential military technologies, but the West is hesitant to have Beijing as a full member of the groups writing these rules. This can be seen in China's nonmembership in the MTCR and in the successor to the COCOM (the New Forum) technology control regime. The United States and others want China to enter global organizations such as the WTO, but seem reticent to concede that the organization may need to appropriately adapt to

China's circumstances as well. And while seeking to extract maximal commitments for change from Beijing for WTO entry, Washington seeks to keep its right of annual review of MFN tariff treatment for China. Doing so is inconsistent with underlying WTO principles, reduces Beijing's incentive to compromise, and represents a land mine in the relationship that can go off every year, resulting in an unproductive, exhausting, and unpredictable debate in the U.S. Congress and between the legislative and executive branches in Washington.

In the environmental area, the Chinese are encouraged to be more environmentally conscious, but they are excluded as a matter of policy from the United States–Asia Environmental Partnership. In addition, the United States has adopted policies that make China ineligible for U.S. development assistance, and even the meager U.S. interagency agreements with Beijing that seek to bolster sustainable development are increasingly starved for funds. Yet by many measures of pollution, including greenhouse gas emissions, the United States is now, and will remain for a considerable period of time, a bigger global "contributor" than China.

Finally, the United States sometimes confuses its own national policy preferences with "international norms." An American domestic law (the Hatfield amendment of 1992) and President Clinton's unilateral extensions of the amendment's moratorium on nuclear testing in 1993 and 1994 do not constitute an international law (or even norm), as the French and Chinese both reminded the world by testing weapons in 1995 and 1996. Liu Huaqiu remarks:

The United States and Russia each prepare a lavish dinner party for themselves that includes numerous tasty courses. Maybe China prepares only one dish, and that is undercooked. If both the United States and Russia say they are not going to eat their feasts after all, China would certainly say happily: "Fine, then I won't do any more cooking either." But now, the United States and Russia say they want to eat their feasts, i.e., they want to keep their huge nuclear stockpiles. This being the case, China has no choice but to say, "Just wait five minutes so I can finish my cooking too."[5]

Americans' argument that China should restrain its international weapons sales (which make it sixth largest in the world) and technology transfers would be taken more seriously if the United States did not have annual sales over ten times as large in the 1990–94 period, making it number one. Indeed, the Pentagon forecasts that the U.S. share of global weapons sales will rise from roughly 50 percent in 1993 to 63 percent by the year 2000.[6]

The age of interdependence, then, is requiring both China and the other major powers to assume greater burdens, modify their behavior in important areas, and cooperate.

Issues for Pacific Basin Neighbors

Pacific Basin nations are sufficiently heterogeneous to defy simple generalization about their foreign, economic, or security policy preferences. Their views of China and its likely role in the world vary widely. Korea, for example, may primarily fear future potential Japanese militarization; Indonesia is far more concerned about the rise of Chinese power. Malaysia publicly distanced itself from the dispatch of two American aircraft carrier task forces to the area near Taiwan in March 1996; most others in the region applauded (some publicly, some privately) the move. Each Pacific Basin member has a different array of perceived economic and security challenges, and each has addressed its challenges in quite different ways.

Given this diversity, the degree to which China's East Asian neighbors agree about two key propositions regarding the role of the People's Republic in global institutions is striking. This identity of views stems from the fact that China is near, China is big, and China's comprehensive national strength is growing rapidly. Agreement is found among East and Southeast Asian societies as small and near as Taiwan and as large and distant as Indonesia.

There are two core elements of common belief. The first is that it is better to get China into international organizations and regimes earlier, rather than later, even at the cost of suboptimal agreements to accomplish this. The thinking is that a China bound by rules and timetables it accepts (even if the rules and timetables have to be generous) is going to be a better, more predictable regional and global citizen than a China that is not bound by any agreed-upon rules. Ambassador Julia Chang Bloch discovered in South Korea in mid-

1996, for example, that observers there believed that "China should be brought into the WTO on relatively easy terms because, once in, it would be easier to pressure China to comply with international rules." In Indonesia, much the same view was expressed to this author in the summer of 1996: "It is important to bring China into the WTO, as its [China's] rules are under formation, at an early date." In the same vein, many in the region believe that China's early admittance to the WTO is desirable, even if longer transition times are given to the People's Republic than many would like. The thinking is that one can argue for years with Beijing about the duration of transition periods, and in the meantime, China is bound by no timetables at all—yet almost any timetable is better than none. One can consume more years in negotiating differences in transition times than are under dispute in the negotiations themselves.

On the subject of China's broader integration into regional and global institutions, I was told in Indonesia in mid-1996: "China needs to integrate into the world, but they don't know how. Engage [Beijing] in all possible ways . . . and we have to be patient—do not coerce them, and do not give the impression that we are ganging up on them."

The second core element of common belief in East and Southeast Asia is that high-level dialogue between China and the United States is essential. There is no support for a strategy of exclusion, humiliation, or stigmatization, and they tend to believe that "containment" is the worst combination of futility and self-fulfilling prophecy imaginable. This consensus extends to Taiwan, where I was told by an authoritative government source in mid-1996:

We don't want to see China as a threat, but the lack of dialogue between the U.S. and China will cause misunderstanding, and better relations are in our interest . . . I have read comments from PLA [People's Liberation Army] generals and they say that they are under pressure. The U.S. should work with the PRC to calm them down. You should have dialogue at the highest level and at the top levels of the PLA. The top brass should understand the U.S. more. That generation [of PLA leaders] engaged the U.S. on the Korean battlefield and those memories linger. You should bring the PLA top brass to see the U.S.

Perspectives on, and
Implications for, Policy

An examination of China's involvement in global governance organizations and norms suggests a number of policy avenues. Consideration of these may aid the United States in developing a sounder basis for its approach toward Beijing.

Although China's unique characteristics require acknowledgment as we think about its participation in international institutions, China fundamentally behaves along recognizable and comprehensible lines. It tends to adhere more tightly to agreements that are in its interest than those that are not. It tends to observe more closely rules that it had a role in making than those in which it did not. It tends to be more willing to negotiate on subjects where there is a clear linkage between Chinese behavior and what its leaders perceive to be the legitimate interests (such as economics and security) of those abroad than on issues concerning its own domestic rule. Beijing makes imperfect calculations about the effects of its actions (perhaps the 1995 and 1996 missile tests near Taiwan and the implied threats against the United States will prove to be examples of this) and fails to coordinate policy among its own bureaucracies. And finally, China tends to be more cooperative when there are positive inducements to compliance—frequently development resources and dignity are more effective than threat and humiliation. Too often we ignore these basic ways in which China is the same as others.

A policy based on unilateral American threats and humiliation will thus fail if those are the primary tools on which reliance is placed—such weapons can be effective only if they are credible. It is tough to be credible when vital interests are not at stake, when allies undermine your threats, and when the threats are aimed at changing fundamental patterns of governance in another country rather than protecting your own demonstrable interests. Winston Lord made clear how important allied support is, and how rare it can be, when he said in 1996: "We want European and Japanese and other help on nonproliferation, trade, or human rights. Good luck. We try very hard; they hold our coats while we take on the Chinese and they gobble up the contracts."[7]

If we desire a productive relationship with China, global institutions, as well as China, will have to adapt in order to accommodate this country's unique circumstances. Although current international rules cannot be distorted beyond recognition simply by reference to China's "special characteristics," neither can we fail to take account of the obvious fact that China is unique in ways of enormous consequence to the world. By unique, I refer not to cultural or historical features (though these are important) but, rather, to the co-existence of China's poverty in per capita terms with the nation's rise to the status of a global trade power in aggregate terms. By unique, I mean China's capacity to develop key technologies, particularly in the defense area, at the same time that it is technologically deficient in many other important domains. By unique, I mean a country with some 800 million peasants, yet a nation with a rapidly growing, globally competitive urban population of over 300 million, a population larger than those of Japan, North and South Korea, the Philippines, Malaysia, and Singapore combined. By unique, I mean the almost *sui generis* combination of administrative control and market impulses in its economy. And by unique I mean the sheer scale of what is occurring in China.

Taking account of the unique characteristics of the People's Republic is not to deny the need for it to make enormous adjustments to the world system as well. China, for its part, must observe its international commitments and cannot expect to remain in the position of having big-nation power and privileges and developing nation responsibilities and burdens. As a great power, China has to recognize that credibly reassuring the world of its intentions is important.

In light of these considerations, Washington (and other G-7 capitals) should attach more importance to China's early entry into the WTO. Involving China in the WTO and obtaining deadlines for compliance (even if allowing for longer transition times than one would wish) is preferable to having China outside the WTO, with no deadlines for compliance whatsoever. Currently the United States is being undermined by its economic competitors who seek to promote their own commercial advantage by portraying Washington as the sole factor preventing China's entry. The worst of all possible worlds results: China outside WTO with no deadlines and the American economic position eroded. The key issue for the world's long-term economic relationship with China is not so much the length of transition periods as openness, or transparency (the ability of outsiders to know the internal rules and processes governing Chinese behavior), and transparency would be promoted by China's early entry into WTO. Washington is not well advised to seek to maintain its right of yearly review for MFN at the same time that it seeks to extract wide-ranging concessions from Beijing for WTO membership. A package deal should be formulated whereby the United States drops its annual MFN threat and China more effectively addresses American and, more generally, Western desires for market access, transparency, protection against potential market disruption and export surges, and better compliance with past agreements. In the same vein, if Russia is an "observer" in the G-7, should not China, with a far more dynamic economy, be involved as well?

In a different realm, serious consideration should be given to making China a full member of the MTCR and the New Forum for technology export control as well as the Australia Group for the Control of Biological and Chemical Weapons. It simply is not feasible to have China perpetually comply with rules it is excluded from helping to draft. For its part, China needs to be effective in its apparent (hoped for) effort to bring greater discipline to its weapons and technology transfers abroad.

China's record in the areas of weapons proliferation and technology transfer is of great legitimate concern to the United States. Yoichi Funabashi, Michel Oksenberg, and Heinrich Weiss observe: "The combination of China's paranoia and the West's hypocrisy has worked against China becoming an effective member of global non-proliferation efforts."[8] This issue must be placed as an overriding objective of U.S. foreign policy (with the implication that attempts to change China's internal political system will be subordinated). China will have to be accorded a seat at all the tables at which nonproliferation rules are adopted, with the United States, China, and others working together to establish effective export control regimes through exchanges and other consultative mechanisms. In addition, the other great powers will have to broaden the scope of the discussion of their own weapons sales and technology transfers. It is not feasible to exclude from the agenda the weapons and particular recipients of concern to China and thus fail to address Beijing's concerns.

We should recognize that international cooperation with China has been most productive in instances in which not only is Beijing part of the group making the rules (for example, at the World Bank, the IMF, the United Nations Security Council, and various environmental undertakings such as the Montreal Protocol), but also where resources are made available to help China address problems of concern to the global community. China still has a very sizable poor population—recent World Bank figures are likely to show more poverty than previously released bank figures have indicated.[9] Moreover, economic progress in China is still tenuous, and exhortation will be more effective if it is linked to tangible resources. In this era of declining support in the United States for development assistance, this will be difficult. But exhortation devoid of assistance will generally be less effective. At a minimum, China should not be excluded from organizations such as the USAID led U.S.–Asia Environmental Partnership; it is manifestly in the United States' interest for China to join. Overall, a glaring contradiction exists between a policy of comprehensive engagement and declining government support for exchanges—both the U.S. government's own bilateral exchanges and private sector exchanges. For example, virtually no added U.S. government resources have been made available for legal and judicial training programs, despite pledges in mid-1994 to do so.

Finally, Beijing has had many motivations for joining international organizations, among which is global standing. When Beijing is a full partner in the global community, it frequently has sought to live up to what is expected of it. This suggests that holding China's participation in major international organizations, regimes, and activities hostage to the behavior we seek to encourage is almost always an unproductive approach. A better path is to seek China's participation in such organizations and activities with the expectation that subsequent behavior will increasingly conform to the norms of those organizations. Here I have in mind the debate (and Senate vote) in the United States over the desirability of China's being host to the Olympic games in 2000. Rather than pushing to have the Olympic games awarded to another nation (in retaliation for Chinese human rights infractions), Washington should not have opposed Beijing's bid. Decision makers might have realized, instead, that China would do all within its power to make the event a success and that such an occurrence would foster many positive trends. By following the path of stigmatization, Washington lost an opportunity to support positive change and fostered resentment throughout the broader Chinese populace.

Notes

1. Poppele (1994), p. 38.
2. Nathan (1996), pp. 8–9.
3. Lord (1996), p. 25.
4. Liu (1995), p. 10.
5. Liu (1995), p. 10.
6. D. Isenberg, "We Arm the World," *Washington Post*, February 18, 1996, p. C5.
7. Lord (1996), p. 29.
8. Funabashi, Oksenberg, and Weiss (1994), p. 57.
9. World Bank (1996), p. 22.

4

How China's Economic Transformation Shapes Its Future

DWIGHT H. PERKINS

Economic growth has been the primary force transforming East and Southeast Asia in the second half of the twentieth century. Because the region's economic growth has been so rapid, an urban society has replaced one dominated by rural villages. An educated middle class has become the dominant political force, replacing a largely uneducated peasant class in that role. Internationally, Asia, which was once the supplier of a few raw materials and agricultural products (silk, tea) to the West, has become an industrial machine providing the world with electronic goods and automobiles. Only in the military sphere has rapid economic growth not brought about

DWIGHT H. PERKINS is a professor of political economy at Harvard University. He authored *China: Asia's Next Economic Giant?* (1986) and other books as well as articles about Chinese and East Asian international and domestic policy. He is a director of the National Committee on U.S.–China Relations and a member of the Board of Trustees of the China Medical Board of New York. He has served as a consultant or advisor on economic policy to the governments of China, Korea, Malaysia, and Vietnam and to many U.S. based institutions, including the Ford Foundation and the World Bank.

profound change. Since Japan's defeat in 1945, Asian military ventures have been confined to localized border disputes or civil wars
(China, Korea, Vietnam). None of the East and Southeast Asian
nations has tried, as yet, to convert economic power into military
might capable of being projected globally.

Prior to 1979 China was not really part of this East Asian transformation. Slow economic growth (3.6 percent per year between
1957 and 1978), together with certain state and Communist party
policies, prevented structural change in the economy and in society more generally. The rural population, for example, was physically blocked from moving to the cities. The heavy industry in urban
areas provided few jobs in any case, so the peasants remained in
place. Education expanded, but only with long interruptions during the Great Leap Forward (1958–1960) and the Cultural Revolution (1966–1976). Average personal incomes rose, but they less than
doubled over a quarter century, and much of this increase went to
a privileged minority, 20 percent of the population, who enjoyed
urban resident status. The history of China in the 1950s, 1960s, and
1970s, as a result, was a history of politics—mass campaigns, power
struggles, and the waxing and waning of Communist party organizational strength. Economics played a role only when political action became so extreme that the economy was severely disrupted,
and, in the case of 1959–1961, widespread famine ensued.

China's history since 1979, in contrast, has been dominated by
economics. The decisions that unleashed the economic engine of
growth were political, but after that, economics drove politics much
more than the reverse. For seventeen years, China's economy has
enjoyed East Asian–style gross national product growth rates of 8
to 9 percent a year, depending on what assumptions one makes
about the reliability of the underlying data used to estimate the Chinese GNP (the official real growth rate over this period is 9.9 percent per year). Seventeen years is a long time when growth rates are
so high.[1] Growth rates of this order of magnitude are what transformed South Korea and Taiwan from poor, rural societies in the
1950s to modern industrial states in the 1990s, a change that occurred in just three decades in Korea's case. China in 1978 was
poorer than Korea and Taiwan in 1960, so the transformation may

take China longer—but only a decade or so longer at these high GNP growth rates.

How much has changed in China since the reforms began in late 1978? If one assumes a GNP growth rate of a little over 7 or 8 percent per capita, per capita GNP in 1995 was three times what it was in 1978. How large is that? Because China has steadily devalued its currency, for trade policy purposes among other reasons, the Chinese exchange rate is a poor guide to putting the Chinese GNP into U.S. dollar terms so that it can be compared internationally. The best "purchasing power parity" dollar estimates suggest that the Chinese per capita GNP in 1991 was a bit above U.S. $1,200 (in 1991 prices), which would make the 1995 GNP (in 1991 prices) a bit above U.S. $1,700.[2] In aggregate terms, China's GNP in 1995 was around U.S. $2,000 billion. In 1978, in comparison, the Chinese per capita GNP using purchasing power parity was somewhat above U.S. $500, and aggregate GNP was around U.S. $500 billion.

The comparable purchasing power parity GNP per capita figures for South Korea and Taiwan when their growth spurts began in the early 1960s were roughly U.S. $850 and U.S. $1400 respectively (in 1990 prices). By the mid-1990s Korea had reached U.S. $10,000 per capita, and Taiwan had passed U.S. $14,000 per capita. Put differently, over the course of three-plus decades South Korea and Taiwan accomplished a per capita rise in income roughly the same as that achieved by the countries of Western Europe over a 150-year span from the 1820s to the 1970s.[3] By way of comparison, if China were to maintain a per capita GDP growth rate of 7 percent per year, roughly the growth rate achieved since 1978, it would take China only thirty more years to catch up to Western European income levels of the 1970s. If China's per capita GDP growth rate fell to 5 percent per annum, European income levels of the 1970s would be attained in just over forty years.

Along with the rise in per capita GNP, China's economy has undergone a profound structural transformation. Chinese urban statistics are particularly treacherous, but China's employment data can be used to tell the basic story. In 1978, 70.5 percent of all people of working age were in agriculture, and the number of workers in that sector was growing by 3 to 4 million people a year, even though there was already a large surplus of workers in the countryside. By 1994 the share in agriculture was down to 54 percent, and after 1991 the absolute numbers of workers in agriculture had actually begun to decline. Many of the other 46 percent were technically still in the rural areas, but they were no longer farmers. Education levels, after two decades of neglect, were also rising rapidly.

As for consumer goods, by 1994 most urban households had color television sets and washing machines, and the majority had refrigerators. A large majority of rural households also had television sets, but most were black and white. Bicycles were universal, with motorbikes just beginning to be a popular purchase (5 percent or less of both urban and rural households). China's cities were jammed with automobile traffic, but only a tiny elite had access to automobiles. Transportation was still mainly public, with China's railroads (in 1994) carrying over 1 billion passengers an average distance of 200-plus miles (355 kilometers). Public vehicles on the highways carried another 10 billion passengers an average of 25 miles: most commuting was by jam-packed buses. Housing space in urban areas, down to a minuscule 3.6 square meters per capita in 1978, had expanded to 7.8 meters per capita in 1994. In rural areas housing space had expanded from 8.1 square meters per capita to 20.2 square meters over the same period, and the quality of housing had improved measurably. If we leave aside large pockets of poverty in the more mountainous and remote provinces, most Chinese were thus a long way from the near-subsistence levels of the past. With television almost universal, they also had more access to information, albeit controlled by the state, than anyone would have dreamed of in the early 1970s.

The central question is whether China will complete this transformation to a modern urban industrial state, and how long it will take to do so. The answer to the second half of the question is conditional on the rate of growth achieved. For China to achieve a purchasing power parity per capita GNP of U.S. $10,000 (in 1991 prices) within twenty years, Chinese per capita GNP would have to rise by 9 percent per year, probably an unrealistically high figure. To achieve that level in thirty years, however, requires per capita growth of only 6 percent per year, a high but by no means unrealistic figure. In absolute terms, at U.S. $10,000 per capita, the Chinese GNP would come to around U.S. $16 trillion, or two and a half times the GNP of the United States in 1995. The answer to whether and under what conditions China might achieve these growth rates is the focus of this chapter.

The Determinants of Chinese Economic Growth

There are two levels on which one can discuss the prospects for Chinese economic growth. One level involves the economic fundamentals of what determines growth—the mobilization of capital, labor, and technology. The other level involves the policies that make it possible for nations to achieve a given level of mobilization of these factors. The policy discussion can be further divided into those policies that the developing nation itself controls and those policies that depend critically on the nature of its relations with the outside world. Policies, of course, do not get made in a vacuum. Social and political tensions create conditions that often dictate a particular policy outcome.

The economic fundamentals underlying China's growth are likely to remain sound. The two key variables for a developing country are physical capital and human capital. In terms of physical capital, China by the mid-1990s had raised its rate of gross domestic investment to 40 percent of gross national expenditure, an extraordinarily high figure for a still-poor country. Prior to the beginning of the reform period in 1979, China already had a high rate of investment and savings, but it was the central government that did most of the savings and made most of the investment. By the mid-1990s the central and local governments' budget allocations accounted for only a tiny part of all investment in new fixed assets (only 3 percent in 1994). A larger portion (22.6 percent) came from the state controlled banking system, but the remaining three-quarters came from Chinese enterprises' own funds, the sale of shares, foreign investors, and other similar sources that were largely beyond the sphere of control of the government.[4]

In addition, savings was based mainly on individual or enterprise decisions. The current account surplus of the government was under 2 percent of gross domestic product in 1994, down from figures near 20 percent in the 1970s. Household savings deposits in 1994 rose by an amount equivalent to 14 percent of GDP. China's high savings rates were primarily generated by forces similar to those behind the high savings rates found elsewhere in East Asia, a low dependency ratio (that is, a low percentage of the population not of working age) and growth in consumption that lagged behind the rapid increases in income.

The central government in China regularly laments its loss of control over much of the nation's investment expenditures, and central government investment goals, as a result, have often not been met. On occasion the failure to allocate investment in accordance with central government priorities may have created transport and energy bottlenecks that slowed economic growth. But the central government's rate of return on investment when it did have full control, as in the 1970s, was abysmal. The net result of the decentralization of savings and investment decisions has been a rise in the overall rate of return on capital and hence a much higher rate of growth. This decentralization of control over investment has significantly weakened the power of the central government in more than just economic terms.

The human capital situation in China has also been changing rapidly for the better. The education system expanded rapidly in the 1950s and then entered two long decades in which the system either stagnated or was closed altogether, while former students roamed the country as Red Guards. Primary education had been nearly universal for some time, but by the mid-1990s junior middle-school education (nine years of education) had become nearly universal as well, and almost half of the graduates of these junior middle schools were going on to senior middle schools. University-level education remained a privilege for an elite of less than 5 percent of the relevant age cohorts, although the absolute numbers (900,000 new entrants a year) were large. What these statistics do not show is the steady improvement in the quality of education taking place in the classrooms. What was once a completely politicized system has been transformed into one that is steadily improving in its capacity to promote skills and knowledge.

As elsewhere in East Asia, the pressure to expand the education system did not come solely or even primarily from the government.

A sizable pent-up demand in the population at large has increasingly been met by private institutions staffed by moonlighting teachers, television courses, and much else.

Education, particularly university and postgraduate education, is also what makes possible the effective use of the other major ingredient in growth, technology. Technology, broadly defined to include improvements in management practices as well as better machines, is what makes possible the more efficient use of capital and labor and hence increases in productivity. In advanced industrial economies, technological change and productivity growth are driven mainly by research and development expenditures by industry and government. This is not the case in developing countries. Except in a few select areas, developing countries such as China do not do much cutting-edge original research. Technology and productivity advances are achieved by importing machinery, equipment, and ideas from the industrialized world and then adapting them to local conditions. The major exception to this rule is the military sphere, where the most advanced technology, and particularly the ability to manufacture advanced weaponry, is often not available on the open market. Agriculture is another area where original research is a necessity if a country is to develop new plant varieties suited to its special soil and climatic conditions.

The continued expansion in the numbers and quality of university and postgraduate students in China is, therefore, central to the nation's economic development strategy. In the 1920s and 1930s, in the critical engineering and natural science fields, China produced around 2,000 higher education graduates a year. Although many of them left China in 1949, of the 47,500 graduates in engineering and the natural sciences in the 1912–1947 period, roughly half remained on the mainland. In the 1950s these numbers expanded rapidly as another 150,000 students graduated in these fields prior to the Great Leap Forward in 1958. In addition, 7,500 students received undergraduate or postgraduate education in universities in the Soviet Union, mainly in the sciences and engineering.[5] China's current political as well as economic leadership, including Jiang Zemin, Li Peng, and Zhu Rongji, comes in large part from these cohorts of Chinese or Soviet trained engineers.

During the 1960s and 1970s Chinese universities, when they were open, continued to produce graduates, but the quality of the education that many of them received is suspect given the long periods of school closure and the highly politicized atmosphere in the classrooms when they were open. After 1978, however, the number of engineering and science students expanded rapidly, and by the 1990s there were more than 200,000 graduates in these fields each year. Over the 1984–1993 decade, China graduated 1.6 million engineers and another 200,000 in the natural sciences[6]—roughly double the number of American students graduating in these fields over a similar period. The average quality of U.S. students was no doubt higher, but the best of the Chinese students were as good as those anywhere. In American graduate programs in fields such as physics, many of the top Ph.D. students are graduates of Chinese undergraduate programs at elite schools such as Tsinghua or Jiaotong universities.

If the 7,500 graduates of Soviet universities have had a major impact on China, how much larger will be the impact of the over 100,000 Chinese postgraduates and visiting scholars who have spent years training in the West since 1978? China does have a problem in getting the best of these to return home from the United States and Canada. Salaries, research facilities, and living conditions are much better in North America, but that was once true for students from South Korea and Taiwan as well. Ninety percent of the Korean and Taiwanese students stayed in the United States in the 1950s and 1960s; in the 1990s, 90 percent or more returned home. The conditions for students returned from the West are beginning to improve in China as well, although the government has yet to initiate the kind of effort undertaken by Korea in the 1970s that persuaded Korean scientists and engineers to begin returning in large numbers. The potential for political instability is a barrier for some potential Chinese returnees, but this problem loomed large in Korea in the 1970s and 1980s as well and was largely surmounted.

The point of this discussion of Chinese engineering and science education is a simple one. China is developing a formidable capacity to adapt modern science and technology to its needs. Given the size of China's industry, there is still a great shortage of qualified engineers, but the gap is closing. In the area of military technology, it is the absolute numbers of qualified scientists and engineers and not the number per capita that matter. A large nation may require ten steel mills or a thousand electronics factories, but it usually requires only one or two nuclear and missile research laboratories. China should be able to staff a sizable military research effort without having to strip industry of the large numbers of engineers and scientists that it requires.

In addition to being able to meet its requirements for trained personnel, China also has created a significant exporting capacity that provides it with the foreign exchange it needs to import the equipment and technology that development requires. From 1960 through 1978 China tried to make a virtue of what originally was a necessity. With limited access to foreign markets and with little ability to borrow abroad, China had to rely on its own efforts for most of its needs, including most machinery and equipment. Mao Zedong and Jiang Qing raised this approach to a matter of principle, making it difficult to import foreign technology of any kind. With the death of Mao and the arrest of Jiang Qing, this policy was decisively reversed in 1977 and 1978, even before the rest of the reform process got under way. The first step taken was to legitimize the importation of foreign technology and equipment, but this action immediately raised the question of how to pay for all of the new imports. That led after 1978 to a concerted effort to promote exports.

As this sequence of events demonstrates, China's initial efforts to promote foreign trade were not motivated by mercantilist dreams of generating large balance-of-payments surpluses. China above all needed the imports; exports were simply a way of paying for them. Initially China had hopes that large new oil discoveries would provide it with an export surplus of petroleum, but these new discoveries never materialized. China then had to follow the lead of its East Asian neighbors and turn to the export of manufactures. But Chinese manufacturers were used to producing low-quality goods for a captive domestic market, not the quality- and style-conscious markets of the United States and Europe. Most Chinese manufacturers had never even heard the word "marketing," but as it turned out, it didn't matter. Hong Kong's entrepreneurs, who were masters at marketing to the West, stepped in to fill the breach. By the 1990s business people from Taiwan were also helping in this area as they moved the production of many of their labor-intensive products to the Chinese mainland.

The net result of these efforts was that Chinese exports, made up mostly of manufactures, rose from U.S. $9.75 billion in 1978 to U.S. $149 billion by 1995. In addition, by 1995 annual foreign direct investment into China was running at a rate of U.S. $37.8 billion, although some of this money was really Chinese domestic funds recycled through Hong Kong to gain tax advantages given to foreign investors. When foreign loans were added in, China had nearly U.S. $200 billion of foreign exchange each year with which to buy imports. China, in effect, was in a strong position to buy most of the foreign technology and equipment that it could efficiently use.

For the most part, China did use this foreign exchange to buy imports. Foreign exchange reserves rose dramatically in 1994 to U.S. $51.6 billion and by the end of 1995 to U.S. $73.6 billion, but prior to that, China had run deficits in its trade and current account balances in ten of the seventeen years since the reforms. Even the recent large buildup of foreign exchange reserves has more to do with capital inflows than it does with what has been happening in the trade sphere. Unless Chinese savings rates continue to rise or investment rates fall significantly, neither a very likely prospect, China will not soon begin running a chronic current account surplus.[7]

The Economic Reform Process

High levels of investment and better technology lead to high GDP growth rates, however, only if the economic system is organized in such a way as to use these inputs efficiently. The alternative is a situation like that found in the Soviet Union in the 1980s or in China before 1978—declining growth rates generated by massive waste in the use of capital and technology.

China began moving away from a Soviet-style command system after the Third Communist Party Plenum of December 1978. When the economic reform process began, the Chinese leadership was mainly interested in improving the performance of the command system, not abolishing it. Seventeen years later, in contrast, there was a leadership consensus that the ultimate goal was a full market economy organized in accordance with international best practice.

There was less than full agreement over just what constituted international best practice, and there was a leadership commitment to maintaining some form of state ownership over at least some industrial and financial enterprises. Beyond that, however, China's goal was an economy that looked much like those of its economically more advanced East Asian neighbors.

The reforms that have taken place have been profound. They have not only improved economic efficiency and doubled the GDP growth rate, but have also fundamentally altered the way in which Chinese society is organized and the way in which the central government relates to its citizens.

The first two areas of reform were in agriculture and in foreign trade and investment. In agriculture, the two major steps were the abolition of the system of collectivized farming based on the rural communes, and the freeing up of rural markets. These reforms, largely completed in the years 1979–1983, had an immediate and dramatic impact on farm output and rural standards of living. Real incomes on average rose by over 60 percent, more than twice the total rise in rural per capita standards of living in the previous quarter century. The growth in farm income leveled off after 1984, but there is no question that most people in the rural areas are far better off today than they were before the reforms started.

The rural population is not only better off in material terms. Government and party cadres no longer have direct control over the way farmers go about their daily activities (with one notable exception in the area of family planning). For the most part farmers can plant what they want, in the way that they want, on their own land, and, after paying taxes, keep what they earn. For some local purposes village leadership is still required, but these leaders are now chosen through a process that has many of the features of genuine democratic elections. The rural population is also free to leave the land, either for nearby township and village enterprises or for jobs in more distant cities. There are an estimated 100 million people in what China calls its "floating population," people who have left their home villages and provide much of the construction, transport, and trading services nationwide.

Given the higher standard of living and greater degree of personal freedom, the rural population might be expected to provide solid support for those who made these changes possible, and in the mid-1980s this was probably the case. In more recent years, however, the government has mishandled the way farmers have been paid for their crops, often using IOUs rather than money in payment. Considerable resentment and even some low-level rural violence have been the result.

We have already considered the impact of the early foreign trade and investment reforms. Changes in this area involved the abolition of the monopolies of the state trading corporations under the Ministry of Foreign Trade and Economic Cooperation (MOFTEC) and the creation of hundreds of provincial and lower-level state trading companies. In principle many of these local trading companies had certain exclusive rights over their local markets, but in practice a considerable degree of competition existed among them. There was also competition for foreign direct investment, with the most economically liberalized provinces, notably Guangdong, getting the lion's share. Success by one area in attracting foreign investment put pressure on the government to allow other regions to follow suit by liberalizing their foreign investment controls and providing tax and infrastructure advantages.

Central control over foreign exchange has also given way to a decentralized system of allocation based on markets. Initially the centrally controlled Bank of China determined company by company who would receive access to scarce foreign currency. The government then created "swap markets," on which a few foreign joint ventures could sell their surplus foreign exchange to other joint ventures that had a shortage. Gradually eligibility to participate in these swap markets was broadened to include more and more domestic Chinese firms. In early 1994 the official exchange rate was made equal to what had been the swap market rate, and China announced its intention of moving to full convertibility of its currency, at least on the trade account. For the considerable number of people and businesses willing to bend the rules, full convertibility was already a virtual reality by the mid-1990s. Hong Kong dollars, for example, circulated widely in Guangdong Province, and billions of dollars of capital flowed readily in and out of Hong Kong. Foreign exchange, which had once been an important mechanism through which the government enforced enterprise compliance with the central plan, had become readily available to almost everyone.

Attempts to reform the industrial, transport, and financial sectors began after the initial successes of the agricultural and foreign trade reforms had been achieved. The task at the outset was to make the state owned enterprises in these sectors perform better. To that end, the government attempted to gradually give these enterprises more autonomy, in large part by allowing firms to sell more of their output on the open market and to buy more of their inputs there rather than relying on allocations through the mechanism of central planning. The government also gave state enterprises greater control over their profits, in part by reforming the tax system so that enterprises paid a fixed rate instead of simply giving all of their profits to the state. Investment, which had been under almost exclusive central plan control, was increasingly turned over to enterprises and local governments, which were now expected to use their own funds or to borrow from the banking system.

None of these state enterprise reforms worked as intended, but their impact on China's economy and society was profound nonetheless. Almost immediately, the reforms gave what are now called township and village enterprises easy access to key inputs if they could afford the market-determined prices. The result was a boom in these enterprises that has continued unabated. This growth, together with the effect of joint ventures, has steadily reduced the share of industry produced by state enterprises from three-quarters of the total to around 30 percent. It is this phenomenal change in the nonstate enterprise sector that has sustained both high industrial and GDP growth rates since 1984.

Formally, township and village enterprises as well as many joint ventures are collectively or state owned, but they differ markedly from the large state firms. They are neither dependent on nor much influenced by the central ministries or the State Planning Commission. They produce for the market and retain their profits after paying taxes, although they often share these profits with their local government patrons. If they run large losses on a sustained basis, they are allowed to go bankrupt. State enterprises, in contrast, despite the existence of a bankruptcy law for nearly a decade, are rarely allowed to fail. One way or another, usually through bank loans that need not be repaid until profitability returns, large state enterprises are bailed out. Some debate whether nonstate enterprises are private or not, but the question may not be that important. These enterprises compete with one another and with the large state enterprises, and they pursue profits with vigor. If they are controlled or heavily influenced by government officials, it is local officials who themselves behave more like managers of a mini-conglomerate than like the regulators and taxers who make up the ranks of higher-level government officials.

State enterprises, for all of their difficulties, are still an essential part of the economy, and China's continuing failure to reform them will ultimately be a drag on the whole economy. In key fields such as steel, automobiles, semiconductors, and railroad and air transport, state enterprises are the central or exclusive actors. Yet one-third to two-thirds of them are running losses. It is not easy to tell how well they are doing because accounting regulations are widely ignored. There is no agreement on how to handle the huge inter-enterprise debt that has accumulated because many state enterprises don't pay their bills. China will be forced to privatize most of them if this situation goes unchanged.

There are several components to a successful state enterprise reform effort, all of which have implications that go beyond the issue of the efficiency of these enterprises. Allowing firms to go bankrupt means that thousands of employees will be put out of work, something that flies in the face of socialist values and carries genuine political risks in China. The workers, furthermore, lose not only their jobs but also their housing and health care, because these are now provided by the enterprise. The government has been experimenting for many years with an unemployment insurance system, national health insurance, and a variety of housing reforms, but the issues are complex and progress on a nationwide basis is slow.

Many other reforms, such as the field of enterprise taxation, exist on paper but not in practice. From local government authorities through the Ministry of Finance, informal means are regularly used to extract additional payments for government coffers, and the problem is not confined to taxation. The rule of law has never been a conspicuous feature of Chinese society. Confucian values have always placed greater emphasis on rule by good men than rule by good laws. The result, both traditionally and at present, is that whatever the formal laws may say, government officials have wide latitude for discretionary action. During the later years of Mao Zedong, who died in 1976, this approach to governance was carried to the extreme: most laws were abolished and lawyers were eliminated. Since 1978 China has been writing and passing volumes full of new laws, particularly in the sphere of economics. The motivation, in many cases, has been to please foreign investors who are uneasy with China's informal methods. More often than not, however, the laws have been made to apply to everyone, not just foreigners. The problem is that China's court system and other mechanisms for implementing these laws fall far short of the objectivity, neutrality, and effectiveness that one finds in societies truly ruled by law. Nor is there any straightforward way of measuring how much progress China is making in this regard.

Not all of the changes brought about by domestic economic reforms have been positive. The decentralization of decision-making authority to local governments, enterprises, and households has certainly expanded human choice and freedoms. The increasing use of law over administrative discretion, however imperfect in its implementation, has been unequivocally positive. And the spread of markets to cover most goods and services means that access to these goods and services is available to anyone willing and able to pay for them, a far cry from the days when most goods were made available through channels directly controlled and manipulated by government and party officials.

But reform has also been accompanied by rising inflation and corruption. A rise in prices was the more-or-less inevitable result of the end of price controls, the presence of suppressed inflationary pressures from the past, and the lax nature of the financial system. As China gradually completes the reform of its financial system and develops more sophisticated financial markets, the management of inflationary pressures will become more efficient and the rate of increase in prices should settle down to single digits.

It is impossible to be so sanguine about the prospects for corruption. Many Chinese blame the reforms for the rising tide of corruption, but the reality is much more complex. People in China were not financially corrupt in the years when Mao Zedong ruled, because there was little to be gained from such activity. If you used your ill-gotten gains, you invited a visit from the Red Guards or the local public security office. If you had valuable possessions, and were not one of the highest officials in the land, you could spend long hours being interrogated about how the items were obtained—only to see them destroyed or confiscated even if they had been acquired legitimately. At the height of the Cultural Revolution such goods were systematically destroyed and their owners paraded through the streets, humiliated, and worse.

After 1978 these practices largely ended, and this change is an important one. People were allowed to get rich and to use their money to buy expensive cars and houses. It was frequently not easy to tell whether the money had been made by legitimate means or not. In a system riddled with licensing procedures, discretionary control over key inputs such as electric power and rail transport, and many other similar practices, the opportunities for corruption were vast. The dual price system instituted in 1984 was a particularly lucrative source of what economists like to call "rents." The system was introduced to bring market forces into the distribution of key industrial inputs without having to take away subsidized inputs from politically powerful plant managers. Anyone who had access to these subsidized inputs and who didn't need them for production could, therefore, resell them at the much higher market price and pocket the difference. Millionaires were created overnight where only a few years before someone with 10,000 yuan was considered rich.

The dual price source of rents has largely been eliminated as the proportion of goods available at subsidized prices has for the most part disappeared. Government discretion in the administration of numerous other controls, however, is widespread. The primary solution to these sources of corruption is to eliminate as many areas of government discretionary authority as possible. This can be accomplished by allowing the market to allocate most goods and services and by using nondiscretionary laws and rules to govern as many other decisions as possible. Both the market and laws that in principle do not allow discretion by officials are expanding their scope in China, but there is a long way to go. Furthermore, there is serious doubt whether the leaders of China truly want to eliminate the power of government and party officials to act as they think best. Corruption is dealt with by instituting vigorous campaigns to root out wrongdoers. These campaigns are not very effective and are sometimes used for purposes having little to do with the control of corruption. Nothing is of greater danger to the leaders of China both individually and collectively than the continuation of this state of affairs.

China and the
International Economic System

How do China's efforts to reform its domestic economy relate to the country's desire to become a part of the broader international economic system? At the most general level, the answer to this question is straightforward. China's decision to create a market economy, albeit a "socialist market economy," is what makes it possible to discuss when and under what conditions China might join international bodies such as the World Trade Organization (WTO). If large parts of the central planning system were to be retained indefinitely into the future, China could not possibly meet the standards for participation in any system of open and free trading.

Having a goal, however, is not the same thing as achieving that goal. A number of major hurdles stand between where China is today and where China needs to be to have a system like those of other nations that are full members of the international economic system.[8] Some of these hurdles are created by the desire of certain Chinese leaders to retain various elements of planning. Other hurdles are deeply rooted in Chinese tradition. The latter are more difficult to deal with than the former.

There are significant differences in view among China's economic leadership over the role that the government should play in guiding the economy. Some of these differences relate to whether or not China should have an activist industrial policy. Others are primarily concerned with the pace of China's move to a market based system. Many among the Chinese economic leadership, for example, are admirers of the role of the Ministry of International Trade and Industry (MITI) of Japan in the 1950s and 1960s or the

Korean heavy and chemical industry drive of the 1970s. In these decades, MITI and Korea's President Park Chung Hee provided high protection of the domestic market, targeted import quotas for favored industries, subsidized loans and special tax treatment for these same industries, and much else. These measures were allowed by the international community largely because the United States was more concerned at the time with the recovery and sustained growth of Japan, Korea, and others than it was with maintaining a completely free international trading system. By the late 1970s and thereafter, however, neither the United States nor Europe was willing to tolerate such practices except among small, poor economies that were bit players in the world trading system.

Another view argues that China should not be trying to follow the path of MITI or President Park. Activist industrial policies are only successful when industrial development decisions are made exclusively on economic and technical grounds, uninfluenced by partisan political advantage or private rent seeking. Japan's and Korea's industrial bureaucracies in the relevant periods were isolated from politics and rent seeking in this way; China's bureaucracy of the 1990s definitely is not. It is hard to imagine a Chinese industrial policy that would not be heavily influenced by politics and efforts to extract rents. China could probably limit these depredations better than, say, the Philippines under President Ferdinand Marcos, but the net result of an activist targeted industrial policy would still be negative.

Many in China who might accept this latter argument in principle are still very concerned with how the country can do without a targeted industrial policy in the short term of the next decade or longer. A third or more of China's state enterprises are in serious financial trouble. Letting these poor performers simply collapse and go out of business is not politically acceptable, as already noted. China, it is argued, needs time to get these firms in a position to compete. The automobile sector illustrates the problem and the approach. Until recently China had dozens of automobile plants scattered around the country, each producing a few obsolete cars and trucks at high cost. In the 1990s China has set out to consolidate these plants into a few that will produce on a much larger and more efficient scale. Agreements have been signed with Volkswagen and other foreign partners to modernize plant technology, but this process takes time. It will be a decade or more before the Chinese automobile industry will be able to stand on its own against competition from foreign imports. Other state enterprises are technologically able to compete but are financially vulnerable because of weaknesses in the financial system as a whole and the accumulation of large unpaid bills. Financial reform too takes time.

The longer-term issue that is only in part under the control of the government is the introduction of the rule of law into all economic transactions. China, as of the mid-1990s, had adopted many of the necessary laws. The problem is enforcement. Economic decisions in China are based first and foremost on personal relationships *(guanxi)*. There has been no tradition of an independent judiciary in Chinese history, nor has there been any meaningful substitute. But the attitude that good governance depends most on the appointment of good people, not the writing and enforcement of good laws, cannot be changed overnight. It is a tradition that was reinforced in post-1949 China for a quarter century by a centrally planned command economy in which plant managers had to be able to pick and choose between the rules and regulations that could be safely ignored and those that had to be enforced. If they had followed all of the rules faithfully, the economy would have ground to a halt.

Some limitations of China's legal system can be corrected easily if the government has the will to do so. The existence of secret rules and regulations not available to foreigners and others can be dealt with by publishing all rules and regulations where publication would not compromise national security. Persuading China's leaders to follow the law even when they believe that some other course of action would be better for the country is going to take time. Until self-restraint of this kind is practiced by the leadership, a truly independent judiciary will be difficult to achieve. An independent objective system for enforcing the law, however, is not an all-or-nothing proposition. It is easier to use law to enforce contracts between small producers than between large ones, and it is easier to enforce almost any business arrangement than it is to restrain extra-legal attempts to control political behavior. If a tradition of law is to be built in China, it is likely to be built first in the economic sphere.

Implications for American Policy

It is in the interests of the United States that China become rich and powerful, provided that this wealth and power are achieved through China's integration into the international economic (and political) system. It is not in America's interest to see China become a great power outside that system, although the United States is probably not in a position to stop China's transformation into a great power by whatever means China chooses.

The desire to have China become a key member of the international economic and political system requires little elaboration. Within the system, China has a stake in maintaining it. Outside the system, it has no such stake. A wealthy China will also be a society dominated by a large and increasingly well-educated middle class. Such a society is much more likely to become democratic than the poor peasant societies of China's past. It is much more likely to respect human rights and to avoid war, however imperfectly.

Several policy measures follow more or less automatically from this broader goal. The easy one is the continuation of most-favored-nation (MFN) treatment for China. Cutting off MFN is tantamount to throwing China out of the international economic system, at least as far as the United States is concerned. If an MFN cutoff hit China's exports hard, as would be likely, it could lead China's government to question key aspects of its outward-looking strategy. China would still seek to acquire advanced technology, particularly in the military sphere, but in ways more consistent than at present with its autarkic past. The likely decision of Europe and Japan not to join in the MFN cutoff would ameliorate but not entirely eliminate this result over the long term.

One sees arguments in the press and elsewhere that the continuation of MFN for China has been a failure because China has continued to arrest people on political grounds. The proper reasons for extending MFN, however, have little to do with short-term negotiating tactics over human rights or weapons sales. It is the long-term goal of a prosperous China integrated into the international economic system that matters.

Trade issues such as intellectual property rights and access for

American businesses to China's services markets, such as insurance, also fit within this framework of interests, although they are of far less importance to either China or the United States. The main issue in negotiations over these issues, fiery as the rhetoric often gets, is primarily money. If the Chinese gain access to the U.S. market, Americans deserve access to theirs for goods and services where the United States has a comparative advantage. If access is not made available, it is appropriate to retaliate and vice versa. The United States is also much less tolerant of those who pirate its intellectual property than it was twenty or thirty years ago, when the practice was widespread elsewhere in Asia but the Asian markets were still small. Some Chinese in positions of influence recognize that protection of property rights is in China's own interest even if they are not willing to expend much political capital to achieve this goal.[9]

China's entry into international economic bodies such as the World Trade Organization raises more fundamental issues, as David Lampton has also indicated in his chapter. The long-term goal is clear. It is in the interests of the United States, of China, and of the rest of the world for China to join the WTO, with China fully abiding by the rules of the organization. Full membership in accordance with WTO rules would further the development of China's foreign trade, both its exports and its imports. Efforts to limit trade, by either China or its trading partners, would be abolished, and violations would be settled through WTO enforcement mechanisms. As China's trade continues to grow rapidly, China would acquire more and more of a stake in the system that made this expansion possible.

Of equal importance is that full WTO membership would require China to set up a system of law compatible with WTO requirements. The WTO is an impersonal rule or law based system. There is no room in it for a high degree of personal discretion on the part of government officials.

The problem is that China does not now have a system that fits the WTO requirements, and many aspects of a system compatible with the WTO cannot be created overnight. The question thus becomes one of what can realistically be expected of the Chinese and whether what can be achieved is sufficient to justify modifying WTO requirements to fit the Chinese reality. In formal terms, the issue is whether to give China developing country status within the WTO or to insist on developed country status. Some modified form of developing country status would give China time to comply with the rules. Insisting on developed country rules within a short time frame is tantamount to vetoing China's entry.

Delineating a full set of goals for negotiations over China's membership in the WTO is beyond the scope of this chapter. If one wants China to become a member, however, some principles are clear. For example, it would not be feasible to negotiate detailed liberalization schedules sector by sector without dragging the process out indefinitely. Nor should WTO negotiations become a vehicle for discussing all kinds of issues unrelated to the international trading system. One can talk about a time frame for the abolition of all nontariff barriers to trade, for the reduction of tariffs, and for compliance with other WTO rules. A realistic time frame will be relatively long for some issues and shorter for others, but even the long term should be shorter than the year 2020, the date by which members of the Asia Pacific Economic Cooperation (APEC) organization, including China, have already agreed to meet liberal trading requirements. Questions that will require a longer time frame include those connected with the liberalization of the trade in grain. Food prices and food availability are very sensitive issues for the Chinese leadership. Crop failures and food price changes are seen as a potential source of major political instability, and no Chinese leader is going to trust the market any time soon to provide the necessary correctives.[10] China will also want to carry out some kind of industrial policy designed to develop certain key sectors such as automobiles and electronics. China should be required to give up infant industry protection of this type, but not until its per capita GDP rises significantly above mid-1990s levels. Realistic requirements of this type will keep the pressure on China to live within the rule of the world trading system, but will give China ample room to carry out its economic development programs.

While an agreement bringing China into the WTO would include provisions delaying the implementation of certain WTO rules, in some cases for as much as a decade, it is in American interests, that is, if China agrees to fully comply with WTO rules by some date certain in the future. Once committed to the principle of abiding by WTO rules, China will be under steady pressure to implement the changes in its economic system that it has agreed to, pressure that is likely to be much more effective than the current ad hoc approach through bilateral trade negotiations.

China's entrance into the WTO will not end all trade friction, any more than has been the case elsewhere. But China and China's trading partners will have a clear view of what the system requires. There will also be a mechanism for dealing with noncompliance that will be less contentious than the current noisy bilateral approach of the United States Trade Representative.

Furthermore, the entrance of China into the WTO will not guarantee that China will avoid a collision course with the United States or other nations. Nor will the rule of law in the trade sphere in China guarantee the spread of the rule of law into the area of civil liberties. But the rule of law must start somewhere. If it works well in one area, it is reasonable to expect that it will be increasingly tried in other areas. If China is not part of the international economic system, it is likely to become more, not less, difficult to deal with as time passes. Even outside the system, China will grow steadily in economic and trading power, but it will have no incentive to play by the rules of the international system. Periodic trade wars may not be as serious as a return to a new cold war in the security sphere, but they will be bad enough. U.S. policy should be oriented toward ensuring that they do not occur.

Notes

[1] In 1981 at a previous American Assembly conference I wrote that Chinese reforms then underway were likely to produce sustained growth rates in GDP of 6 to 8 percent per year. While these projections met with considerable skepticism at the time, China's actual growth rate has been at or above the upper end of this range. See Solomon (1981), p. 120.

[2] These calculations are based on data in Ren Ruoen and Chou Kai (1995). See also Keidel (1994).

[3] The data for Western Europe are from Maddison (1995).

[4] Official data used in this chapter, unless otherwise noted, are from State Statistical Bureau (1995, 1996).

[5] The data in this paragraph are from Orleans (1961), pp. 68–75, and Cheng (1965), pp. 72, 198.

[6] These totals were derived from data in State Statistical Bureau (1995), p. 590.

[7] In the discussion of the American Assembly group with Vice Premier Zhu Rongji, the vice premier put particular emphasis on the importance he placed on the buildup of China's foreign exchange reserves. This emphasis may reflect a shift in thinking among Chinese leaders toward the kind of mercantilist policies practiced by Japan and South Korea at various times, but whatever the wishes of Chinese policy makers, it will be Chinese savings and investment rates that will determine whether or not China will continue to accumulate foreign reserves.

[8] For a more in-depth discussion of China's international economic policies, see Lardy (1994).

[9] During the American Assembly group's June 1996 visit to China, more than one of its Chinese hosts, themselves authors of books and other publications, mentioned that they personally had lost significant amounts of income because of the publication of pirated copies of their books.

[10] There are individuals in the Chinese leadership who would be comfortable relying on the international market for significant amounts of grain, but there are many others who want to limit such dependence as much as possible if it can be done at an acceptable level of cost.

5

Breaking the Impasse over Human Rights

HARRY HARDING

E ver since the mid-1980s, and especially since the Tiananmen crisis of 1989, human rights has been one of the most prominent and contentious issues in U.S.–China relations. The U.S. government, many American nongovernmental organizations, and much of the American press have repeatedly criticized the absence of democracy and the violations of human rights in China. The United States has employed a variety of measures—from private diplomacy to public criticism to threats of economic sanctions—to try to force change in China's system of governance and to gain greater respect for human rights in China.

HARRY HARDING is dean of the Elliott School of International Affairs and professor of political science and international affairs at the George Washington University in Washington, D.C. Dr. Harding is a specialist on Asian affairs with a particular interest in China. He is a trustee of the Asia Foundation, a director of the Atlantic Council of the United States, a director of the National Committee on U.S.–China Relations, and a director of the U.S. Committee of the Council for Security Cooperation in the Asia Pacific. He is the author of *A Fragile Relationship: The United States and China Since 1972* (1992), other books concerning China's domestic issues and foreign relations, and numerous articles.

Unfortunately, none of these measures has achieved significant or lasting results. The Chinese government has occasionally made a few gestures to mollify American critics, such as releasing a few dissidents from prison, or promising to allow international inspections of its prisons. In general, however, China's treatment of political dissent, autonomous labor unions, or independent religious organizations has not improved since 1989. Indeed, most human rights organizations in the United States would say that the human rights situation in China has continued to deteriorate.

But examining the same record, many Chinese would come to a different conclusion. They would argue that, despite the Tiananmen crisis, the last two decades have seen marked progress in promoting human rights in their country. The overall political situation has remained stable. The standard of living for the majority of the population has improved, in many cases dramatically. Ordinary people have greater freedom from government or party intervention in their daily lives. There has been widespread progress in enhancing the rule of law, in enlarging the power of legislative bodies, and in popularizing competitive local elections. Chinese find it difficult to understand why American observers fail to acknowledge that these improvements have taken place.

Thus China and the U.S. have reached an impasse over human rights. Where Chinese see progress, Americans see stagnation, even retrogression. Where Americans see grounds for criticism, many Chinese find reasons for satisfaction.

This impasse over human rights has undermined the broader Sino-American relationship. The perception that China systematically violates the human rights of its people has greatly exacerbated American concerns about a number of other issues. Many Americans now worry that China will drastically limit the exercise of political freedom in Hong Kong, once it regains sovereignty over that territory. Others believe that the absence of democratic institutions in China makes it more likely that China will engage in aggressive or uncooperative international behavior as its economic and military power grows. Still others argue that Beijing's growing trade surplus with the United States is the result of the use of child and prison labor to produce goods for export, as well as the maintenance of artificially low wages through the chronic suppression of independent trade unions.

At the same time, the human rights issue has also significantly damaged Chinese perceptions of the United States. Many Chinese, ordinary people as well as government officials, believe that the American preoccupation with human rights is the latest evidence that the United States remains a hegemonic power, which tries to interfere in the internal affairs of other countries in order to impose its political system and cultural values on them. The purpose of that intervention, many Chinese now believe, is to keep China weak and divided, by undermining the central government, by encouraging regional separatism, and by fomenting social unrest. In this way, American policy toward human rights in China is perceived not only as ill-informed, but also as ill-intentioned.[1]

The impasse over human rights is thus a highly emotional one. It touches some of the core values in each society: the American values of freedom, individualism, and democracy, and the Chinese values of sovereignty, national pride, and self-determination. It evokes each society's core myths: America's missionary responsibility to carry freedom and democracy overseas, and China's struggle against foreign intervention in its internal affairs. Increasingly, too, it is related to the shift in the relative power of the two countries: China's determination to become strong, and America's desire to maintain its leadership role in international affairs. Managing this complex and controversial issue will test the two countries' ability to develop and maintain a stable and cooperative relationship. How can China and the United States avoid chronic tension, let alone acute confrontation, over the issue of human rights?

Some observers, both Chinese and American, argue that the only way out of this conundrum is for the United States to abandon its attempt to promote human rights in China. They share the conclusion that a concern with human rights represents a residual commitment to ideology, in an era when international relations are increasingly preoccupied with such pragmatic questions as economics and security. They believe that only when questions of human rights are set aside can Sino-American relations become more stable.

This chapter adopts a different approach. It begins with the assumption that the United States is unlikely to abandon its interest in promoting human rights abroad, as a strong strain of idealism continues to run through much of American thinking on international affairs, and as Americans increasingly believe that respect for human rights is strongly correlated with responsible international conduct and with an attractive environment for foreign investment. But if the human rights issue cannot properly be set aside, at least it can be managed more successfully and more productively than has been the case in recent years. To do so, however, will require several conditions: China must embrace a program of gradual political reform and acknowledge the legitimacy of international concern about its human rights practices; the United States must adopt a broader definition of human rights and take a longer-term approach to the promotion of democracy. On that basis, there is the possibility that the two countries can work cooperatively to promote greater respect for human rights in China and elsewhere, and can reach an understanding about how to manage their remaining differences.

The Impasse over Human Rights

The Maoist era in China, especially the period of the Cultural Revolution (1966–1976), witnessed massive violations of Western concepts of human rights, as well as a significant departure from China's own traditions of humane governance. The widespread popular violence against alleged "class enemies," the forced relocation of millions of youth into the Chinese countryside, the millions more arrested or sent to labor camps, the dissolution of China's legislative and judicial institutions, the assault against the practice of religion, the assertion of total control over the press—all these developments constituted one of the most brutal episodes in either Chinese history or modern world history.

Even so, China's poor record on human rights was not an insuperable obstacle to the improvement of Sino-American relations from 1969 through the mid-1980s. At first, both countries agreed to set aside their ideological differences for the sake of their common interest in opposing Soviet hegemonism. Then, in the post-Mao era, China embarked on a program of both economic and political reform, with some intellectuals calling for fuller democratization, and even for the adoption of some American political institutions and American political practices. As a result, many Americans concluded that China was evolving in positive directions, particularly as compared with other Communist countries, and were willing to work together with the Chinese government to promote further change.[2]

By the mid-1980s, however, Americans had become increasingly concerned about the violation of human rights in Tibet, the suppression of dissent among Chinese intellectuals, and the use of coerced abortions in China's family planning program.[3] For the first time since the Sino-American rapprochement of the early 1970s, human rights became a controversial and contentious aspect of the bilateral relationship. Ironically, this was so even though China's overall human rights record had been substantially improving in the course of economic and political reform. Not only were living standards rising, but Chinese were freer to explore new ideas and travel abroad.

This paradox can be explained in several ways. Although Chinese leaders relaxed many administrative controls over their society, they simultaneously reasserted limits on political expression through campaigns against "spiritual pollution" and "bourgeois liberalization." And with more foreigners—including American journalists—allowed to reside in China, these remaining limitations on political, religious, and social freedoms became increasingly visible. Thus even as conditions in China improved, Chinese intellectuals came into more frequent conflict with government restrictions on their freedom of speech, and American criticism of China's human rights record became more intense.

Still, the concern with human rights was only one strand in the broader tapestry of Sino-American relations in the mid-1980s. Most Americans remained convinced that China was moving in the right direction, both economically and politically. Other aspects of the relationship, especially in the cultural and economic spheres, remained highly cooperative. Even though Soviet foreign policy under Gorbachev was becoming more accommodative, China and the United States shared a major common strategic interest in securing the withdrawal of Vietnamese forces from Cambodia.

It was the Tiananmen crisis that brought the human rights issue to the very center of the Sino-American relationship, and transformed it into a subject for confrontation rather than cooperation.

The massive demonstrations in the heart of Beijing in spring 1989 convinced many Americans that the Chinese people wanted more democracy than the regime had been willing to provide, and raised the expectation that there would soon be further political reform. The suppression of the protests on June 4 was televised extensively in the United States, and many Americans concluded that the Chinese government was simultaneously brutal (because of the severe crackdown on the demonstrations) and weak (because of the scope and duration of the protests).

Meanwhile, developments elsewhere—particularly the fall of the Berlin Wall, the collapse of the Soviet Union, and the further democratization of Taiwan—suggested to some observers that the world was experiencing nothing less than the "end of history." Democratic institutions were on the ascendant, and democratic ideology had overcome its last authoritarian challenge. From this perspective, China seemed a far less admirable place than only a few years before. It had moved from the vanguard of political and economic reform to the rear. It now seemed to be one of the few countries in the world in which authoritarian impulses remained strong. At the same time, the disintegration of the Soviet Union and the withdrawal of Vietnamese forces from Cambodia also removed the common overriding strategic interests that might otherwise have placed the issue of human rights in a broader perspective.

As a result, American policy on human rights in China changed fundamentally, with regard to both ends and means. American policy now focused on promoting political and civil rights, even democracy, rather than on the broader objective of encouraging the reform and opening of China. And American strategy emphasized the use of coercive, rather than cooperative, means. The U.S. hoped that threatening economic sanctions—such as revoking China's most-favored-nation status, imposing tariffs on state owned or military owned enterprises, or withholding economic and technical assistance of various kinds—would have a positive effect, given China's growing dependence on the American export market. U.S. policy was also based on the assumption that China simply needed a push from abroad for the democratic impulses evident during the "Beijing Spring" to succeed.

The transformation in U.S. policy was catalyzed by American domestic politics. The Bush administration's attempts to stabilize Sino-American relations between 1990 and 1992 were condemned by many congressional Democrats and by much editorial opinion as "coddling dictators" in Beijing. The Clinton administration came into office in 1993 committed to a tougher and more vigorous policy of promoting human rights in China, including the linkage of the renewal of China's most-favored-nation status to Beijing's human rights record.

At first, many Chinese seemed to welcome American pressure on human rights. But as time went by, persistent American criticism increasingly appeared to deny China's continuing progress in the 1990s. After the Tiananmen crisis, Chinese leaders placed the highest emphasis on regaining political legitimacy by promoting rapid economic growth. By the mid-1990s, they had made remarkable progress in combining high rates of growth with relatively low rates of inflation. More and more Chinese gained access to higher incomes and a broader array of consumer goods. Economically, the way of life of ordinary Chinese continued to improve.

At the same time, although the Chinese government continued to crack down on individuals and organizations that it feared might pose a challenge to stability—particularly political dissidents, labor organizations, independent religious groups, and the press—it also permitted the formation of a large number of apolitical non-governmental organizations, as well as the expansion of the role of private entrepreneurship in the Chinese economy. In addition, the Chinese government undertook a modest program of political reform, with a particular emphasis on increasing the consultative role of legislative bodies, conducting competitive elections at the grass-roots level in rural areas, and enhancing the authority of the legal system to handle civil and criminal cases. It said relatively little about this political reform program publicly, largely out of fear that excessive propaganda would raise public expectations that could not be fulfilled. But still, political reform continued in the post-Tiananmen period.

In this context, the steady American criticism of China's human rights record struck many Chinese as being both uninformed and unreasonable. The United States appeared to be interested in a relatively small range of political freedoms—especially the rights of free speech and of independent organization—while ignoring China's progress in the social and economic spheres. Americans also seemed preoccupied with the rights of a small number of political dissidents, rather than the overall condition of the Chinese public as a whole. As Chinese saw it, the U.S. ignored the progress that China was making in other areas of human rights.

Indeed, American human rights policy suggested to many Chinese that the U.S. wanted China to follow the path of the former Soviet Union and Eastern Europe—toward economic decay, social unrest, and political instability. Many Chinese saw the American preoccupation with the human rights issue as a pretext for refusing to cooperate with China's continuing economic development, rather than as a sign of sincere concern for the well-being of the Chinese people. They interpreted American support for political dissidents and promotion of democracy as an attempt to induce unrest, instability, and even political collapse in China. The result was a decline in good will toward the United States and a rise in nationalism among many urban Chinese. Even those who acknowledged the violations of human rights in China still resented American pressure and questioned American motives.

Thus the American pressure failed to achieve significant results in those areas of greatest concern to the United States. Pressure secured the release of a few political dissidents, promises to participate in bilateral or multilateral discussion of human rights issues, and pledges to allow international inspections of Chinese prisons. But the release of a few prisoners did not presage any increase in Beijing's overall tolerance of dissent; and China's promises to engage in international dialogue or to permit international monitoring of its human rights record remained unfulfilled once it was clear that the sanctions would not be imposed. This pattern of behavior reflected China's calculation that the cost of compliance with American pressure was high, while the cost of defiance was low. The U.S. failure to fulfill its threat to revoke China's most-favored-nation status in 1994 simply confirmed Beijing's calculations.

The lack of progress on human rights, in turn, did great damage to China's reputation in the United States. At the time of the Tiananmen crisis in 1989, China's growing role in the global strategic balance and in the international economy was not fully perceived in the United States. As a result, its violations of human rights were regarded as deplorable, but not especially dangerous internationally. By the mid-1990s, however, China's expanding economy, its growing trade surplus with the United States, and its program of military modernization placed its human rights record in a very different, and even more negative, light. Now, its lack of democratic institutions made its growing military power appear far more threatening. In the eyes of many Americans, the way in which the Chinese military had treated its own people in the streets of Beijing in June 1989 provided an alarming forecast of the way it would treat the rest of Asia once it had acquired sufficient force projection capability. And the rising tide of Chinese exports to the United States, once seen as evidence of Chinese diligence and entrepreneurship, was now interpreted as the result of the repression of workers' rights and the mobilization of prison and child labor.

In short, America's approach to the promotion of human rights in China has failed. Not only has it failed to achieve any significant improvement in China's human rights record, but, equally important, it has damaged America's reputation in the eyes of many Chinese, including those who are committed to reform. They have concluded that the American position on human rights in China is ill-informed and insincere, and that it masks the intention of blocking China's rise to power by undermining China's social stability and political order. At the same time, the failure to make any progress on the human rights issue is exacerbating other tensions in U.S.–China relations, especially by heightening concerns that China is becoming a major threat to American economic and security interests.

Managing the Human Rights Issue

Breaking this impasse requires a fresh approach to the human rights dimension in Sino-American relations. This new strategy will not enable the two countries to reach complete consensus on the issue of human rights. But it will permit them to *identify their common interests* on the issue of governance in China, to *develop cooperative programs* for pursuing those common interests, and to *identify appropriate strategies* for addressing their remaining differences. The overall aim of the approach is to transform the human rights issue from confrontation to at least partial cooperation.

1. *The United States should adopt a more comprehensive definition of human rights, so as to include social and economic rights as well as political and civil freedoms.*

In recent years, the United States has been preoccupied with the state of individual political and civil freedoms in other countries: freedom of expression, freedom of organization, freedom of protest, freedom of religion, the existence of opposition political parties, free and competitive elections, freedom from torture, the right to legal counsel, and the right to a fair and speedy trial.

These are, to be sure, important rights. They are the core values of the American Revolution, and the values that attracted so many immigrants to the United States. They are also universally recognized, enshrined in the International Covenant on Civil and Political Rights. But they are not the sum total of any reasonable international definition of human rights. Equally important are social and economic rights: the rights to subsistence, to development, to employment, to education; and the special rights of women and children and the elderly. These, too, have international standing, in that they are embodied in the International Covenant on Economic, Social, and Cultural Rights. Moreover, political and civil freedoms are not the only things that people value in their political lives. Other political goods, including stability, effective governance, and absence of corruption, are also worthy of pursuit.

The American preoccupation with political and civil liberties has several shortcomings. The U.S. appears indifferent to the concerns of people of poorer countries for subsistence and development. And by focusing on the fate of a relatively small number of political dissidents, the U.S. may give the impression that it is in favor of instability and disorder. Such a narrow definition also minimizes the areas of common interest between the United States and countries like China, and magnifies the areas of disagreement.

Thus the United States should adopt a broader concept of human rights. Specifically, it should pay as much attention to the protection of social and economic rights as to the promotion of political and civil liberties. And in the sphere of political and civil lib-

erties, it is preferable for the U.S. to focus on the promotion of institutional reforms, rather than on the fate of individual dissidents.
As important as the release of political prisoners may be to the individuals and their families, it does nothing to reform the political
and legal institutions that imprisoned them in the first place.

Redefining our human rights agenda in this way will have several advantages. Not only will our policy come into greater con-
formity with the way in which much of the rest of the world, and
much of international law, defines the question of human rights. It
will also lay the basis for a more comprehensive and more balanced
assessment of China's human rights record, and for a more cooperative approach to the promotion of human rights in China.

2. *The United States should adopt a longer-term perspective toward the issue
of democratization.*

Most Americans naturally equate the promotion of human rights
with the promotion of democracy. Ultimately, they believe, the establishment and protection of human rights require the creation of
a more responsive and accountable government and a more pluralistic and independent society. Democracy embodies the set of institutions that best guarantee political responsiveness and social
pluralism. To most Americans, the sponsorship of democratic reforms seems to be a reasonable, even unassailable, position for the
United States to take.

But Americans need to understand the limitations to this definition of the problem. First, successful and sustained democratization requires a variety of accompanying institutional and cultural
preconditions. Higher levels of income, the emergence of a middle class independent of the state, higher levels of education, the
development of a culture of mutual tolerance (what is often called
a civic culture[4]) are all preconditions for democratization, and take
time to develop. In short, although democracy is not necessarily a
prerequisite for economic modernization, economic development
and the cultural changes that such development produces may be
a condition for successful democratization.

Thus democratization is usually a long-term process. Taiwan
and South Korea—two societies smaller and less complex than
China and with higher levels of American aid—required around

thirty years from the beginning of their economic takeoff before
they embarked upon democratization. There is no reason to believe
that China's progress can be significantly accelerated by external
pressure. It can, however, be facilitated by external assistance. In the
promotion of democracy, patience is truly a virtue.

Second, Americans should not be naive about the consequences
of democracy. There is a strong tendency in the United States to
believe that "all good things go together"—that democratization
will promote free markets, free trade, and peaceful foreign policy.[5]
Indeed, the Clinton administration's rationale for its efforts to "en-
large" the number of democracies around the world has been the
assertion that democratization will promote international stability
and prosperity. And yet, more recent research suggests a different
possibility. Democratization, especially in immature societies, can
permit the expression of nationalism that authoritarian regimes
once suppressed, and thus may not lead to peaceful foreign policies.
Moreover, democratic states can well adopt protectionist measures,
high corporate and societal subsidies, and other policies that can
contradict the principles of free trade and can restrict economic
growth. And, if not conducted properly, democratic reforms can
lead to social disorder and political instability. Thus democratization should be regarded as only one objective of American policy
toward China, not as the only one. In particular, the U.S. should be
sensitive to the traditional Chinese preoccupation with maintaining political order during periods of dynamic societal and economic change.

Third, Americans should realize that many foreigners, including
Chinese, view American-style democracy as having serious flaws.
They believe that pluralistic, competitive democratic institutions
tend to exaggerate the differences among political forces, rather
than building consensus. As a result, the policy-making process can
become fragmented, contentious, and eventually gridlocked. In addition, they also believe that the high cost of lobbying and campaigning in the United States produces a kind of "money politics"
that advantages the wealthy and powerful, while handicapping the
ordinary citizen. To those who view democracy, like any other political system, as a means to an end, rather than an end in itself, those
are powerful objections. American refusal to acknowledge these

problems makes the United States appear insincere and highly ideological.

Finally, Americans will also have to acknowledge that their own model of democracy has such unusual features that it may not be frequently replicated abroad. The American system—a directly elected president combining the roles of head of state and head of government, a considerable sharing of power between the executive branch and the legislature, a strong independent judiciary, a federal relationship between the central government and the states, and single-seat districts in the legislature—is highly distinctive. As China embarks on political reform, it is highly likely that it will look elsewhere for models of political structure. Indeed, for a transitional period, it may look to quasi-democratic, quasi-authoritarian political systems, including those in South Korea and Taiwan in the 1960s and 1970s, and those in much of Southeast Asia today. A program of gradual reform will keep the Chinese Communist party—or at least a reformed version of that party—in power for many years to come. Even at later stages of reform, China may develop political institutions that are unfamiliar to Americans. Still, this will represent progress, albeit with Chinese characteristics.

3. *Beijing should acknowledge that the international community is governed by an international regime on human rights, in much of which China already participates.*

Matters of governance can no longer be considered to be protected by the principle of absolute sovereignty. There is a growing body of international law, including several international conventions, that specifies the human rights that should be universally protected. There are both global and, in some places, regional institutions that assess the performance of national governments in protecting and advancing human rights. There is also ample precedent for the international community to take action, including sanctions, against governments that engage in gross violations of human rights.

China has already accepted the legitimacy of much of this international regime. It has ratified several of the most important international conventions on human rights. It participates in the United Nations Human Rights Commission, and engages in that body in critical assessments of other nations' human rights records. And by implementing international sanctions against the former apartheid regime in South Africa, China has accepted the appropriateness of sanctions against governments that severely infringe on human rights, and the legitimate authority of intergovernmental organizations to impose such sanctions.[6]

It would be extremely helpful to the management of the human rights issue in Sino-American relations if China were to accede to the remaining international covenants on human rights, particularly the International Covenant on Economic, Social, and Cultural Rights and the International Covenant on Civil and Political Rights. Americans should be aware that their own government ratified the second of these two international conventions only recently, and has not yet ratified the first. As signatories to those conventions, both China and the United States would have to engage in regular self-examinations of their own human rights records, as well as criticize the records of other states. They would also have to subject their behavior to potential scrutiny by the United Nations Human Rights Commission. This would place the issue of human rights in a more multilateral setting, and would provide a common set of criteria for discussions of each other's human rights record.

4. *China should continue a gradual program of political reform, based upon the realization that genuine stability in advanced societies is rooted in responsive political institutions.*

The recent history of Sino-American relations shows that the human rights issue can be more easily managed if China is implementing a program of political reform, albeit gradual and even halting. In the mid-1980s, as noted above, China's violations of human rights began to become an issue in Beijing's relations with the United States. And yet the human rights issue was manageable at first, among other reasons because Chinese leaders before the Tiananmen crisis appeared committed to steady political reform.

It would be helpful, therefore, if Chinese leaders were to recommit themselves to a program of political reform, such as that approved by the 13th Congress of the Chinese Communist party in 1987. Such a program would be intended to build more responsive, more effective, less corrupt, and less arbitrary political institutions.

These institutions would include competitive elections for government positions, a more powerful legislature, a stronger judicial
system, a better trained civil service, a freer press, and nongovernmental organizations with access to decision makers. An appropriate program of political reform would also allow the emergence of
a more pluralistic society, with greater autonomy from government
control. As noted above, some of these reforms are already underway, but they have not been combined into a comprehensive package.

Beijing should not undertake political reform simply to appease
or mollify the United States. Instead, it should do so from an understanding that political reform is a necessary concomitant of successful economic modernization, especially when economic
development results from a strategy that allows private enterprise,
integration with the outside world, and extensive market forces. By
denying the need for such a program of political change, Chinese
leaders are only exacerbating the danger that their political system
will eventually be swamped by social and political contradictions.
Conversely, as will be noted below, by launching such a program,
Chinese leaders will be building the institutions that are the key to
genuine stability and that increase the prospects for maintaining
long-term public support.

At the same time, renewing a genuine commitment to political
reform will carry significant international benefits. Not only will it
tend to reduce foreign criticism of China, but equally important, it
will create opportunities for Beijing to cooperate with other countries interested in promoting political reform and human rights in
China. Thus human rights issues can become the focus for cooperation, not just confrontation, in China's relations with the United
States and other Western countries.

5. *China and the United States should identify areas of common ground on
human rights, and work together to promote human rights in their two countries.*

On the basis of the preceding four points, China and the United
States would have begun to transform the human rights issue from
disagreement and confrontation to partial consensus and cooperation. They would have agreed that governments are responsible for
promoting a wide range of human rights—social, economic, polit-

ical, and civil. They would have agreed that those human rights are identified and protected by a body of international law. They would have agreed that governments are obliged, under that system of international law, to engage in self-criticism of their own human rights record, as well as being empowered to criticize the human rights violations of others. They would have agreed that the evaluation of any country's record must take all those human rights into account, not just a few. And they would have agreed that China needs both stability and gradual political reform.

On that basis, the two societies—including both governments and nongovernmental organizations—could engage in collaborative activities, both conceptual and practical, on the issue of human rights:

- On the conceptual level, Chinese and Americans could engage in a dialogue on the most appropriate definition of universal human rights, and on the institutional mechanisms for protecting and promoting them. The aim would be to contribute to what the Japanese scholar Onuma Yasuaki has called an "inter-civilizational consensus" on human rights, in which Asian and Western societies reach a new agreement on the matter, rather than simply adopting Western values and institutions to Asian circumstances.[7]

- Chinese and Americans could undertake more balanced and comprehensive assessment of the state of human rights in their two countries, featuring not only criticisms of each others' shortcomings, but also self-assessments of their own records.[8] The United States should, to the greatest degree possible, avoid double standards in its evaluations of China's human rights records. That is, it should not criticize China for suppressing dissent in Tibet if it ignores the similar suppression of separatism by the Russian government in Chechnya. Nor should it fail to praise China for the economic achievements that it would recognize in other countries.

- Chinese and Americans could also develop cooperative programs to promote human rights, building on some activities already underway. This could involve promoting the rule of law, civil service reform, local elections, and legislative development in China. It could also involve joint efforts to develop poorer regions, to protect the rights of children, and to enhance the status of women and minorities. In this way, the United States will be seen as providing significant assistance to support positive developments in China, not just offering criticism of the remaining shortcomings.

Such a strategy would enable dialogue and cooperation to replace criticism, pressure, and sanctions as the principal mechanism for promoting human rights in China and the United States. It would show that we are sincere in desiring progress for China and its people and not, as some Chinese believe, intent on destabilizing China's political system.

To make this strategy work, however, the U.S. will have to find the public and private resources to support these common efforts. The American government, American foundations, and American nonprofit organizations will have to finance collaborative programs to promote human rights in China. Otherwise, Chinese will call American sincerity into question, much as they did when the U.S. government offered meager material aid to the victims of flooding in China a few years ago.

6. *Both countries should also develop guidelines for managing the disagreements over human rights that will inevitably remain.*

If adopted by both governments, the approach outlined above would help ameliorate the human rights issue in U.S.–China relations. Still, it would be naive to believe that the issue could be eliminated completely. Americans will continue to perceive human rights abuses in China and will want to criticize them; and Chinese will continue to resent American criticism and pressure as evidence of American arrogance and even as American hegemonism. It is also unlikely that the two countries can come to complete consensus over the relative weight to be assigned to civil and political rights as against social and economic rights.

In addition to these chronic disagreements, even more contentious human rights issues may reemerge in Sino-American relations in the years ahead. Other than the emergence and suppression of political dissent in Hong Kong after the return to Chinese sovereignty in 1997, the most likely circumstance would be serious instability in China, accompanied by calls for more rapid political reform and democratization, followed by suppression of dissent in the name of stability. Given the uncertainties surrounding the succession to Deng Xiaoping, the possibility of a downturn in the Chinese economy, and the grievances produced by inequality, inflation, corruption, and unemployment, such a scenario cannot be ruled out.

In the event of such a crisis, it is important that the two countries—and especially the United States—keep the broader picture in mind. In particular, since the crisis would likely feature the suppression of political freedoms and civil rights in China, Americans should continue to weigh the importance of economic growth, social progress, and political stability in determining the welfare of the Chinese people. Americans also need to consider whether such a crisis involves sustained retrogression from political reform, or only a temporary setback. At the same time, given that the United States will be attempting to determine the significance of a domestic political crisis in China, it is important that Chinese leaders reconfirm their commitment to gradual but sustained political reform as soon as it is feasible to do so.

If such a crisis occurs in China, it is inevitable that Americans will express disappointment, and even outrage and shock, much as occurred after the Tiananmen crisis of 1989. It may also be appropriate to examine the situation in China in relevant international forums, such as the United Nations Human Rights Commission. Individual countries and international organizations may choose to suspend official development assistance or high-level ceremonial visits for a suitable period of time. And the international community would be far less forthcoming on global or regional issues of importance to China.

But the United States and the rest of the world should consider the use of trade sanctions only as a last resort, in those extreme cases when it is clear that there has been a severe, sustained, and deliberate retrogression in China's human rights record. Even then, it would be extremely unwise to suspend official dialogue altogether, especially given that it is possible to conduct relatively high-level, substantive discussions in ways that do not imply that the U.S. is disregarding or condoning the suppression of dissent. And it is always necessary to keep in mind the fuller range of economic, security, and other interests inherent in relations with China, so that human rights considerations do not inappropriately dominate American policy toward Beijing.

Conclusion

At present, the human rights issue is one of the most difficult elements of the U.S.–China relationship. The goal should be to transform the issue into an area for cooperation, rather than confrontation. To do so requires reconsidering our two countries' definitions of human rights so as to identify common interests; finding areas in which the two countries can work together to promote human rights; and identifying rules for managing the differences that will inevitably remain.

This recommendation will doubtless strike some observers as either excessively cautious or extremely naive. The proponents of realpolitik in both China and the United States may argue that it would be better for the two countries to remove human rights from their bilateral agenda altogether, and to focus exclusively on commercial relations and security questions. But given the enduring role of values in American foreign policy, such an approach is unlikely to be politically sustainable in the United States. Moreover, it ignores the fact that political reform will be necessary if China is to remain an attractive environment for foreign trade and investment and avoid the international security concerns that are produced by political repression and decay.

Other observers may doubt that either country will be able to take the approach to the human rights issue that is recommended here. They point out that Americans will find it difficult to adopt a broader definition of human rights, or to accept the possibility of cooperating with Beijing in promoting political reform in China, especially if that entails the continued rule of the Chinese Communist party. For their part, Chinese leaders may find it hard publicly to acknowledge the need for gradual political reform, for fear that this will encourage political protests from those groups and individuals who may want deeper change than the government is prepared to consider. And they may continue to resist any outside criticism of the remaining flaws in their human rights record.

Still, I am persuaded that the approach outlined in this chapter is the only feasible way to manage the human rights issue in Sino-American relations. If we cannot do so, the prospects for U.S.–China relations will remain guarded, given the contentious quality of the human rights issue and the way in which it is linked to virtually every other aspect of the Sino-American relationship. Since human rights cannot be set aside altogether, it must be managed effectively.

Conversely, if our two countries can adopt the kind of strategy proposed here, we can take a giant step toward transforming the human rights issue into an arena for cooperation, rather than confrontation, between China and the United States. And if these two great nations can reach a more constructive approach to the question of human rights, they will have taken a giant step away from provoking what Samuel Huntington has called a "clash of civilizations" between East and West,[9] and toward promoting an "inter-civilizational consensus" on human rights.

Notes

[1] Information Office of the State Council (1996).

[2] During the Carter administration, in fact, some argued that China was the beneficiary of an "exception" on human rights. If so, these factors may explain why. See Shirk (1977–78) and Cohen (1987).

[3] See Harding (1992), pp. 198–206, for a discussion of the rise of the human rights issue during this period.

[4] Almond and Verba (1963).

[5] This concept is discussed in Packenham (1973).

[6] See Kent (1995).

[7] Yasuaki (1996).

[8] China's most recent effort in this regard is the second white paper on human rights, published by the Information Office of the State Council in December 1995. It is useful as an indication of the Chinese government's definition of human rights, as well as evidence of China's recognition of an international regime governing human rights. Still, it is largely self-congratulatory, rather than self-critical. See "The Progress of Human Rights in China," in *Newsletter [of the] Embassy of the People's Republic of China*, no. 25 (December 28, 1995).

[9] Huntington (1993).

6

Commercial Diplomacy

JULIA CHANG BLOCH

R ising powers challenge the established international order,"
Thucydides tells us. China's rise to world power status is not
a question of "if" but "when." Its economic resurgence, followed
by its growing political influence and its potentially huge military
presence, is a certainty the world must deal with in the next century. China's economy doubled in size between 1985 and 1993, an

JULIA CHANG BLOCH is president of the United States–Japan Foundation and most recently was group executive vice president and head of
Corporate Relations for BankAmerica Corporation in San Francisco. Prior
to joining BankAmerica, she served as the United States ambassador to
the Kingdom of Nepal, becoming the first Asian American ambassador
for the United States. She was also a Peace Corps volunteer in Malaysia,
chief minority counsel for a Senate Select Committee, a Senate professional
staff member, and the deputy director of the Office of African Affairs at
the U.S. Information Agency. Ambassador Bloch is a member of the Council on Foreign Relations and the U.S. National Committee for Pacific Economic Cooperation. She is author of *A U.S.–Japan Aid Alliance*. She has
received numerous awards including the Hubert Humphrey Award for International Service (1979).

extraordinary achievement. Fully half of the growth in worldwide demand for products and services in the decade following 1996 will come from Asia, much of it from China.

At the same time, the inevitable bumps along the road to prosperity, which might be ignored or easily absorbed in another country, cannot be ignored with respect to China or, more generally, the nations of Asia as a whole: the sheer size of their economies commands attention. Together, Asian countries make up the largest consumer market in the world, and by the mid-1990s more than a third of the world's trade took place between Asia Pacific Economic Cooperation (APEC) countries. For the first time in several centuries, many East Asian economies have caught up with the West and cast off their earlier sense of inferiority. Throughout the region, therefore, Asians are saying good-bye to Western domination, politically, culturally, and economically. Asia is prepared to join the world as an equal partner, making its own decisions and deciding for itself the role it will play in the global community. Any policy maker, whether government or private, who fails to see this fundamental change and respond appropriately will risk the loss of an unparalleled opportunity; those who do not work *with* Asia will be excluded from the largest single event in the development of the world economy and from what the *New York Times* has called the "defining international political event of this era."

Huge Economy, Huge Market

A Quickly Expanding Economy

With over a billion citizens, China represents approximately one-fifth of the world. It has a population roughly five times larger than that of the United States and nearly twice that of all Western countries combined. Although China's annual population growth is a modest 1.01 percent, over 120 million Chinese children are in primary school, which indicates future growth in both human resources and consumption.

China's economic reforms, launched by Deng Xiaoping in 1978, have turned the country into the fastest growing economy in the world. With the growth of its gross domestic product in double dig-its for much of the 1980s and 1990s, China already has become an economic power. Using measures of purchasing power parity, the World Bank in 1993 estimated that China was the world's third largest economy after the United States and Japan. Although ques-tions about the continuity of reforms in the post-Deng era make China's future growth rate uncertain, Marcus Noland of Wash-ington's Institute of International Economics has calculated that even under a slow-growth scenario, China would emerge as the world's second largest economy in the decade to follow.

China's economic achievements have not been confined solely to growth. Progress in overcoming economic overheating has been stunning. From 1994 to 1995 inflation dropped from 24 percent to 17 percent and is expected to continue falling. A "soft landing," a gradual rather than sudden drop in its growth rate to about 10 per-cent, is now taking place.

Having reversed its trade balance by turning a record $12.2 bil-lion deficit in 1993 into a $5.3 billion surplus in 1994, China's 1995 trade surplus grew to $16 billion, or 2.6 percent of GDP. This trade surplus, coupled with a strong inflow of foreign investment, up 10 percent over the previous year to $37 billion, raised foreign ex-change reserves to more than $73.5 billion by the end of 1995. *Busi-ness China* estimated then that China represented approximately 3 percent of world trade, making it, as Xinhua News announced, the world's eleventh largest trading nation.

Chinese consumption as a measure of the market is another way to consider China's economic scale. The total work force numbered 615 million in 1994, and the per capita income is expected to rise to $6,000 by the year 2000. A Gallup poll of China, the first of its kind, concluded that a billion Chinese want to become rich and buy televisions, washing machines, refrigerators, and video cassette recorders. The Chinese appetite for Western consumer staples such as McDonald's and Coca-Cola, Marlboros and Proctor and Gam-ble shampoo runs high.

By anyone's measure, China should become the largest market in the world in the twenty-first century. The experience of the mar-ket leaders has shown that even modest inroads can reap great re-wards. McDonald's senior vice president Richard Starmann has recalled, "People said, why expand to China? Only 10 percent of the Chinese population can [currently] afford a Big Mac. Well, that's 100 million people. That's 5,000 stores." At the time, McDonald's operated approximately 11,400 stores in the United States. Entire industries are being sucked into China as companies transfer production. While they used to move jobs to take advantage of the cheap labor, many companies now go to China simply to supply its burgeoning middle class.

Sales of capital equipment are jumping as factories have to be equipped, roads built, and communication and transportation systems improved. In telecommunications alone, China plans to install almost 100 million phone lines over ten years, which will only begin to make a dent in the demand. The dimensions are staggering: such a project is the equivalent of creating a new phone system for the United Kingdom every three years, for over a decade.

However one counts or measures, China's sheer size means that the United States and the rest of the world must take China seriously. Where economics are concerned, China is a competitor, to be sure, but it is also an opportunity not to be missed.

Opportunities for the United States

Since China's economic reforms began, the United States and China have developed strong and significant commercial relations. Although China and the United States take different approaches to measuring their trade, by most reckonings, China is the United States' fifth largest trading partner, and the United States is China's third largest partner. U.S. and Chinese trade figures differ greatly because the United States includes reexports via Hong Kong; China does not. Annual bilateral trade rose to over $40 billion in 1995.

The United States is China's single largest export market (excluding Hong Kong), buying shoes, textiles and apparel, and, increasingly, electronic equipment. In the early 1990s China became the single fastest growing overseas market for U.S. exports, increasing at an annual rate of 21 percent, from $5 billion in 1988 to over $10 billion in 1995. U.S. exports, up 16 percent in 1995, showed a strong performance in aviation, power generation, telecommunications equipment, chemicals, and agricultural products such as grain and cotton. According to Chinese sources, China imported

$1 billion worth of cereal and $800 million worth of cotton from the United States in 1995. U.S. figures indicate that cereal exports to China increased 570 percent from 1994 to 1995.

Long-Term Direct Investment

U.S. companies have made investment commitments in approximately 20,000 projects worth $26 billion in China, focusing on long-term, fixed, high-tech investment projects. As of 1994 this made the United States the largest foreign investor in China, although technically it was the second largest after Hong Kong/Macau. U.S. annual investment has risen 620 percent since 1990, with the U.S. share of total foreign direct investment (FDI) in China rising compared with other countries' investments in 1995. By 1995 the U.S. share of projects accounted for 9.6 percent of total investments that year. Despite such increases, Japan overtook the United States in late 1995 as the largest foreign investor in China.

According to the United States–China Business Council, "The commercial relationship has brought important benefits to both countries. U.S. companies, facing mature markets at home (and in Europe), need access to the Chinese market to grow and remain competitive throughout the world. China needs the experience, technology and markets the U.S. has to offer. U.S. consumers benefit from China's low-cost products."

Despite the mutual benefits from trade, U.S. exports to China have not expanded as quickly as China's exports to the United States, resulting in a trade imbalance that has become a flashpoint in U.S.–China bilateral relations and is prompting a negative reaction in the United States.

Most American firms are generally satisfied with the current status of their investments in China. Virtually all respondents in a 1994 survey by the U.S.–China Business Council reported that they were either profitable or at least meeting their long-term profit expectations. Questions on market penetration also drew generally positive responses, with more than half the respondents reporting that their ventures had met market-access goals.

Department of Commerce data confirm the profitability of U.S. direct investments in China, indicating an average return of 9.6 percent in 1993 versus a negative 5.6 percent in 1992. Returns in the manufacturing sector rose to 20.8 percent in 1993 from 9.1 percent in 1992.

Manufacturing concerns made up the majority of these "foreign-invested enterprises" (FIEs), with over half in the coastal areas, including Beijing (19 percent), Shanghai (26.2 percent), and Guangzhou (10 percent). All respondents noted that conditions had changed since they began doing business in China, an indication that Beijing had made some progress in addressing FIE concerns.

In the council's 1993 investment survey, member companies reported primary concerns regarding foreign exchange, housing, and labor practices. The foreign exchange issue improved dramatically after the January 1994 currency reforms. The top three concerns by mid-1994 were inflation, rising accounts receivable, and as expected, bureaucratic interference. At the same time, the FIEs characterized their relationships with their Chinese partners as positive to valuable, with only a minority (8 percent) registering them as counterproductive. They clearly value their Chinese counterparts' sales channels and ability to cut through the red tape.

Because of the small size of the sample (thirty-one FIEs), the survey cannot be considered definitive. It provides an overview of China's foreign investment environment, however, and reflects the concerns that foreign investors in China have had for a number of years. At the top of the FIEs' wish list for improving the business environment were specific suggestions for greater transparency in the Chinese legal system, streamlining the relationship between the Chinese bureaucracy and investors, and uniform fees and treatment of foreign nationals in China. But if the growth of U.S. direct investment in China is any indication, the continuing difficulties of doing business in China will not deter American investors.

Convergence of Commercial and National Interests

Emerging China: Danger or Opportunity

Despite the lure of China's huge market for U.S. business, most Americans still have two questions about China. Does China's economic resurgence present a danger or an opportunity for the United States? And is its rise good or bad for Americans?

Americans worry about job loss to cheap labor overseas, and the seepage of technology to a potentially powerful competitor. Patrick Buchanan's vitriolic attack against foreign trade, particularly trade with China, during the 1996 presidential campaign found ready supporters and touched a sympathetic chord among many Americans angered by international trade's perceived harmful effects on U.S. workers. Although experts debunked his rhetoric as self-defeating protectionism, the fear was real, and at least some jobs are lost to "cheap labor" overseas. Even the chairman of the Federal Reserve, Alan Greenspan, has spoken of the insecurity Americans feel in the national climate of layoffs. George David, president of United Technologies, which has successfully begun investing in China, admits that from 1990 to 1996 his firm has eliminated 33,000 jobs in the United States while creating 15,000 abroad.

But many experts feel the danger is overstated. The economist Paul Krugman argues that far more jobs are being lost to technological changes in the United States than through the export of jobs overseas. In addition, like trade itself, job loss is not a bilateral or zero-sum game. Overall, the creation of jobs overseas may have a net positive effect on Americans and the American economy. The U.S.–China Business Council estimates that "U.S. trade with China supports more than 200,000 high-wage American jobs, as well as tens of thousands of additional jobs in U.S. ports, retail establishments, financial institutions, and consumer goods companies [that support trade]."

Obviously, the more the U.S. exports to China, the greater is the U.S. involvement in that market and the greater the number of jobs in the United States that will be supported by the Chinese market. The real question is whether a company like Boeing best serves the interests of U.S. citizens by employing them in the short run or by maximizing profits worldwide so that ultimately it can hire more workers—even if in the interim, global expansion costs some jobs at home.

As for technology transfer, China is a master at exacting foreign technology as the price for access to its market. American corporations such as General Motors, McDonnell Douglas, and AT&T

have scrambled to win lucrative rights to operate in China by building sophisticated research facilities and factories there—the only way to get a share of the future Chinese market. There is increasing concern that such transfers to China may ultimately create a formidable competitor.

Although competition and job loss are issues Americans cannot ignore, the reality is that U.S. influence on China is limited. Where business is concerned, America's European and Asian rivals are only too eager to intensify the competition to win China's business at U.S. expense. Assistant Secretary of State Winston Lord confirmed this widely held view in his remarks to the House Ways and Means Committee during a 1996 hearing on China's most-favored-nation (MFN) status, as David Lampton, author of chapter 3, has also noted. Lord's image of the Europeans and Japanese first "holding American coats" to allow the United States to take on the Chinese with regard to a variety of issues but then stepping around America to "gobble up the contracts" is a powerful one.

Commercial Engagement Supports Change and Reform

Successive U.S. administrations from Nixon to Clinton, supported by proponents of U.S. business and trade, have consistently pursued commercial engagement as a stabilizing force in U.S.–China bilateral relations and as a liberalizing force within Chinese society. From the standpoint of U.S. national interests, this policy of engagement has helped secure Chinese cooperation in meeting vital regional and international security challenges, including those posed by the Gulf War, the Cambodian peace accords, and nuclear proliferation on the Korean Peninsula.

On the Bush administration's China policy, former Secretary of State James Baker wrote, "Economic reform, we believed, would in the long run lead to political liberalization, the surest way to ensure human rights for all in China." President Clinton went on to explicitly link economic and political liberalization when he said, "American jobs and prosperity are reason enough for us to be working at mastering the essentials of the global economy. But far more is at stake. For the new fabric of commerce will also shape global prosperity . . . and with it, the prospects of people around the world for democracy, freedom, and peace."

American business strongly agrees with this linkage. Nine chief executive officers of Fortune 100 companies (AT&T, Boeing, the Chrysler Corporation, Digital, General Electric, Honeywell, Kodak, Motorola, and TRW) wrote President Clinton in May 1994 arguing that U.S. trade and investment promote direct Chinese exposure to American companies, values, and ideas and contribute to economic freedom and economic choices for the Chinese people. They spoke from experience:

> U.S. companies operating in China bring with them management, personnel, ethical, environmental, manufacturing, quality and many other traditional and innovative business "best practices." These practices often have a profound and positive impact on the lives of Chinese employees and other Chinese with whom our companies interact. We believe . . . the benefits of the technology, practices and services which American companies bring to China continue to work to further open Chinese society.

These executives made the case that U.S. companies have been agents for positive change in China, greatly expanding the exposure of ordinary Chinese to Western influences. According to an industry paper, "Global Practices by U.S. Companies in China," U.S. companies are changing the environment and condition of the Chinese people, as they

- Promote American ideals through (1) human resource policies and practices that base advancement and reward on merit, performance, and productivity; (2) grievance systems that redress wrongs by petition; (3) business practices that eschew illicit payments; and (4) good corporate citizenship and corporate-community relations.
- Advance a more open Chinese society through the technologies utilized internally by the companies operating in China, as well as through the high-technology products and services that these companies sell to Chinese industries and consumers, exposing Chinese citizens to new information, ideas, values, behavior, and international standards.

- Accelerate Chinese exposure to the West. Through the technical and management training of employees and foreign travel by customers or government officials, Chinese visitors are exposed to market economies and to Western social and political processes.
- Provide and promote high standards in environmental, health, and safety practices through the example of company standards and practices as well as through technical assistance and the introduction of environmental technologies and industrial systems that minimize waste, control emissions, and enhance safety.
- Train local employees and suppliers in Western management and technical skills by (1) establishing technology laboratories in Chinese universities; (2) offering scholarships for Chinese students; and (3) teaching participatory management, empowered work force, employee teaming, total quality management, and just-in-time systems.
- Provide better employment alternatives for the Chinese by offering wages that are the highest available in China, benefit packages that exceed local Chinese requirements, and general physical working conditions that are higher than local standards.

Commercial Relations Increase
China's Stake in the Global Community

For over two decades the U.S. policy of engaging China and encouraging China to integrate itself into the global community has been largely successful. Most Chinese enjoy far better standards of living and human rights than they did two decades ago. As the Chinese economy developed closer ties with the West, supporters of commercial engagement believed that China would further liberalize its economy, increasingly submit to the rule of law, allow the free flow of information, and become a more responsible global citizen. Although there may be some ups and downs, in the long run, as suggested by recent experience in Asia, economic prosperity and the rise of a middle class would inexorably lead to a more pluralistic political system and eventually to a more favorable human rights environment and multiparty democracy.

Some major changes did occur. From the time of the major reforms launched in 1978 until the events in Tiananmen Square in

1989, China put economics in command of politics. China explicitly modified its global political policies in return for economic benefits. It declared peace with its neighbors, including traditional adversaries such as India, Vietnam, and the Soviet Union. It also improved its relations with Hong Kong and Taiwan and halved its military budget. Evidence of China's pragmatism can also be seen in its membership in the Pacific Economic Cooperation Conference (PECC) and the Asia Pacific Economic Cooperation forum, organizations that also count Hong Kong and Taiwan as members. Although China failed in its bid to join the World Trade Organization (WTO) before the group's formal launch in January 1995 to replace the General Agreement on Tariffs and Trade (GATT), it has continued access negotiations to become a member. Significant domestic changes in this period occurred as well; they are considered in chapter 4 of this volume.

By the mid-1990s, however, detractors of the engagement policy were gaining momentum as China increasingly appeared to be at odds with the West, particularly the United States, on key issues. Even as U.S.–China trade soared and foreign investment poured into China at the rate, some say, of $100 million a day, China continued to violate intellectual property rights (IPR) agreements, flaunt nonproliferation commitments, and rattle nerves around Asia by intimidating Taiwan with missile tests and war games.

China experts have been disheartened but not surprised by the changing signals from Beijing. By the mid-1990s, Deng Xiaoping had not been seen in public for two years. Beijing's leaders, intent on preserving their positions in the post-Deng era, were retreating from economic policies to concentrate on maintaining social stability. As President Jiang Zemin has tried to consolidate power, he has played a balancing act but has increasingly taken a hard line, appealing to Chinese nationalism and hanging tough on sensitive issues such as Taiwan and human rights.

China, however, has not entirely abandoned its economic pragmatism. In the midst of the worst crisis in U.S.–China relations since Tiananmen, China bought 400,000 tons of U.S. wheat. It also offered to finalize $4 billion in orders for commercial jets from Boeing and McDonnell Douglas, but linked the orders to a delay in U.S. sanctions on the intellectual property rights dispute. Beijing's interest in keeping its commercial relationship with the United States on track provides an opportunity for America to find the convergence in the two nations' commercial and national interests to stabilize a critical bilateral relationship.

Flashpoints in Commercial Relations

Commercial diplomacy, generally less contentious than its political or strategic cousins, could serve as a leading edge to stabilize U.S. bilateral relations with China. To do so, however, the flashpoints in U.S.–China commercial relations must first be managed. The flashpoints are driven by the uniquely American practice of linking noncommercial objectives to trade and economic policies and by the age-old Chinese tactic of holding business hostage to political interests. Since the events of 1989 in Tiananmen, the annual rite of renewing China's most-favored-nation trade status has become the greatest source of friction and mistrust in relations between Washington and Beijing.

Most-Favored-Nation Status

As other chapters also note, under U.S. law the president must extend MFN status to China as a "non-market economy" on a year-by-year basis only. The Jackson-Vanik amendment to the Trade Act of 1974 made MFN for "non-market economies" conditional on freedom of emigration, a move then aimed at restrictions on Jewish emigration by the Soviet Union. Although Chinese emigration to the United States is limited more by U.S. law than by Chinese government action, the classification of China as a "non-market economy" subjects it to an annual process of presidential certification in order to have its MFN status extended.

What is little understood is that MFN is the basis of normal trade relations between the United States and other nations, not an award of special favor to China. Over 160 countries have MFN trading status with the United States, and only six countries— Afghanistan, Cambodia, Cuba, Laos, North Korea, and Serbia/ Montenegro—are denied MFN status. Nonrenewal would bring into question the consistency of U.S. policy, given that the United

States extends MFN status to many countries that have abhorrent human rights records—for example, Iran, Iraq, and Libya. Moreover, nonrenewal would not serve the strategic interests of the United States and is highly unlikely to serve its stated purpose—an improvement in human rights in China.

Since Tiananmen, however, the annual certification process for China's MFN renewal has grown increasingly contentious. President Clinton renewed MFN status for China in May 1993, but, going beyond the requirements of Jackson-Vanik on freedom of emigration, linked further renewal to "significant overall progress" on human rights. This new stipulation proved temporary. Recognizing that democracy and human rights could be better served by "engagement" and by the integration of China into the global economy, President Clinton delinked human rights from the annual extension of MFN for China in May 1994.

The 1995 debate was brutally divisive, pitting an unholy alliance of the left and far right, who fought to relink MFN renewal for China with human rights and a host of other issues, against the president and a broad coalition of business and trade interests. Finally, the forces for renewal won in a cliffhanger congressional vote.

The 1996 debate, compared with those of previous years, covered the same ground but was relatively mild. As expected, President Clinton announced in May that he was renewing China's trade status, which was due to expire on July 3. Congress had sixty days to reject the decision. On June 17, the United States and China achieved a major breakthrough on intellectual property rights and averted a multibillion-dollar trade war at the eleventh hour. The resolution of the IPR conflict eased tensions in overall bilateral relations and smoothed the way for congressional approval in a bipartisan vote to extend MFN to China by an unusually large margin.

Intellectual Property Rights

There was high anxiety but no real surprise that the United States and China would reach agreement over copyright piracy just hours after the deadline to do so had passed. Too much was at stake for both countries. U.S. business did not want to lose deals or to be edged out of China's market, and China could ill afford to be shut out of the U.S. market, which absorbs a third of its exports. Even the *China Daily,* the official English news service of China, editorialized, "A trade war will benefit neither side."

The tit-for-tat threats of sanctions and retaliation, orchestrated for domestic political consumption, titillated observers, belying the gravity of the negotiations. Intellectual property rights is a serious problem with long-term consequences for global commerce. It is not a problem solely with China, however; the United States and other Western nations have similar concerns with most of the capitalist Third World. China, in fact, is a latecomer to the game, following the Third World practice of duplicating computer software without paying royalties, copying and exporting legally protected hardware, infringing trademarks, copying and distributing chemicals and pharmaceuticals without paying for them, exploiting access to trade secrets—in short, taking full advantage of Western products without paying the companies that own them.

The original commitment to mutual protection of intellectual property rights was included in the United States–China Bilateral Trade Agreement of 1979, although no serious followup was attempted until 1985. Additional measures followed in the 1990s, including the "Special 301" investigation of IPR protection by the United States in 1991, which resulted in a joint Memorandum of Understanding on IPR in January 1992. In 1994 another "Special 301" investigation of China was launched, after which the two sides reached a new agreement in February of 1995 to improve enforcement under growing pressure to do so.

Although there is wide agreement that the Chinese have improved certain aspects of IPR protection, notably at the retail level, enforcement at the production level remains limited. China has at least nominally complied with all aspects of the IPR agreement, including establishing a legal and judicial framework for IPR enforcement. Despite these efforts, however, piracy of U.S. software, videos, and sound recordings remains a serious problem.

The International Intellectual Property Alliance, a group of movie, recording, software, and book producers, reported that losses from Chinese piracy increased to $1.1 billion in 1995 from $866 million in 1994. If the $1.2 billion in China related losses claimed by the entertainment software industry are also included, the actual losses estimated by the industry for 1995 would amount to $2.3 billion.

The most graphic illustration of such piracy was provided by the compact disk industry. The alliance claimed that China's CD factories have a capacity to produce a total of 100 million CDs annually, but sell only 5 million to 7 million legitimate units domestically. Pirated products account for the remainder, with half being sold in China and half overseas.

In a U.S.–China Business Council survey, one-third of the participants reported experiencing some form of IPR infringement in China, whether patent, trademark, or copyright problems. Of those who had registered their intellectual property with China, only 11 percent reported infringement, but one-third still reported trademark problems. Most typically, companies "on the ground" seek negotiation or an administrative solution, and apparently these efforts have been largely successful, with most reporting satisfaction with the outcome.

From the Chinese perspective, the concept of intellectual property is new, and incorporating Western capitalist concepts of ownership into Chinese socialist law is a complex process. As a signatory of the 1992 Memorandum of Understanding and the 1995 joint agreement, China has essentially accepted the West's definition of intellectual property, agreeing to very broad protection of copyrights, patents, and trade secrets. This puts China in the vanguard of the Third World in intellectual property rights. Taiwan, for example, still refuses to accept such sweeping agreements.

The 1996 IPR agreement notwithstanding, the United States needs to hold China to its commitments, and China needs to enforce those commitments more vigorously. The conflict over intellectual property is about theft and how to establish a legal framework in which companies can trade and invest with confidence. What is at stake is whether China, already one of the world's largest trading nations, will agree to abide by the basic rules that govern international trade.

Technology Transfer

A potentially more serious problem for industrialized countries and the international system is China's appropriation of proprietary technology. In the long run this issue is more serious than the pirating of computer software, movies, and music. Because China maintains tariffs that average 30 percent and may run as high as 100 percent for products such as automobiles, foreign companies are forced to build factories in China if they want access to the Chinese market. Beijing often very successfully and skillfully plays off one multinational against another. In 1995, for example, General Motors competed with Mercedes Benz to see who would give China the most technology in return for the right to manufacture and sell cars in China. In the end both companies committed sophisticated technology to design and build new models. What makes this a particularly serious problem is that the technology is often then stolen.

In a well-publicized case, the DuPont Company found that one of its major herbicide products was being made by thirty different Chinese state owned companies. Not only were those companies squeezing DuPont out of business in the China market, but they were also crowding DuPont out of markets elsewhere in Asia. Seven of the Chinese companies were exporting, some using the DuPont packaging and brand name. But as is true for other major corporations, competition and the lure of the Chinese market keep DuPont in the game; it continues to invest heavily in China.

The World Trade Organization

Global commerce can ill afford to have a major player like China not playing by market rules and conventions. If China is allowed to pirate whatever products and technology it chooses, the international system could well break down. The system might withstand infractions by small trading nations, but it would be overwhelmed by piracy on the scale and volume of China's, if left unchecked.

The exclusion of such a large economy from the rules-making body for global trade, therefore, would spell failure for the organization. At the same time, the WTO is a rules based organization, and it behooves a nation of China's size and stature to meet the criteria for membership. As other chapters also emphasize, the disagreement over the terms of China's membership needs to be worked out—whether China joins as a developing or developed nation.

During its consultation trip through Asia in June 1996, the American Assembly group found broad support for admitting China to the WTO on its terms and as soon as possible. Even the APEC Business Advisory Council (ABAC), whose executive membership is generally averse to controversy, has taken the position that APEC should push for China's admission. Although the United States is being painted as the obstructionist, this stalemate cannot be broken unless both sides come to a meeting of the minds.

U.S. Trade Deficit

Business Week appeared prophetic when it noted in October of 1995 that "China may already have eclipsed Japan as America's number one trade headache." The United States has had a consistent trade deficit with China since 1983. The growth of the deficit from $2 billion to $33.6 billion in 1995 had made it the second largest, after Japan's. But in June 1996 China surpassed Japan as the country having the biggest trade surplus with the United States. China's surplus had climbed to $3.3 billion, while Japan's had decreased to $3.24 billion from $5.3 billion a year earlier.

These figures, however, must be kept in perspective. Chinese analysts persistently told the American Assembly group in Beijing and Shanghai in June 1996 that "U.S. statistics have greatly exaggerated the trade deficit with China." They point to the studies of Nicholas Lardy of the Brookings Institution, which show that our bilateral trade deficit may be overstated by as much as 40 percent. The problem centers on how trade figures are kept.

Analysts agree that the accuracy of the figures is suspect because a great deal of Chinese trade passes through Hong Kong and may be mislabeled. U.S. Commerce Department data do not fully take into account that half of what U.S. companies sell to Hong Kong is subsequently reexported to China, while two-thirds of what the United States buys from China also passes through Hong Kong entrepreneurs, who make at least a quarter of the gross profits from these goods. Also, a large portion of China's export earnings goes to foreign firms who process about half of all Chinese exports.

Moreover, much of the reason for the rise in the U.S. deficit with China can be attributed to a displacement of U.S. imports from

Hong Kong and Taiwan because of production shifts from those countries to China. The U.S. deficit with Hong Kong and Taiwan decreased by about $13 billion between 1987 and 1992; for the same period, the U.S. deficit with China rose by $15.5 billion. In effect, Hong Kong and Taiwan shifted their surpluses to China.

China protectionist trade secrets, however, cannot be discounted as a cause for this surplus. Commerce Secretary Mickey Kantor, further blaming Chinese trade policies that maximize exports and limit imports, attributed the persistent deficit with Beijing to "unfair practices on the part of China, not only the piracy of U.S. products but also keeping U.S. products out of the Chinese market."

At the same time, it must be recognized that U.S. policy constraints against American exports have also exacerbated the deficit. The annual MFN debates have fed concerns in China about the reliability of U.S. companies as long-term suppliers. The fact that the United States has maintained economic sanctions against China far longer than any other country has also depressed U.S. exports. A U.S. embargo against China was in effect from the onset of the Korean War until 1971, the beginning of normalized relations, and many of the sanctions initiated in 1989 because of Tiananmen remained standing even in 1996, when all other major exporting nations had long since abandoned them. The provisions of the 1989 sanctions, for example, prohibited the sale of steam turbines and generators to China. It is estimated that U.S. firms such as Westinghouse and General Electric lost sales in what is anticipated will be a $200 billion market over the next ten years, of which at least 25 percent will consist of new generation capacity ordered from foreign suppliers.

In addition, most of the big procurement deals go to non-American companies because U.S. export credits are traditionally less generous and less predictable than those of other nations. In the case of the Three Gorges Dam project, the largest civil engineering project in the world with a price tag of at least $24 billion, the U.S. Export-Import Bank decided after much delay against export financing for U.S. equipment because of environmental concerns, effectively leaving American companies like Caterpillar and Rotec out in the cold.

In sum, in an era of mobile capital and global trade, where economics and politics are increasingly linked, simple bilateral calculations of trade deficits are less meaningful and may be misleading. Nevertheless, the trade deficit is a sensitive issue for the United States and adds fuel to demands for counterprotectionist measures as well as to demands for further opening the Chinese market and increasing transparency.

Nonproliferation

U.S.–China commercial relations were further aggravated by alleged Chinese sales of nuclear and missile technology to Pakistan and Iran. On February 5, 1996, the *Washington Times* revealed that a Chinese government owned company had sold Pakistan specialized magnets for use in equipment that enriches uranium for nuclear weapons. Shortly after, another lead divulged that the Chinese were providing Iran with the technology for advanced chemical weapons factories.

Under U.S. laws, these sales—if proved—could trigger economic sanctions unless the president issues a waiver for reasons of national interests or national security requirements. Nonproliferation experts calculate that these Chinese actions may have violated the nuclear Non-Proliferation Treaty and four U.S. laws. Two laws from the 1970s were passed by Congress to deter the spread of nuclear technologies from Europe to Third World countries, while two later laws were a response to revelations that Washington had maintained close economic ties with Iraq while it was developing nuclear arms. The sanctions spelled out by the laws include: a ban on economic and military aid, a cutoff of international loans or loan guarantees, and a deferral of any sensitive U.S. commercial exports to China.

Even as President Clinton ordered a suspension of $10 billion in Export-Import Bank financing of U.S. business deals in China, pending further investigation of the Pakistan and Iranian deals, the administration quietly approved Beijing's participation in developing the world's most advanced nuclear power reactor in the United States. Six Chinese nuclear engineers were granted visas to work with Westinghouse Electric Company on the reactor program. Officials justified the visa decision as securing a job-producing piece of China's multibillion-dollar civilian nuclear technology market. China already operates two French-built reactors and has purchased two more. It is also purchasing two each from Canada and Russia. In this case, economics and the lure of China's huge market won out over nonproliferation concerns.

Washington, however, has been trying for fifteen years to stop the flow of Chinese nuclear technology to Pakistan, twice imposing limited economic sanctions against China, which were withdrawn after China promised to stop such deliveries. After spending months investigating the most recent Pakistan sale, Secretary of State Warren Christopher decided in May of 1996 that the U.S. would not impose sanctions on China because the U.S. accepted Beijing's explanation that the Chinese government was not aware of the sale, and further, that China would take steps to stop such a sale from recurring. No sooner was this protracted decision made, but news leaked again that Pakistan was secretly building a medium-range missile factory near Islamabad using Chinese blueprints and equipment.

The dilemma of these cases often boils down to an impenetrable question: were the state controlled companies operating on behalf of the Chinese government, or were the sales simply the work of greedy or corrupt officials? If there is no proof of direct government involvement, sanctions cannot be imposed on a nation for the corruption of a few.

Moreover, there is increasing recognition that even the threat of sanctions can have severely negative effects on U.S. commercial interests, including the shift of contracts to U.S. competitors. There are well-publicized cases in which export controls were unilaterally imposed by the U.S. at high cost to U.S. companies. The predicament of nonaction in such cases is that the Chinese may believe they can act with impunity or turn a blind eye. And despite the costs, some experts believe that the threat of sanctions is about the only leverage the U.S. has to keep Chinese markets open over the long run. The trick, however, is not to impose unilateral sanctions but to galvanize multilateral action, since everyone, including the Chinese, has a stake in nonproliferation.

Sanctions

The U.S.–China Business Council comments that "there is little evidence that unilateral U.S. sanctions can effectuate policy changes in other nations," particularly when so few goods produced by the United States are not produced elsewhere. Unilateral sanctions tend to hurt only U.S. interests without any guarantee of change.

Whether it is human rights, intellectual property rights, or non-proliferation, many economists and diplomats argue that China's huge domestic economy and ready access to alternative markets insulate it from U.S. economic pressures. The days when the United States could threaten to cut off access to its market and forget about the consequences are long gone. In the mid-sixties, exports accounted for less than 4 percent of America's GDP; that figure more than doubled in the 1990s. As the growth prospects for the U.S. economy, as for all other industrialized economies, have become increasingly dependent on exports, unilateral sanctions have their costs.

For example, halting Export-Import Bank loan guarantees to China has blocked or jeopardized deals for U.S. companies such as Boeing, AT&T, and Westinghouse. When the United States imposed new sanctions on technology exports to China in August 1993, it banned the sale of almost $1 billion in high-technology goods to China over two years. Companies that were affected included Hughes Aircraft and Collins Avionics, a unit of Rockwell International.

Sanctions, moreover, once unleashed, are difficult to sustain. President Bush first imposed sanctions tied to proliferation concerns in late April 1991, when his administration denied an export license for the sale of U.S. components for a Chinese domestic communications satellite. In early February 1996, however, President Clinton, looking at the bottom line, cleared the way for Hughes Electronics, Lockheed Martin, and Loral to sell hundreds of millions of dollars worth of satellites to the Chinese.

Despite the fact that such sanctions may have caused as much, or more, damage to American economic interests as to China's, some experts argue that sanctions are the principal weapon available to persuade China to live by international norms. Yet sanctions have not retarded China's impressive economic growth, and elsewhere they have not been very effective even when applied against small impoverished countries like Haiti. According to Gary Hufbauer of the Institute for International Economics, co-author of a book on sanctions, "The efficacy [of sanctions] isn't better than one in four, and [is] getting weaker over time."

Unless Washington receives support from other major industrial countries, the Chinese government will react to sanctions by becoming even more hostile to the United States and by switching from U.S. products to European and Japanese ones. Unilateral sanctions, in fact, isolate the United States, because other nations normally do not link trade and noncommercial objectives.

Indeed, where sanctions are concerned, the United States appears increasingly alone. Recent U.S. laws that would punish companies (whether American or not) for doing business with Cuba, Iran, and Libya have triggered a chorus of criticism from friends and foes alike, with the European Union, Australia, Canada, and Japan all voicing objections.

Hardening Attitudes

This vicious cycle of sanctions and retaliation, added to a relationship increasingly characterized by mistrust and mutual recriminations, has produced a hardening of attitudes that can be seen both in the China-bashing that is becoming more common on the floor of the U.S. Congress and in changing Chinese public opinion.

In a recent survey of Chinese youth, 90 percent said they feel that the United States behaves "hegemonistically." According to the *China Youth News*, which published the results of the youth poll, more than 94 percent believe that the United States is blocking China's entry into the WTO; 91 percent feel that the United States has been "unfriendly" in handling the issue of Taiwan. The best-selling book in the summer of 1996, according to a survey of bookstores in thirty major Chinese cities, was *China Can Say No*, written by a group of young journalists and scholars. The book has chapters entitled "We Don't Want MFN" and "I Won't Get on a Boeing 777." Its main theme is that China should take its place as a world power and "say no" to America.

At a U.S. embassy briefing for the American Assembly group in June 1996, there was recognition of the negative turn in Chinese attitudes toward the United States. The concern was also expressed that the United States needs to better manage its relations if it doesn't want the "deep well" of good will for Americans in China to be eroded.

U.S.–China Trade and Investment

Politics appears to have a chilling impact on American business in China. Members of the U.S. Chamber of Commerce in Beijing told the American Assembly group that Sino–U.S. frictions have cost them business, as sales were lost to competitors. A Chinese diplomat asked the group what kind of relationship the United States really wanted with China. He cited the statement of Joseph Nye, former undersecretary of defense: "If the U.S. considers China an enemy, she will become an enemy." And as Vice Premier Li Lanqing put it in an interview with *Business Week,* "The basic American policy toward China is not clear . . . I'm not sure whether 'engagement' means to fight or to marry."

Whether American or Chinese, however, everyone the American Assembly group met in China seemed to understand the importance of the U.S.–China relationship. One Chinese official emphasized, "The healthy development of our bilateral economic and trade relationship is in the fundamental interest of the people in both countries." American business, at the same time, feels strongly that it cannot be successful in China unless it is involved in normalizing U.S.–China relations. In a grassroots project led by Boeing, American business is mounting a nationwide public information campaign to educate Americans about the country's stake in U.S.–China relations.

What Is at Stake for the United States?

A recent public opinion survey found that a substantial majority of the American people believes that the United States has vital national interests in China. And clearly the United States currently has an enormous stake there. China is America's fifth largest export market. U.S. exports over the period 1990–95 increased at an annual rate of 21 percent, creating 200,000 U.S. jobs. China's massive demand for capital goods is unparalleled; its future demand for infrastructure, estimated by the World Bank at $750 billion in the next decade, is largely untapped at this time. In addition, U.S. firms plan nearly $26 billion in direct investment in China, strategic investments that require a long-term time line to pay off. Already, however, the U.S. Department of Commerce data show an average return on investment of 9.6 percent (in 1993) for investment in China, as compared with 9.1 percent in the manufacturing segment overall.

U.S. trade with Asia is now over 50 percent larger than its trade with Europe, and the potential future growth in Asia far exceeds that in Europe. Many have been concerned by America's trade deficit with China, but the U.S. economy depends heavily on exports to developing countries; the latter were more than 60 percent of exports to developed countries in 1992. The growth of developing country exports far outpaces that of developed country exports, at rates of 13.7 percent and 1.8 percent respectively in 1992. And China is the fastest growing market of all, growing at around 20 percent over the same time period.

What does corporate America stand to lose if relations break down? In addition to the loss attributed to sanctions, China's response to the visit to the United States by Taiwan's President Lee Teng-hui in May 1995 offered another taste of potential damage. Chinese officials shifted procurement trips from the United States to Europe, canceled top-level meetings with U.S. chief executives, and told U.S. companies like Greiner Engineering that they had lost major deals because Beijing disapproved of U.S. policy toward China. At the same time, the European Union (EU) wasted no time in unveiling a program to improve the EU's relations with China.

A further indication came when the United States threatened sanctions over intellectual property rights. Premier Li Peng went to France and signed a $1.5 billion order for thirty short-haul Airbus planes. Boeing chief executive officer Phil Condit called the purchase in part a political decision, prompted by troubled Sino–U.S. ties. After agreement was reached in IPR, China also made good a letter of intent signed during Premier Li's visit to France, giving a European consortium the rights to develop a new hundred-seat airliner. Although there may have been good commercial reasons for China to buy Airbus planes to diversify its largely Boeing fleet, its message, nevertheless, was loud and clear—we have alternatives.

More insidious than these headline cases, however, are the day-to-day bureaucratic actions that hold back, divert, or delay action on U.S. companies' permits, applications, and bids whenever U.S.–China relations sour. Chinese bureaucrats play it safe and turn away American business.

The Europeans and Japanese are only too happy to criticize America's tactics with China, while turning the tensions to their own benefit. Japan has said openly that unilateral sanctions are a bad idea, while EU Commission president Jacques Santer said before the Europe-Asia conference in Bangkok, "We're not going to engage in any sort of confrontation . . . it's only when bridges are built and partnerships are established that we can talk frankly about all subjects." Among the biggest beneficiaries of America's crackdown on copyright piracy in China, however, are Bertelsmann of Germany and Sony of Japan.

Although the consequences of these losses for the overall U.S. economy were minimal, the effect on particular corporations, industries, and states could be substantial. But as important as the two nations' trade and investment relations may be, the U.S.–China relationship extends far beyond the commercial opportunities that may be lost. With its seat on the United Nations Security Council, China has influence over international security. As a nuclear nation, it is a player in proliferation policies. It is a power to be reckoned with in Asia, holding sway over North Korea, Cambodia, and the Spratley Islands in the South China Seas. Given China's size, its policies toward global issues of migration, narcotics, and the environment could overwhelm the rest of the world. At the same time, if the commercial relationship deteriorates, China will have less incentive to work cooperatively on noneconomic U.S. concerns.

What Is at Stake for China?

China, singularly obtuse in reading American public opinion and political processes, cannot afford to push U.S. businesses too hard over political tensions. Otherwise, it risks alienating the companies who make up the most potent constituency for maintaining a U.S. policy of engagement with China. Corporate America is characteristically risk averse and can easily get cold feet in any high-profile confrontation.

The loss of most-favored-nation status, according to a recent World Bank estimate, could cause China's exports to the United States to fall by at least 42 percent and perhaps by as much as 96 percent. No matter how hard China works to improve trade ties with Europe and Asia, the United States absorbs at least one-third of China's exports. Without the United States, China would have an enormous current account deficit.

Under the loss of MFN, American exports to China would undoubtedly fall as well, as China would retaliate and buy elsewhere whenever possible. The United States would absorb the decrease much more easily, however, as its exports to China make up only 2 percent of total U.S. exports. The resulting downward spiral in commercial relations and the deterioration of overall relations would reduce the flow of U.S. foreign direct investment into China. In retaliation, Chinese officials might make it difficult for U.S. joint venture projects to be approved. At the same time, U.S. companies that have the telecommunications, electronics, aviation, and other technologies critical to China's modernization might decide that investment in China is not worth the risk, and shift capital to other emerging Asian markets such as Indonesia and India.

Over the long run, without MFN, American companies would lose out in getting their share of the rapidly growing China market. China would be hit much harder. Without the U.S. market, or U.S. technology and capital, Beijing would find it difficult, if not impossible, to reach its growth and infrastructure goals.

Indeed, a trade war with the United States would devastate Hong Kong and the economies of the five coastal provinces that have most benefited from trade, particularly Guangdong and Fujian. Nearly half of all Chinese exports pass through Hong Kong. According to the Hong Kong government, its gross domestic product would be slashed by half if China lost its MFN status.

A stable trade and investment relationship is clearly in the interest of both China and the United States. It is also a precondition for strengthening regional trading ties and promoting broader economic cooperation within the region.

Policy Recommendations

Economics is where the interests of the United States and China intersect. There is more common ground between the two countries here than in many other areas. Beijing's leaders are desperate for economic growth, because China's stability and survival depend on it. The United States, at the same time, is desperate to take advantage of the greatest commercial opportunity of the next century. China's enormous need for investment and technology to fuel its growth coincides perfectly with America's hunger for exports and new markets to create profits and jobs. Normalizing U.S.–China commercial relations, therefore, ought to be a priority for both countries. It is in their mutual interest to do so.

Normalize U.S.–China Commercial Relations

In U.S. foreign policy, economic interests have always been subordinated to geopolitical objectives. Until Tiananmen, the geopolitical consideration of using China as a counterbalance to the former Soviet Union overshadowed human rights and economic concerns. Since Tiananmen, however, human rights concerns have dominated U.S. economic policy toward China, and without the Soviet threat, China has receded in importance in U.S. foreign policy. American attitudes toward China have also had their ups and downs over this period. Ironically, just as the human rights of Chinese citizens expanded during the 1980s, Tiananmen ended whatever romance the Americans may have had with China. Repeating a pattern of the 1940s and 1950s, U.S. policy has swung from idealizing to vilifying China.

It is time for the United States and China to establish a framework for bilateral relations that removes the vicissitudes in their relationship. And it is time, in this post–cold war era when economics are increasingly in command in international relations, for the United States to rethink the subordination of economics to political concerns in its foreign policy. There is no better place to start than normalizing U.S.–China commercial relations, an area where mutual interests outweigh differences.

Priorities for the U.S. Government

In considering the priorities for the U.S. government toward China, the recommendations of the United States–China Business Council, the Coalition of Business for U.S.–China Trade, and the Business Roundtable are helpful. Four areas of U.S. government policy are most important.

• *MFN Status.* MFN is the cornerstone of U.S.–China commercial relations. Every effort must be made to find an alternative to the annual MFN certification process. Various options exist: do away with the Jackson-Vanik amendment as a relic of the cold war that is no longer needed; grant China permanent MFN status; or reclassify China as a market economy. The threat of MFN denial, instead of achieving its intended objective of pressuring China to improve its human rights performance, actually harms U.S.–China relations and serves no identifiable U.S. national interests. The annual series of divisive and politicized congressional debates has undercut U.S.–China commercial relations and given the Chinese the deadly impression that the United States is trying to contain China's economic and political resurgence.

• *World Trade Organization.* The United States should support China's accession to the WTO with the understanding that China agrees to the commercial terms that apply to other nations. China, however, insists on being admitted as a developing nation, a status that would allow it to follow less stringent rules for opening markets. A high-ranking Chinese official told the American Assembly group quite frankly that China wanted to join the WTO but that the "hurdle rate" was too high. To make an exception for China carries risks, but to delay too long may mean losing an opportunity for integrating China into the global trading community. In the long term, no global trading system will work if one of the world's largest economies does not subscribe to the rules. As some of our Chinese interlocutors suggested, a workable compromise might be to agree on a transition period, with a specific timetable for China to meet the required commercial terms. China then would gain the prestige it seeks in entering the WTO, and both sides would get the international integration they seek for China.

• *Human Rights.* U.S. business recognizes that human rights is a core American value and an essential element of American global diplomacy. Moreover, the principle is a universal one and, therefore, is conducive to multilateral action. Persuasion rather than sanctions, private negotiation rather than public sermonizing are more likely to achieve the objective of improving human rights for the Chinese people. The U.S. government, therefore, should discontinue its policy of linking noneconomic issues, such as human rights, to economic initiatives. It should return to the principle of pursuing trade and investment agreements to liberalize trade and investment and further economic growth, while promoting human rights through independent cooperative efforts. The North American Agreement on Labor Cooperation and the North American Agreement on Environmental Cooperation may serve as models for a similar cooperative effort on human rights with China. At the same time, the United States should continue to push hard for a China resolution in the U.N. Human Rights Commission. Less confrontation does not mean appeasement.

• *U.S. Trade Restrictions and Regulations.* In some significant instances, because foreign competitors are not encumbered by the same rules and regulations, restrictions imposed by the U.S. government seriously disadvantage U.S. companies' ability to compete in China. Although some restrictions may continue to be justified on national security or foreign policy grounds, many of them are left over from the cold war and are no longer needed. The regulations that most concern U.S. companies operating in China concern export controls, embargoes, sanctions, and restrictions on financing by the Overseas Private Investment Corporation (OPIC), the Export-

Import Bank, and the Trade and Development Agency (TDA). The U.S. government should:

(1) Reassess and rationalize the U.S. export control system. In general, unilateral export controls should be eliminated, the speed of licensing decisions should be increased, and predictability and accountability improved.

(2) Extend eligibility for OPIC insurance and Export-Import Bank and TDA financing to all countries in the Asia Pacific region, including China. The only effect of the six-year U.S. OPIC and TDA sanctions has been to restrict efforts by U.S. companies to establish a presence in China, handicapping U.S. exports. Expanding Export-Import Bank export financing and guarantees is essential for American companies to participate in major infrastructure projects in China and would boost U.S. companies' competitiveness.

(3) Eliminate or rationalize country-specific policies. As part of step-by-step normalization, Congress should revise trade law provisions that single out China for less favorable treatment, particularly in the areas of export controls, peaceful nuclear power plant construction, aerospace, and special import safeguards.

Priorities for China

Normalization of commercial relations is a two-way street. Policy priorities for China in part mirror those of the United States. Four of the most important need urgent attention.

• *World Trade Organization.* Clearly China has the right to take its place among the trading partners of the world. Accession to the WTO, however, is a commitment to be bound by a set of rules. China needs to agree to a commercially acceptable protocol. Commitments should include eliminating the restrictions on foreign investment and trade contained in China's industrial policies, extending full trading rights to foreign companies, and eliminating protectionist tariff and nontariff barriers to trade. If China needs more time to achieve the protocol than that allowed for a developed country member, a reasonable alternative timetable ought to be proposed.

• *Market Access.* China needs to implement all phases of the 1992 bilateral agreement and phase out quotas, import licensing restrictions, and other administrative barriers that act as effective market barriers. Currently China, like many other Asian nations, maintains significant barriers to entry by foreign financial services providers and telecommunications companies. Given China's need for increasingly sophisticated financial services and telecommunications infrastructure, it is in its interest, when it joins the WTO, to work within the APEC framework and the General Agreement on Trade in Services (GATS) to remove market access barriers.

• *Intellectual Property Rights.* Although the United States and China have entered into agreements regarding intellectual property rights standards (1992) and enforcement (1995 and 1996), piracy of U.S. software, videos, and sound recordings remains a serious problem. China's credibility is on the line when it does not adhere to agreements that it signs. It must follow through on its IPR commitments, crack down on piracy, and vigorously enforce IPR regulations.

• *Transparency.* Foreign corporations doing business in China overwhelmingly suggest the need for transparency, or openness, in Chinese regulations and laws. Lack of transparency involves the nonpublication and nonavailability of laws, regulations, and related measures and procedures, as well as the use of informal administrative "guidance" or "approval" as a form of rule making. Lack of transparency harms both foreign and domestic businesses by increasing uncertainty, complicating business planning, and facilitating corruption. Establishing greater transparency in regulations and laws not only would strengthen investor confidence but would help China succeed in its anticorruption campaign.

Conclusion

As members of the U.S. business community told our American Assembly delegation in Beijing in June 1996, their success in China is hostage to U.S.–China relations. These relations are too important to be left to the unpredictable fluctuations of case-by-case confrontations over Taiwan, human rights, nuclear proliferation, intellectual property rights, most-favored-nation trade status, and similar high-profile issues. The common interests between China and the United States are far more numerous than their differences. What is needed is a more coherent long-term framework for a new bipartisan China policy. The United States needs to revamp its approach.

First and foremost, the U.S. government needs to recognize China's emergence as a regional and world power. The United States should increase China's importance on the U.S. foreign policy agenda, and this should include engaging China's leaders through exchanges of high-level visits.

Second, the United States must help to integrate China into the international community and induce it to abide by a reasonable set of principles and rules in both its economic and its political actions. Just as Russia has been invited as an observer at G-7 economic summits, so China, a much more important economy, might also be included.

Third, wherever possible, the United States should pursue its economic, political, and strategic objectives with China through multilateral efforts. Such an approach should lessen U.S.–China bilateral tensions and increase the probability of a positive outcome.

Fourth, the United States must identify and forge links of common interest, engage China appropriately, and build ties that will bind China to international norms of behavior. The stalemate over China's accession to the WTO must be resolved as soon as possible.

Fifth and not least, the United States should promote opportunities for U.S. trade and investment, not only because to do so helps the U.S. economy, but also because such actions will also advance economic reform and lead eventually to political reform in China.

7

Energy, Agriculture, and the Environment: Prospects for Sino-American Cooperation

MICHAEL B. McELROY
AND CHRIS P. NIELSEN

The many avenues for cooperation between the United States and China in the areas of energy and environment provide great potential for mutual benefit. The emphasis in this chapter is on a number of challenges and opportunities related to air pollution and climate. China, a nation moving swiftly from an inward-looking planned economy to one that is a major competitor in global markets, may be able to learn from the mistakes made ear-

MICHAEL B. McELROY is chairperson of the Department of Earth and Planetary Sciences and chairperson of the University Committee on Environment at Harvard University. In 1970 Professor McElroy was named Abbott Lawrence Rotch Professor of Atmospheric Sciences at Harvard and in 1975 was appointed director of the Center for Earth and Planetary Physics. Professor McElroy's research interests range from studies on the origin and evolution of the planets to, more recently, an emphasis on effects of human activity on the global environment of the earth. He is a fellow of the American Academy of Arts and Sciences and the International Academy of Aeronautics. He was the recipient of the Macelwane Award of the American Geophysical Union in 1968 and the NASA Public Service Medal in 1978.

lier in Western energy development. If Americans of today were transported back to the 1940s, is there any doubt that they would choose to modify their path of energy development to protect the environment in a more efficient and integrated manner? In effect, China faces such an opportunity, but could well squander it.

China also confronts challenges in ensuring the security of its food supply while protecting the interests of its 800 million rural citizens, the majority of whom still earn their living in agriculture. China must feed a growing population, already numbering 1.2 billion, primarily from its own limited arable land. An efficient, productive agricultural sector is possible only with a healthy natural environment.

The Chinese government knows that both sound energy development and a sustainable environment are vital to their future. On the books, environmental law and policy are extensive and ambitious. But these measures falter in implementation and enforcement owing to a host of societal, political, and legal factors. In the near future it is unlikely that either the Chinese or Westerners can offer policy prescriptions on China's air pollution problems that deal realistically with all these factors. On a more optimistic note, the impediments to China's environmental policy performance may well diminish as the country continues to restructure its institutions in its transition to a market economy and a modern state.

Meanwhile, energy strapped and capital constrained, Chinese leaders and economic actors feel compelled to opt for choices in the

CHRIS P. NIELSEN, since its inception in 1993, has coordinated and now serves as executive director of the Harvard University Committee on Environment China Project, a collaborative program of energy, economic, and environmental research between Harvard and five research institutions in the People's Republic of China. Currently participating in the project are forty-five American and Chinese professors and senior researchers from the natural and applied sciences, public health, medicine, economics, law, business, political science, public policy, anthropology, and East Asian studies. The research used in this chapter was partially supported by the U.S. Department of Energy, as part of the Harvard University Committee on Environment China Project, under contract #DE-FG02-95ER62133.

energy sector with low initial investment, despite burdensome environmental externalities and higher long-run monetary cost. China could, by contrast, draw on the know-how, experience, and investment capital of Western countries to develop its energy needs in a way that is more efficient and less polluting, addressing a host of severe environmental concerns at the same time. Constructive Western inputs could also offer significant opportunities to U.S. companies for trade and investment, while fostering a spirit of mutual respect and confidence. Where cooperation appears feasible, however, it must be well targeted and conducted in a manner mindful of differences in local conditions and prerogatives.

In political terms, dialogue and cooperation in the relatively value-neutral fields of energy and environment could offer some welcome counterweight to the disputes on human and intellectual property rights, Taiwan, Tibet, arms proliferation, and trade that currently dominate relations between the two countries. The tenor of cooperation in energy, environment, and agriculture could diverge significantly from the contentiousness of Sino-American politics-as-usual. Overall U.S.–China relations could gain from a major new conduit of economic, technological, and scientific engagement promising benefits to both nations.

There is ultimately an even more powerful reason to advocate cooperative Sino-American relations in these fields. The hazards of the intellectual disconnect between science and policy making are growing ever more acute as the challenges posed by atmospheric pollution expand to planetary scale. A potent though undervalued time bomb in Sino-American relations, as in the international order at large, ticks quietly: the threat of global climate change. The United States and China, the two largest contributors to emissions of the gases responsible for the threat to climate stability, will encounter international pressures to lead equitable but effective global strategies to respond to the threat. Taken in isolation, forging U.S.–Chinese engagement on climate change appears difficult and unlikely. But cooperation in energy development pursued on other environmental, economic, and political grounds can simultaneously yield benefits for protection of global climate stability and would be a major step in the right direction.

Energy Use in China

Economic growth in China has notably outstripped growth in energy consumption since the late 1970s, reflecting a reduction in the energy intensity of the Chinese economy. Yet the pace of expansion of fossil fuel use is nevertheless swift and its scale immense. Coal provides the dominant source of primary energy in China, as it has for most of this century. In 1992 it accounted for almost two-thirds of the total consumption of primary energy, followed by biomass (chiefly crop wastes and firewood in rural areas), oil, hydroelectricity, and natural gas, with a minor contribution from nuclear fuel.[1] The biomass share has been falling, and the combined contribution from hydroelectricity and natural gas has been relatively constant at 7 percent for the past two decades, reflecting continued priorities assigned to investment in thermal power generation and oil.

China has abundant sources of coal. It contains approximately 11 percent of the world's total supply, sufficient to fuel its current energy demand for more than 100 years. Production of coal increased in China by a factor of close to forty between 1949 and 1994. It has almost doubled since 1980 with an increase of about 12 percent between 1990 and 1994. In 1985 consumption of coal in China surpassed that of the United States. China is already the world's largest producer and largest consumer of coal and, after the United States, the world's second largest consumer of primary energy.

Industrial boilers are responsible for the largest share of coal use in China, approximately 33 percent of the total consumed in 1990. Electric power generation accounted for an additional 26 percent, with the balance attributed to household use (9 percent) and other industrial uses. A growing proportion of China's primary energy is employed in the production of electricity. Gross generation of electricity increased by more than 46 percent from 1990 to 1994, with coal the major fuel. By comparison, total primary energy production rose over the same time period by less than 13 percent.

Oil is the fastest growing component of the energy consumption mix in China, accounting for 40 percent of the increase in primary energy between 1990 and 1993. Most of this growth was supplied by imports. China is now an important net importer of oil, having been a net exporter during much of the 1970s and 1980s. Gasoline use increased by more than 32 percent between 1990 and 1992, and primary energy employed annually for transportation doubled over the period 1980 to 1992. Despite this increase, the proportion of total energy consumed by China's transportation sector remains small compared with that in the United States (7.5 percent as compared with 27 percent). Per capita energy use for transportation in China is far less than that in the United States (by a factor of forty-four). If China's per capita energy use for transportation were to grow to even half the value in the United States, energy demand in China would almost triple.

The Environmental Impacts
of China's Energy Use

In the West, problems related to the use of fossil fuel were obvious even in the early years of the Industrial Revolution. Accidents, the increase of black lung disease, and accumulating slag heaps extracted a heavy toll on communities engaged in coal mining. The connection between burning coal and the prevalence of dirty air in industrial cities was inescapable, but until recent decades these environmental problems drew relatively little attention from national policy makers. Impacts of fossil fuel use tended to be accepted as the inevitable cost of progress. In the middle of the twentieth century, well-publicized episodes of deadly smogs in Pennsylvania and London killed thousands, escalating calls to action. While similar incidents have not yet occurred or at least been identified in China, echoes of the same concerns can be heard there today.

Coal burning is associated with the emission of finely dispersed materials with diameters in the range 0.1 to 100 microns.[2] Xu Xiping, in a chapter for a forthcoming volume from the Harvard University Committee on Environment China Project, has described how breathing this material can induce a variety of respiratory problems, including emphysema, asthma, bronchitis, and lung cancer. Particles in the smallest size range are capable of penetrating deep into the lung, sometimes for life, and are judged most serious in terms of their impact on public health. One study of annual mean concentrations of air-borne particulates in five major Chinese cities from 1981 to 1991 showed Xian with the highest and Guangzhou the lowest average concentrations, at five and two times the maximum deemed acceptable by the World Health Organization, respectively.

Although cost-effective means to alleviate particulate emissions for small sources may be more elusive, relatively straightforward technological strategies are available to reduce emissions from large industrial sources. Strategies include the use of electrostatic precipitators, wet scrubbers, fabric filters, and mechanical precipitators. Efficient electrostatic precipitators are installed currently on only a small number of the most modern coal-fired thermal power plants in China. Industrial boilers are infrequently equipped with mechanical dust separators, and most small coal-consuming devices are operated without any control on emissions.[3] National data for 1985–1993 on China's total discharge of particulates from combustion show general stability, however. Such data are not always reliable in China, but this nevertheless suggests some progress in abatement, given that total use of coal rose over the same period by 24 percent.

In addition to particulates, gaseous compounds like sulfur dioxide are also emitted in combustion of fossil fuels. Inhalation of sulfur dioxide has been demonstrated to have a direct effect on acute and chronic health problems in China, including loss of pulmonary function and assorted respiratory disease. Additionally, secondary reactions with these gaseous combustion products create a number of environmentally harmful components of the atmosphere, notably sulfuric acid formed by the oxidation of sulfur dioxide. The evaporation of cloud particles containing sulfuric acid leads to the production of small sulfate-rich aerosols (air-borne particles), which in turn significantly affect the reflective properties of clouds. There are reasons to believe that a high abundance of sulfate aerosols over China may be responsible for a significant drop in daytime temperatures there. This situation poses a dilemma for policy makers: a reduction in emissions of industrial sulfur, required both for reasons of public health and to lessen the impact of acid rain, may result in an increase in temperature, exacerbating additional warming anticipated from higher levels of greenhouse gases such as carbon dioxide.

Acid rain, by which we mean precipitation with pH below about

5, is another challenge for China. By-products of combustion (oxides of nitrogen and sulfur) are the primary precursors for the formation of acid rain in polluted environments. In China acid rain is a problem primarily in the southwestern and south central regions (the provinces of Sichuan, Guizhou, Hunan, Guangxi, and Guangdong), where soils are naturally acidic. It is less serious in the north, where soils are more alkaline and where other factors help neutralize the rain's acidity. An annual average of 3.2 was reported for the pH of rain in Guiyang, Guizhou in 1993, while the average for suburban Chongqing, Sichuan was only slightly higher, 4.18.[4] Acid rain has been implicated as a cause of serious damage to structural materials in cities and has also been blamed for the decline of forests over extensive regions of the southwest. Leaching of aluminum by acid rain percolating through soils can lead to toxic concentrations of this element in lakes, with serious consequences for fish. Despite the high priority attached to the issue of acid rain by the Chinese government in the Seventh and Eighth Five Year Plans, it appears that the situation has deteriorated and that the area affected by acid rain in China has actually expanded in recent years.

A number of approaches are available to reduce emissions of sulfur compounds associated with the combustion of coal. The simplest involves pulverizing and washing the coal, but water requirements for the process pose a limitation in China, and it also introduces a waste water problem. For large-scale industrial applications including power generation, fluidized gas desulfurization (FGD) can be used. It involves exposure of stack gases to a spray of chemicals, usually a slurry of lime and limestone, which acts to convert volatile forms of sulfur to less volatile products.[5] Emission of sulfur compounds to the atmosphere can be reduced by as much as 95 percent with current FGD technology. Costs of FGD systems can add as much as 30 percent to initial investment in a power plant, and thus there is only one large such system installed currently in China, and even it apparently is not always operational. There is an additional cost in terms of energy use and a consequent increase in emissions of carbon dioxide. Overall, aggregate emissions of sulfur dioxide in China rose 35 percent between 1985 and 1993. In contrast to particulates, the growth of sulfur dioxide emissions has been higher than that of coal use over the same time period, suggesting in broad terms that abatement is not spreading.

The Potential for Future Climate
Change and the Impact on China

Although technologies are available to reduce local and regional air pollution, it is difficult, if not impossible, to cut back through "end-of-pipe" solutions on emissions of the primary product of fossil fuel use, carbon dioxide. Coal burning in China resulted in the emission of more than 2.7 billion tons of carbon dioxide in 1992. Carbon dioxide is the largest single waste product of modern global society. China is responsible for approximately 12 percent of the world's total today, and its contribution is steadily increasing. Notably, the U.S. produces 22 percent of global carbon dioxide, though its emissions are currently growing only slowly. We consider now the possible effects of increased emissions of carbon dioxide for the global and regional climate, or what has come to be known as the greenhouse effect.[6] (Included as an endnote is a brief introduction to global climate change for readers interested in gaining a background understanding of the science and its current limitations.)

The Intergovernmental Panel on Climate Change (IPCC) concluded that the increase in greenhouse gases anticipated to occur over the next century may cause a rise in global average temperature of between 1 and 3.5 centigrade with an associated increase in global average sea level of between 15 and 95 centimeters.[7] It also concluded that the temperature increase that has already taken place in this century "is unlikely to be entirely natural in origin" and that "the balance of evidence suggests that there is a discernible human influence on global climate." There are, of course, uncertainties and disparate views on this. Mahlman classifies as "very probable" the prospects for future increases in global average temperature and precipitation and as "probable" the odds that continental areas will be drier and warmer in the future, especially in summer.[8] Others, notably Richard Lindzen of M.I.T., are more skeptical. But the 2,500-member IPCC, formed by the United Nations and the World Meteorological Organization, carefully seeks a broad consensus on the most up-to-date peer-reviewed research on climate science, impacts, and potential response strategies. Its reports, though based largely on studies using general circulation models, are accepted by most as a reasonable summary of present understanding of climate and the prospects for future change. (We strongly recommend to those interested in summaries of recent scientific advances regarding the risks of climate change and associated policy issues to consult the "Summary for Policymakers" for each of the three IPCC working groups, available at the IPCC World Wide Web site.)

The consequences of climate change for developing countries, including China, are potentially serious. Expressed as a global average, the surface temperature of the earth has increased by about 0.5 degrees centigrade since the middle of the last century. The increase for China has been even larger, about 1 degree centigrade. Fed by melting glaciers, amplified by thermal expansion of warmer water, the level of the ocean has risen globally by between 10 and 20 centimeters over the past 150 years. It is unclear whether the changes in temperature and sea level recorded to date reflect the natural variability of the climate system or, more ominously, a response to an additional burden of greenhouse gases. In general, though, they are consistent with predictions of models simulating the response of the climate to increasing levels of carbon dioxide and other greenhouse gases.

The global increase in sea level associated with a doubling of carbon dioxide could ultimately be substantial. The geologic record suggests that changes in sea level can occur rapidly, influenced by processes that may not be included in current models. Some researchers conclude that "the potential for future catastrophic sea level rise also exists—especially now that catastrophic rises have been recorded from the recent past."[9] China would be especially vulnerable. A large proportion of its population, agriculture, and industry is sited on the low-lying alluvial plains and deltas of its major rivers. An increase in sea level by as little as 50 centimeters, without accounting for the effects of storm surges, could inundate an area as large as 40,000 square kilometers.[10]

Possible impacts of climate change on Chinese agriculture could be highly disruptive, though its effects on yields might be either negative or positive depending on type of crop, geographical region, and the ability of management systems to adapt quickly to changing and unpredictable conditions. Warmer summers in the future, with an increase in evaporation, are likely to result in significant reductions in the moisture content of soils in China, especially in the north. This will impose an increased demand for water by agriculture, adding to existing shortages. A comprehensive study, based on one of many emissions and population scenarios of the IPCC, projects major changes by 2050 in cropping systems throughout China, with the greatest changes in the crucial eastern agricultural belt.[11] This analysis suggests that diminished availability of water would be the most important factor in projected agricultural impacts, through disruption in precipitation, evaporation, permanent ice and snow melt, annual runoff patterns, and flow of river systems. While warming might permit crop diversification, the water supply for essential paddy rice would decrease. Areas suitable for rice cultivation would increase, but average yields would likely decrease. Wheat cultivation would be severely affected by diminished water availability, requiring increased irrigation water demands from major river systems. In colder agricultural areas of northeast China, yields might increase significantly due to less likelihood of crop freezes. While projections such as these should be considered speculative, it is clear that climate change at minimum would introduce new uncertainties and immense management challenges into China's agricultural production. And there is a significant risk that it could have much worse agricultural implications, undermining China's ability to produce food to feed its growing population.

There are other, less dramatic, reasons why prospects for future climate change should be taken seriously by policy makers in China. The country is already vulnerable to extremes of weather, such as floods in the south and droughts in the north. Floods in south and central China were responsible for more than a thousand deaths in each of the summers of 1994, 1995, and 1996. Over the same period, large portions of northern China experienced drought. In 1996 the Yellow River was dry in more than 370 miles of its lower reaches for more than 127 days. Between 1990 and 1995 the river ceased flowing eighteen times and was dry a cumulative total of 333 days. A change in the frequency, duration, intensity, or spatial distribution of precipitation and/or extreme weather events can place serious burdens on the infrastructure of even the richest countries, a point demonstrated forcefully in the United States and elsewhere by disasters such as Hurricane Andrew.

It is customary in the West, in building bridges, roads, dams, or other construction projects, to refer to 100-year flood data in formulating cost-effective, but safe, plans for development. In the face of a changing climate, however, the historical data may be insufficient to guide planning. China is currently engaged in a massive program of infrastructure development. It must make a conscious decision either to overdesign to ensure safety in the future or to take a chance and risk serious political, economic, and human consequences.

High temperatures can also have a direct effect on public health, with symptoms ranging from fatigue to serious cases of heat stroke and even death. Climate change has been implicated in the spread of diseases such as malaria and dengue fever, and there are suggestions that it may contribute to the emergence of entirely new strains of disease. The implications are potentially serious, not just for China but for the global community.

If we are to limit the risks and adapt to the consequences of the accelerating release of greenhouse agents such as carbon dioxide, there is a need for a serious, coordinated global response. China is now the second largest national source of greenhouse emissions, surpassed only by the United States. Ho Mun, Dale Jorgenson, and Dwight Perkins, in the forthcoming China Project volume, describe how emissions of carbon dioxide in China, given current trends, will inevitably grow swiftly, potentially exceeding those from the United States in the next couple of decades. Emissions from developed countries are still growing, but at a much slower rate. Future increases depend largely on what will occur in the large expanding economies of the developing world, and China's path is critical. Yet on a per capita basis, American industrial emissions of carbon dioxide are nine times those of Chinese emissions. The United States and other industrialized countries of the West and former Eastern bloc, furthermore, are responsible for the vast majority of historical emissions to date. The United States and China, as the two leading contributors to the greenhouse threat, will thus be expected to take "common but differentiated responsibilities," in the language of climate diplomacy, to lead the international effort to slow the growth of carbon dioxide emissions. The two nations' disparities will make some contention over the issue nearly unavoidable, but without greater bilateral exchange and understanding, the discord could become acute.

Chinese Agriculture and the Demand for Food

We have emphasized the challenges China must address to ensure a supply of environmentally sound energy to fuel its developing economy. A related issue is the supply of food, as China seeks to accommodate the demands of its increasingly affluent citizens.

A gloomy perspective has been presented by Lester Brown.[12] Citing experience in Japan, South Korea, and Taiwan, he argues that rapid industrialization in China will inevitably lead to a transfer of large areas of crop land to other purposes (power plants, factories, warehouses, and roads, for example). He points out that over the last few decades, land conversion combined with a decline in multiple cropping has led to a decrease by 40 to 50 percent in the area harvested for grain in Japan, South Korea, and Taiwan. Grain production in Japan dropped by 32 percent from its peak in 1960 and has declined by about 24 percent since 1977 in both South Korea and Taiwan. At the same time, demand for grain has risen in all three countries, driven in part by shifts in dietary preference toward more meat, poultry, and fish. Increases in the demand for grain have been met by a corresponding rise in imports. Brown argues that China will similarly be unable to satisfy its demands for grain domestically and draws an extreme conclusion: "In an integrated world economy, China's rising food prices will become the world's rising food prices, China's land scarcity will become everyone's land scarcity, and water scarcity in China will affect the entire world." Yet Brown may have underestimated three factors: China's capacity to expand production; the inevitability of precipitous rises in demand; and the capacity of world markets to respond to meet the demand. In addition, he may have overestimated the accuracy of official agricultural statistics.

Experience in Japan, South Korea, and Taiwan may not be a reliable guide to China's agricultural prospects. On a per capita basis, the land available for agriculture in China, though much less than that in the United States, is significantly greater than that in Japan, South Korea, or Taiwan. Brown's pessimism about China's ability to expand its production of grain is based in part on his view that prospects for future increases in per hectare yields of grain in China are limited. Yields per hectare doubled between 1950 and 1977, and they rose at an astonishing annual rate of over 7 percent following the introduction of economic reforms in 1978. But the rate of increase has dropped since 1984 to a current rate of less than 1 percent per year. The growth in production since 1978 is attributable largely to increased production and to the use of chemical fertilizer, especially nitrogen. Applications of chemical fertilizer in China tripled between 1978 and 1986—China is now the world's largest producer of chemical fertilizer, having surpassed the United States in 1986. Brown concludes that China may have reached a point of diminishing returns in terms of the response of grain production to increasing applications of chemical fertilizer.

Several researchers, in contrast, suggest that the problem may have less to do with fertilizer use per se than with inefficiencies in its distribution and with suboptimal applications of its key components.[13] Historically, nitrogen has been the limiting nutrient for growth in Chinese soils, but phosphorous and potassium may now have become more important. Domestic sources of phosphate in China are of relatively low quality and not widely available. Although China may be forced to rely on international markets for high-grade phosphate, doing so may allow it to achieve significant additional yields in grain.

Still more important in refuting Brown's productivity analysis, however, is that the Chinese government itself has recently acknowledged that cropland acreage may be significantly underestimated in the official figures that Brown used, perhaps by as much as 40 percent less agricultural product than Brown estimated. The new numbers immediately undermine his conclusion that Chinese agriculture already approaches world-class productivity levels and his pessimistic view of the prospects for significant future gains.

Brown may be on sounder ground, on the other hand, when raising the potential effects on agricultural production of a number of environmental factors. The disruptions from climate change mentioned earlier could be a critical long-term consideration for China's agricultural future but are rarely acknowledged in debates on the topic. Many of China's hydrological systems are overtaxed; agriculture in the vital northern plains, for instance, depends increasingly on irrigation supplied by mining of ground water resources. Most experts agree that the biggest unknown in China's future agricultural production is the ultimate success of securing adequate water resources through rationing of use or, of greater apparent appeal to Chinese planners, increases in supply. A massive scheme for interbasin transfer of water from the Yangtze River to the north of China is being developed and promoted without serious thought to the potential significance of changes in precipitation regimes arising as a consequence of climate change.

In addition, other environmental factors may also affect agricultural production. Deterioration of air quality in China's large cities may have contributed to the recent drop or slowdown in agricultural yields. Of particular concern is the possibility of a significant increase in the abundance of ozone, the primary ingredient of Los Angeles–style photochemical smog, as China develops its urban transportation sector. To a large extent, China's agriculture and its major centers of population and industry are located in the same areas, and the impact of industrial emissions on agricultural productivity may be important. Even in the United States, where major centers of agriculture are generally removed from centers of industry, some suggest that crop losses from pollution can be significant, more than 5 percent and perhaps as much as 10 percent. Concerns in the United States have primarily emphasized the effects of elevated levels of ozone, which so far is a relatively minor contributor to air pollution problems in China. The situation could change quickly, however, as emissions from chemical factories, refineries, and automobiles supplement those from coal-fired power plants and industrial boilers. By cleaning up industrial emissions and by taking early action to forestall problems associated with development of high levels of ozone, China has the opportunity to achieve not only improvements in public health but also gains in agricultural productivity. A comprehensive strategy is required, however, if China is to avoid the complications that arose elsewhere, notably in the United States, as solutions to one problem (air-borne particulates) set the stage for another (ozone).

Per capita annual consumption of grain in China, 300 kilograms, is 50 percent higher than that for India though significantly less than the 800 kilograms consumed in the United States. Annual consumption of meat per capita in China rose from 8 kilograms in 1977 to more than 32 kilograms in 1994. Brown argues that per capita annual demand for grain in China could grow to at least 400 kilograms by 2030. He suggests that production is likely to decline over the same period by as much as 20 percent. Given the expected growth in China's population, this would dictate an increase in the annual demand for grain from the present level of about 350 million tons to close to 480 million tons, implying an excess of demand over domestic supply by as much as 200 million tons per year.

Brown's alarmism depends significantly on the demand side of his analysis, which is based on a simplified linear projection of future requirements. An examination of consumption patterns can suggest other possible scenarios. The growth in meat consumption in China in recent years is due largely to increased production of pork, which accounts for close to 75 percent of meat consumed. But compared with pork, only half as much grain is needed to produce poultry, the consumption of which has tripled in China in the past seven years. Continuation of trends such as this, which incidentally might also have public health benefits, would decrease Brown's estimates. More broadly, should growing scarcity of grain arise, this would simply increase its price and that of meat products, dampening demand. Brown's projection may thus be too high.

International markets are another source of supply. World trade in grain rose from about 60 million tons per year in 1950 to close to 250 million tons per year in the early 1990s. To place China's influence on agricultural world trade in context, the total value of Chinese agricultural imports in 1994 was less than the value of U.S. imports by almost a factor of four. Most economists believe that, given a market, the major grain-producing countries of the world have the capacity to markedly increase production.[14] It may make sense for China to rely on international markets to offset shortfalls in domestic production of grain. Grain can be produced more efficiently in countries such as the United States, Canada, Argentina,

Australia, and in the European Union. China could benefit from efficiencies of resource use that could be captured by trade. Experience suggests that despite occasional attempts by one country to exploit grain shortages in another for political advantage, notably efforts by the United States to apply pressure to the Soviet Union in the 1980s, international markets are reliable. Ideally China could concentrate its resources on the production of agricultural commodities where it might have an advantage, such as fruits and vegetables, and rely on international markets for commodities such as grains.

China's Domestic Environmental Policy and Its International Context

China faces a variety of environmental challenges as it develops its industry and infrastructure. With the exception of the food issue, the problems examined here all relate directly to the consequences of China's reliance on coal to fuel its economic growth. Even with food, the state of China's environment may influence its ability to sustain its rate of economic expansion.

In the West, the consequences of fossil fuel use were recognized in a piecemeal fashion, as we moved from the problems of particulate emissions, to high levels of ozone, to acid rain, and now to carbon dioxide and other greenhouse gases. In contrast, China has an opportunity to confront all of these issues in concert. In the process it may avoid inefficiencies inherent with the response that developed in the West. It can opt for the piecemeal solutions that mitigate the impact of particulate emissions, acid rain, and ozone now but may result in a decrease in overall energy efficiency with a consequent increase in emissions of carbon dioxide. Alternatively, it can learn from the West's experience and adopt a more comprehensive approach to deal with all of the environmental consequences of energy use simultaneously. A Sino-American initiative targeting specific areas of energy and environmental cooperation could help China build comprehensive long-term solutions into its development, with political and economic benefits for both countries.

China's government has demonstrated significant commitment to environmental protection, particularly so if judged by the standards of other developing countries. China expended 0.8 percent of its gross national product on environmental protection in the first three years of the Eighth Five Year Plan, a comparatively high figure for a lesser developed country. In the years since the Cultural Revolution, moreover, it has built an extensive body of environmental law. Based currently on the 1982 Constitution that declares the state responsible for protecting the environment and controlling pollution, the framework for environmental regulation includes the comprehensive Environmental Protection Law of 1989 and a multitude of sector-specific environmental laws, provisions of the civil and criminal code, regulatory enactments, national and subnational standards, and cases. These enactments make use of various policy instruments, including command and control regulations, moral suasion, and economic incentives. The Environmental Protection Law exemplifies the use of eclectic approaches in a single law, encompassing instruments such as siting prohibitions, requirements for environmental impact assessments, exhortations, promotion of environmental technology development, discharge standards, and collection of fees for the emission of pollutants exceeding state standards.

As William Alford and Shen Yuanguan, in research conducted for the China Project, have described, despite the fiscal commitment and the good intentions and breadth of environmental legal enactments, Chinese environmental law and policy are regrettably deficient both in implementation and in enforcement. It is as important to understand the structural deficiencies and societal conditions that undercut enforcement of environmental laws in China as it is to understand their content, for the success of policy-driven pollution control is likely to depend ultimately on progress toward broader reform. This wider perspective is important in considering which options for foreign cooperation will have the greatest impact on China's environmental conditions.

The recently amended Air Pollution Prevention and Control Law resembles the overarching Environmental Protection Law, with deficiencies that are common in Chinese law more generally. One flaw, reflecting the era in which these laws were originally developed, is the assumption of a planned economy composed only of individuals and enterprises with a formal relationship to the state. The original 1987 air pollution law requires the government to consider the environment in "planning out a rational distribution of industry," even though that distribution is now increasingly determined by unplanned market forces. Another assumption is that of vertical cohesion in the governmental administrative system. Many of the laws require subnational units to follow requirements set on the national level, especially the extensive network of provincial and local environmental protection bureaus that are to be guided by the National Environmental Protection Agency (NEPA). Yet NEPA's authority over the environmental protection bureaus is not clearly specified in the law. In practice, bureau officials principally report to, are budgeted by, and have job promotion paths linked to local government units that sometimes view environmental protection as an impediment to economic growth. Given the flexibility accorded subnational officials and their authority to relax compliance schedules and to allow exemptions in view of local conditions, the local enforcement of national requirements is understandably muted.

The air pollution law and supporting statutes are frequently couched in imprecise or very general aspirational language; for instance, enterprises shall "give priority to clean production technology" or "gradually take measures to control nitrogen oxide generated by coal burning." One relevant policy (now possibly revised) gives thermal power plants the option of using either high smokestacks or fluidized gas desulfurization to meet a local acid rain standard. Given that fluidized gas desulfurization can add as much as 30 percent to the cost of a plant, it is hardly surprising that plant managers take advantage of the law's flexibility to simply build higher stacks. The larger the installed capacity, moreover, the higher the stack. This decision transfers sulfur dioxide downwind, thus expanding the aerial extent of the region subjected to acid rain.

Partly in recognition of these deficiencies, reform of the framework of environmental law has begun, including passage in 1995 of a number of incentive oriented amendments to the air pollution law. The revisions include enhanced criminal penalties, greater adherence to the "polluter pays" principle, and movement toward systems of tradable emission permits. Beginning with the original Environmental Protection Law of 1979, China initiated incentive based instruments with a system requiring that a fee be paid for emissions over a specified standard. Levies, however, are set far below control costs, which leads firms to simply pay the fee as a matter of course, when enforced, rather than control emissions. The law also has budgetary effects that may influence enforcement choices. Subnational environmental protection bureaus fund their operations in part on the basis of the 20 percent of the fees they are allowed to retain and from additional collections of fines. The remaining 80 percent is perversely allocated back to the fee-paying enterprise ostensibly to invest in pollution control, which further dilutes the incentive.[15]

To be broadly successful, economic instruments require market-like operating conditions for the polluting enterprises, an adequate exchange of information, and a clear distinction between regulating and regulated entities. Large, polluting, state owned enterprises typically do not face budgets that are stringent enough to force them to respond as intended to economic penalties and fines, the levels of which are in any event too low. Township and village enterprises are often directly linked to political authorities who have responsibilities over the enforcement of relevant regulations. This is not to suggest that incentive based instruments for pollution control are generally ill-conceived, and at least some inadvert forms in China, such as energy price reform, surely yield environmental benefits. For more complicated incentive based pollution control policies, however, the prerequisites for their successful implementation on a broad scale may be lacking in China. Opportunities for U.S.–Chinese cooperation yielding direct environmental benefits in the immediate future are unlikely to come from Western policy concepts and more likely to come through direct investments in the energy sector, which yield local, regional, and global pollution control benefits simultaneously.

In accord with an international commitment signed at the U.N. sponsored Earth Summit in Rio de Janeiro in 1992, China was the first country to announce a national plan for sustainable development, "China's Agenda 21." This book-length white paper, approved by the State Council in 1994 and intended to "guide" the Ninth Five Year Plan (1996–2000), seeks "a path for development, wherein considerations of population, economy, society, natural resources, and the environment are coordinated as a whole, so that a path for non-threatening sustainable development can be found which will meet current needs without compromising the ability of future generations to meet their needs." It includes a "Priority Programme" of sixty-two proposed projects targeting international assistance in support of its overall aims; twenty of these projects were under way by December of 1995.

Developed under vice ministers at the State Science and Technology and State Planning Commissions, led apparently by the former, the actual influence of Agenda 21 on the Ninth Five Year Plan is uncertain. Of more fundamental concern is how such a sweeping and comprehensive planning document might influence the most dynamic enterprises in China's market economy, the private firms and the township and village enterprises that are chiefly responsible for the nation's explosive growth. Operating largely beyond both the state plan and effective law, such enterprises are collectively evolving into China's most inefficient energy consumers and its most uncontrolled polluters. Nevertheless, Agenda 21 represents a commitment by China's leadership to find ways to integrate environmental considerations into national development. It is also important in that it identifies a variety of opportunities for cooperation with international partners.

International strategy with respect to climate change is being developed under the Framework Convention on Climate Change (FCCC), reflecting a consensus reached by 155 nations at the 1992 Rio Earth Summit. The FCCC calls on Organization of Economic Cooperation and Development (OECD) and former Eastern bloc nations to reduce emissions of greenhouse gases, including carbon dioxide, to 1990 levels by the year 2000. As of the fall of 1996, only Germany and the United Kingdom appeared to be on track to accomplish this objective, the former because of the historical accident of German reunification and retirement of inefficient energy systems in the east. All parties to the convention, including developing countries, are obliged to report "national inventories of anthropogenic emissions by sources and sinks" and to adopt "measures to mitigate climate change," requirements that are neither specific nor onerous.

For a variety of reasons China has often, though not always, taken a contentious stance in negotiations regarding the FCCC, as Abram Chayes and Charlotte Kim describe in the China Project volume. The common view in China is that because industrialized countries of the West are primarily responsible for the majority of greenhouse gas emissions to date and because their per capita contributions are much higher, they must take the lead. Until recently, U.S. administrations have also been reluctant to embrace aggressive action in FCCC negotiating sessions, and responses in terms of domestic policy have been muted and largely ineffective.[16] In the summer of 1996, however, a major change in the U.S. position allowed the FCCC's Conference of the Parties to commit to enacting binding greenhouse gas emission targets for industrialized nations at its next meeting, scheduled for the end of 1997 in Kyoto, Japan. Because of the stakes involved, the Kyoto session and the meetings leading up to it represent a crucial but potentially contentious step in advancing the FCCC to greater effectiveness. A provision of the FCCC that may prove central for Sino-American cooperation is termed "joint implementation." Policies and projects designed to reduce net emissions of greenhouse gases can be administered jointly by two or more signatories to the convention. Because long-lived greenhouse gases reside in the global commons of the planet's atmosphere, a ton of carbon dioxide abated in Sichuan, for example, has the same environmental benefit as one saved in Michigan. Joint implementation was proposed and promoted by the United States and other OECD countries as a formal mechanism by which developed countries could utilize private capital to meet limits on national emissions through credits for greenhouse gas abatement or for the sequestration of carbon (such as programs for reforestation) in developing countries. Joint implementation has a powerful economic rationale, given the relative costs for the mitigation of greenhouse gas emissions in developed as compared with lesser developed countries.

There has been much international debate on the effectiveness and fairness of the joint implementation strategy, however, raising skepticism about its ultimate viability. Officials in many developing countries charge that it provides a mechanism for major industrialized countries to escape responsibility for controlling profligate per capita emissions in their own economies. Sovereignty concerns play a part, because joint implementation requires monitoring emissions in host countries, presumably involving foreign institutions.

Also controversial is the calculation of baseline emission trajectories in lesser developed countries, against which joint implementation reductions need to be measured. Chinese officials have been vocal in expressing these concerns. Because of these objections and in the absence of binding emission constraints, a permutation of joint implementation was adopted on a pilot basis in 1995, under the name "activities implemented jointly" (AIJ). The key difference is the omission of a system of credits for greenhouse gases abated or sequestered, despite the fact that in theory it is precisely those credits that should provide the additional incentive for investment. Nevertheless, as of September 1996, twenty-eight pilot projects for AIJ have been initiated, the majority in countries of central and eastern Europe and in Central America. As of the fall of 1995, an official Chinese stance on AIJ had not yet emerged, and there has been no formal designation of a government agency to oversee Chinese AIJ activities, though Sino-Japanese and Sino-Canadian AIJ projects or agreements have already been reported.

Meanwhile, as a major proponent of both joint implementation and "activities implemented jointly," the United States pursues pilot projects through the U.S. Initiative on Joint Implementation (USIJI), a multi-agency working group. Although the USIJI has encountered interbureaucratic difficulties, fifteen pilot projects have been announced to date, most with enthusiastic but small host countries such as Costa Rica. Recognition is emerging that the initiative must evolve to include partnerships with larger host countries such as China, where opportunities for abatement and sequestration are more significant.[17]

Cooperation in Energy Development

The experience of Western countries can inform China's development of an air pollution control strategy that comprehensively targets local, regional, and global hazards. Because of the scale of this undertaking and the many impediments already described, an integrated policy strategy for air pollution control will imply a long-term endeavor at best. For more immediate results, China can address key segments of its energy use and development for which "no regrets" options exist, yielding benefits that outweigh costs even without consideration of non-market local and global environmental impacts. To be sure, a number of such options are probably unsuitable for foreign participation, for a variety of complex reasons. A noteworthy example is the case of industrial boilers, which consume a remarkable 33 percent of all coal in China and typically lack controls on pollution. Although Chinese boilers average only 50 percent efficiency of energy conversion, compared with 75–80 percent for systems employing best Western technologies, the lack of a foreign market and unprotected intellectual property rights severely limit the potential for joint venture manufacture. Here we focus on a few specific areas of energy supply and demand in which American firms could play an effective role.

Boom economies such as China's require major investments of capital for the development and delivery of energy. One recent consultancy assessment projects investment needs across China's energy sector of $1 trillion to the year 2015, with more than $550 billion for electric power generation; $180 billion for the exploration, production, refining, and distribution of oil; and $90 billion for the development of an adequate supply of natural gas.[18] The United States could make an important contribution in terms of both capital and technology to the development of China's energy market. Foreign capital, it is forecast, could account for 20 percent of the $1 trillion needed and could be particularly important for power generation, in exploration for oil and gas, and in refining.

Much of China's expanding appetite for energy is being met today by low-cost, conventional means: domestically produced industrial boilers and power plants burning coal, with little or few controls on pollution. Without effective mechanisms to internalize environmental costs, other options for satisfying the demand for energy services—efficiency and conservation measures, natural gas, hydroelectricity, and many other types of nonfossil energy supply—are typically overlooked because of high initial capital costs, lack of credit, the unavailability of suitable technologies, or lack of familiarity with them. This situation arises despite the existence of a variety of options for which long-term internal rates of return should be attractive; managers of enterprises in China's rapidly expanding economy are often disposed to embrace only investments for which payback periods are exceptionally short. By capitalizing on foreign participation, China would have an opportunity to employ strategies that could allow it to leapfrog the inefficiencies and environmental consequences inherent in a more traditional energy path constrained by an over-reliance on coal. The benefits to China are obvious: an opportunity to learn from Western mistakes and to take advantage of foreign capital, technology, and expertise. For the United States, beyond the political benefits of integrating China further into the global economy, direct economic benefits could accrue to the private sector, which would gain a foothold in investment and trade of advanced technologies in a primary sector of the world's largest growth economy.

Many of the fields for potential cooperation outlined below have the potential to moderate growth of greenhouse gas emissions and could be suitable for pilot AIJ projects under the aegis of the FCCC. Even in the absence of binding emissions constraints in the United States and incentives to earn credits abroad to meet them, private firms in the West may have reasons to undertake AIJ projects in other countries for the practical and institutional experience they could provide. This could prove valuable as the FCCC process becomes more rigid. Pilot AIJ projects could prove attractive for additional reasons to American private investors eyeing Chinese energy markets. With high-level bilateral political endorsement and preferential government loan guarantees, AIJ could smooth the approval process for individual projects and could reduce political and investment risks that currently force private firms to demand returns on investment that Chinese authorities and partners can find excessive. Although AIJ faces unresolved challenges and may in time be supplanted by an alternate scheme, a bilateral initiative targeting projects with local, regional, and global benefits in terms of air pollution could be attractive to China's leadership and could induce a more proactive role by China in the FCCC process.

Roughly 80 percent of electric power in China is generated through the thermal combustion of fossil fuel, mainly coal. Additions to power generating capacity have totaled 10,000 megawatts per year since 1988, reaching an installed capacity of 195,000 megawatts in 1994 with production of approximately 900 terawatt hours of electricity. In their China Project research Fiona Murray and Peter Rogers describe how power sector investments recently have emphasized large, domestically built, steam turbine plants with thermal efficiencies superior to the outmoded technologies of the past but still less efficient than new plants constructed in OECD nations. At the same time, investment in smaller, comparatively inefficient units continues. Chinese authorities have announced optimistic plans in recent years to add approximately 15,000 megawatts of electric power generating capacity annually. China's program to boost electric power generation and to replace antiquated facilities is equal to the construction of twenty-five large power plants per year, an annual increment nearly equivalent to the total installed generating capacity of Taiwan or Belgium.

Needless to say, the scale of power sector development required to satisfy China's appetite for energy has attracted considerable attention from abroad, particularly in the early 1990s. Official Chinese estimates of investment needs in the electric power sector are placed at $15–$20 billion per year, with demand for foreign capital of about $5 billion a year. Following early announcements of a number of high-profile joint venture power projects, however, Fiona Murray, Forest Reinhardt, and Richard Victor have shown how most of these deals were either delayed or collapsed because of problems that included financing, contract disputes, and onerous requirements for permitting. The central government, by offering inadequate guarantees for repayment of loans and by capping guaranteed rates of return at levels that are not competitive with returns from investments in other high-risk overseas markets, enacted policies that effectively immobilized new foreign equity investments. Domestic political objection to "excessive" foreign profits may have played a role. But the central government may also have simply decided in 1994 to regain control of the helter-skelter development of its power sector, seeking time to find its own formula for build-operate-transfer (BOT) foreign equity arrangements that could meet local conditions. The hiatus on foreign investment negotiations in the power sector may soon be at an end. The State Planning Commission is developing a BOT decree that will standardize requirements for participation in foreign equity ventures, and has sponsored a 700-megawatt power station in Guangxi as a means to experiment with a formula to be employed elsewhere.

A great deal of attention has been focused on Integrated Gas

Combined Cycle (IGCC) technology, which has the potential both to increase efficiency, cutting back on emissions of carbon dioxide associated with a given yield of electric power, and at the same time to reduce emissions of nitrogen and sulfur oxides and particulates. The United States and China signed a high-level agreement in 1994 to cooperate on a demonstration plant employing IGCC, though it has subsequently been delayed. This, however, is still an expensive technology that has been demonstrated only on a pilot basis and has not yet been applied commercially.

Despite the existence of many alternatives, coal is certain to continue to form the foundation of China's electric power sector at least in the medium term. Even in the absence of enforcement of stringent measures for pollution control, investments that include foreign coal combustion technologies are likely to yield environmental benefits over the domestic technologies that would otherwise be installed. Foreign units can be imported at sizes up to 600 megawatts, with combustion efficiencies in the range of 33–37 percent, compared with the Chinese efficiencies of 29–32 percent. As a consequence foreign units are capable of delivering more useful electricity for a given input of fuel.

Of all the major fossil fuels, natural gas emits the fewest pollutants. Gas use, concentrated in Sichuan Province, currently provides only 2 percent of China's primary commercial energy production. Up to 35 percent of natural gas production is used as a feedstock for production of chemical fertilizer.[19] Whether the development of natural gas can provide a significant opportunity for China to reduce its current reliance on coal is a matter of debate. The conventional opinion in China is that the country is simply geologically "gas poor," and that opportunities for development of the gas option are limited unless the country should decide to invest in expensive imports of liquefied gas or in transnational pipelines. Others, however, question this view. They point out that the geological processes that produce fossil fuels are linked, and given that China has the largest coal reserves in the world and is the fifth ranking producer of oil, it is unlikely to be as gas poor as the conventional view would suggest.[20] Exploration for natural gas has received relatively little priority, with investment totaling only approximately 10 percent of that for oil. Explanations for this disparity appear to include limited expertise and political favoritism toward the development of other energy resources, particularly oil. Given that natural gas now accounts for 23 percent of the supply of primary energy in the world (including 46 percent of Russian and 29 percent of American production), it is surprising that it has not attracted greater interest as a potential source of relatively clean fuel for energy-constrained China.

Development of pipeline distribution systems would be part of the challenge and the opportunity. Beyond domestic extraction and distribution, options may exist for importing gas from Siberia and Central Asia through regional pipelines that could serve demand not only in China but also in Japan and Korea. The abundant expertise of American firms in exploration, extraction, and distribution of natural gas could prove attractive should China seek greater exploitation of this environmentally advantageous fossil fuel. One study of energy sector markets projects investment in natural gas development in China, even under current plans, at as much as $90 billion through 2015. The full potential for the market, however, depends significantly on the scale of the development of the accompanying distribution infrastructure.

It is generally accepted that the Three Gorges Dam is an ill-conceived showpiece for which better alternatives exist, such as a series of less monumental hydroelectric projects along the Yangtze River and its tributaries. Not only would this option rest on sounder technical grounds, it could provide the same benefits in terms of electric power generation, flood control, and navigation at much lower costs in terms of capital, human resettlement, and environmental damage. The recent decision by the U.S. Export-Import Bank not to support the project appears justified. However, the Three Gorges project has been politicized at high levels of the Chinese government for decades, in ways Westerners may not fully appreciate. External pressures opposed to the dam may now be irrelevant or perhaps even counterproductive. Depending on further developments in China, internal opposition may still have an opportunity to stop construction of the dam, which will take more than twenty years to complete. At some point, however, the scale of the investment will reach a level that makes completion of the dam inevitable. If the Chinese government is resolved to complete this politically charged project using its own financing, there is little outside actors can do to influence it, beyond refusing to participate.

Overwhelming attention to Three Gorges has diverted attention from China's other prospects and efforts in hydroelectric development, including its successful domestic programs for construction of small- and medium-scale facilities. Considered one of the most environmentally benign sources of electric power, small- and medium-scale hydro could be particularly advantageous for remote communities in China's mountainous southwest provinces and in Tibet. Hydroelectric potential in this region is among the largest in the world. Electrification of remote towns and villages in such imposing terrain through conventional power transmission links is prohibitively costly; small-scale hydro offers opportunities for affordable off-grid supply of power. In Yunnan, for instance, a third of all villages and 11 million of its 37 million residents were unconnected to the provincial power grid as of 1992. A cooperative effort to adapt advanced U.S. small- and medium-scale hydro technologies to local conditions could provide environmentally sustainable electrification to some of China's poorest rural inhabitants and would appear to be justified on both political and economic grounds. Similar opportunities exist for other forms of renewable energy such as wind power and biomass and for improvements on the demand-side such as investments in building efficiency, end-use technologies, and energy use management strategies.

China's nuclear power program is surprisingly undeveloped, given the country's depth in associated scientific fields, directed to date mostly toward research and development of nuclear weapons. Expansion of nuclear power development is probably inevitable given the perceived lack of viable alternatives to coal, the associated environmental costs, and intensifying bottlenecks impeding the transport of coal from mines to demand centers. At present China has only one major operational nuclear plant constructed with foreign participation, although plans have been announced for a number of others. Westinghouse in particular has been active in lobbying for the lifting of trade constraints so that it may participate in China's nuclear power program. Despite the flagging fortunes of nuclear power in the United States and most Western countries, its continued development in France and in East Asian nations such as Japan and Taiwan serves as a model to Chinese energy planners. Construction of nuclear plants itself produces appreciable carbon dioxide emissions, but nuclear power is free of greenhouse gas emissions. If climate fears continue to mount, nuclear power could enjoy an international resurgence. While issues relating to proliferation, safety, and waste management are obviously of concern, any efforts to oppose the peaceful development of nuclear power in China are unlikely to be successful. In the China Project volume Fang Dong, Debra Lew, Li Ping, Daniel Kammen, and Richard Wilson suggest that to the extent that China remains steadfastly committed to its nuclear power program, including the import of inherently less safe Russian designed reactors, Western cooperation could have a positive influence in raising standards for safety and encouraging proper recognition of environmental costs in China's nuclear program.

The importance of end-use energy efficiency at the household level should not be overlooked in prospects for cooperation. There are implications here not only for the environment but also for public health. Some of the greatest gains in reducing the health impacts of energy use, particularly among women and children, may occur through improvements in the utilization of household energy. Space heating and cooking with coal expose urban residents to high concentrations of sulfur dioxide, carbon monoxide, particulates, benzopyrene, and hydrocarbons in addition to the contribution they make to emissions of carbon dioxide. In their China Project research Peng Ruicong, Wang Lihua, Wang Hong, He Kebin, and Xu Xiping have implicated indoor pollutants as a reason for the elevated urban incidence of respiratory diseases, pulmonary and heart diseases, and lung cancer in China. Poorly understood and underappreciated are the health effects of indoor air pollution on China's immense rural population. Attendant environmental impacts of rural energy use are also acute, including pervasive deforestation and depletion of agricultural soils through widespread combustion of nutrient containing crop wastes as heating and cooking fuel. Low-cost partial solutions to the problems of indoor air pollution include the introduction of stoves designed for more efficient combustion. An aggressive program to improve the health and environmental consequences of household energy use could have the related benefit of raising awareness of the importance of energy efficiency; such awareness could transfer to nonresidential settings. Other options in household energy use include switching to higher-quality or renewable energy sources such as natural gas, biogas, and even solar radiation.

China's transport sector is notably undeveloped, accounting for only 7.5 percent of total commercial energy consumed in 1989. Of this, 30 percent was employed for transport by rail with 47.6 percent and 18.2 percent for the road and water sectors, respectively.[21] A World Bank team has projected that the transport sector will almost quadruple from 1990 to 2020 in terms of its demand for primary energy, at which point transport would account for 5 percent of net emissions of carbon dioxide in China.

In developing its transportation sector, China has the opportunity to integrate strategies for appropriate urban development and mass transit into its plans at an earlier stage than was the case in the West and to downplay the role of the personal automobile. By pursuing this strategy, China could also reduce the massive investments required to develop a large-scale system of highways and the loss of arable land this would imply. While the auto industry conventionally has been viewed as an engine of growth in the economy, it was downgraded recently from the number one position on the government's "key industries" list, and some urban planners concerned about infrastructure development have begun to question the official priority accorded it. Nevertheless, all of the signs indicate that China is still likely to follow a path similar to that pursued in the West and newly industrialized countries of Asia. Automobile ownership has assumed a symbolic importance as a measure of economic success and as a signal of the nation's material promise. Lesser goals in the management of transportation intensity and modal composition may yield environmental benefits, but it is likely that the Chinese demand for cars and motorcycles will continue to rise steeply.

Car manufacturers from around the world, including the American Big Three, hope to enter and/or expand operations in China. A sensible approach for the Chinese government, if it continues a long-term embrace of motor vehicles for personal transport, would be to set and enforce high fuel efficiency and emissions standards for its entire vehicle market, but then open it widely to foreign investment and technology transfer. By doing so, China could reduce emission of pollutants from its expanding new vehicle stock by as much as a factor of two, while simultaneously reducing what could be its huge future demand for imported oil.

Research Initiatives

Enhanced Sino-American research collaboration could form a valuable part of cooperation in energy development and environmental protection. We focus here on one small but critical area. It would be advantageous to strengthen underdeveloped Chinese research capacities and involvement in atmospheric chemistry, physics, computer modeling, and other key fields of climate and environmental science and in the impact assessments that drive public understanding of the greenhouse effect. The effects of this proposal could be profound. There is evidence that Chinese policy makers are beginning to associate costly weather anomalies with global change, particularly with regard to the increasing instability of China's hydrological systems. Strengthening scientific understanding of the domestic impacts of prospective climate change may be the most potent means to heighten concern and motivate proactive responses. Further, one should not discount the potential of Chinese scientists to contribute significant new perspectives and resources to climate science. China's unique historical record of data on changes in climate, land use, hydrology, sediment flux, and sea level can provide valuable assets for some forms of climate research. It is likely also that China could offer experience, expertise, and perspective lacking in Western countries to assess the socioeconomic impacts of potential climate change and to identify response and adaptation options that could be useful for the developing world in general, the countries most vulnerable to potential greenhouse impacts.

Less obviously, few appreciate the political relevance of the overwhelmingly Western origins of the empirical studies, complex atmosphere-ocean-biosphere modeling, and impact assessments that propel current concerns about climate change. Key Chinese policy makers cite paleoclimatic studies undertaken within China to cast doubt on greenhouse conclusions by a scientific community drawn largely from OECD countries. To some, this emphasis may be interpreted as driven simply by trust in indigenous scientific capacities and methodologies. To others it may reflect a politicization of science akin to the convenient but often simplistic arguments sometimes advanced to inhibit actions to address environmental challenges in the West. There are powerful incentives unrelated to informed scientific dissent for leaders to remain skeptical, or even to envision Western initiatives as strategies for containment masquerading as climate science. This is not to say that Chinese officials are exclusively greenhouse skeptics, or that those who are have political motivations. But to bolster acceptance by decision makers of greenhouse evidence and thus to enhance prospects for agreement on potentially difficult response strategies, there is a clear incentive to build indigenous capabilities and to give China a greater ownership of the relevant international science through accelerated joint research.

Conclusions

China's rise to superpower status will mark the end of an era, the centuries-long monopoly of world economic and political power by nations of the West. Evaluating the prospects for Sino-American cooperation in energy and environment to play a role in easing this transition, it is essential not to dismiss China's significant accomplishments in development, achieved despite great pressures of demography and resource scarcity. Making such respect contingent on wholesale adoption of Western environmental values, some of which are culturally alien, is a recipe for failure. Moreover, environmental concerns cannot be used to deny Chinese their right to the material benefits of economic development that Westerners already possess, conceivably in overabundance. It is an unfortunate truth that, like for most countries including the U.S., fossil fuels will unavoidably form the backbone of China's expanding energy system for the foreseeable future. Ultimately, within the limits of international norms to which it is bound, China will make its own decisions regarding energy use and environmental protection.

The U.S. and China are unlikely to resolve all of their disagreements in the near future. But today nations with gaping differences simultaneously engage closely with each other through shared economic and other interests and through modern technological connectivity. Sino-American relations will take place through a tangle of conduits, some heated with contention but others cooled by common interests. Prospects for the latter type must not be neglected, even when national values come into conflict. Still greater potential for engagement exists, moreover, in those areas in which basic values coincide. Addressing the challenging and interrelated problems of urban, rural, indoor, and regional air pollution, where the impacts on human health, economic development, and agricultural productivity are perceived quite similarly around the world, is just such an opportunity. At the same time, cooperation with China in energy and environment could offer substantial benefits to American firms seeking a foothold in this great, expanding economy.

Overshadowing the transition to a new international order caused by a rising Chinese superpower, however, may be a historic challenge transcending the conventional political and economic calculus: insuring the integrity of the global atmospheric commons itself. It is a potentially monumental task, pregnant with discord between the two largest, but very different, national contributors of greenhouse gas emissions. Yet it would be a mistake to assume that meeting the challenge of the confluence of Sino-American relations and global environmental change must occur in isolation of other national interests. Respectful American engagement with China to address its domestic air pollution problems through better use of energy resources—and perhaps to learn in the process about our own energy profligacy and global environmental responsibilities—can readily coincide with great gains in greenhouse gas mitigation. If these two powers of the early twenty-first century do not seize the opportunity to establish and cultivate cooperative relations in these areas, the costs to both nations—and to the rest of the world—may be higher than most currently appreciate.

Another U.S. interest concerns the security of China's food production and its openness to trade in agricultural commodities. To the extent that China will embrace the comparative advantages of world food production, greater bilateral trade in grain and other foodstuffs may arise between the two countries. Even deep uncertainties about China's agricultural production caused by environmental and other factors, however, could cause wide fluctuations in global grain markets. It is thus important to the United States that China be able to produce enough food that its demand for imports does not unexpectedly destabilize world markets. The United States needs reliable information on food production and food policies so that there are no sudden shocks in international grain markets that might cause hoarding and speculative activity interfering with the smooth flow of food trade. Activities that strengthen U.S.–Chinese cooperation in Chinese agriculture would contribute to these goals.

We must acknowledge that it is not possible for one nation to impose its views and practices in environmental protection on another. Significant progress requires sustained national commitment that cannot be achieved through the use of sanctions. The Chinese government will make its own decisions about environmental policy and projects, and has already proven its desire to develop appropriate technological and policy strategies with regard to energy and the environment. It is in the United States' and other nations' interest for China to develop its capabilities to address its air pollution problems and to be receptive to cooperative and equitable strategies to limit its emissions of greenhouse gases. Sino-American engagement in these areas could contribute directly to the overall protection of the global environment and indirectly to the same goal by proving to other nations that they too should now act aggressively in the effort. And successful U.S.–Chinese collaboration in areas of energy and the environment may also have a positive impact on the two nations' relationship in managing issues where interests and values diverge more sharply.

Notes

[1] Much of the material in this section is taken from Sinton et al. (1996).

[2] The composition of coal-derived particulate emissions varies depending on the nature of coal used and details of the combustion process. In addition to unsightly black soot, emissions from coal contain a mix of organic and inorganic substances including sulfates, metal oxides, various naturally occurring radionuclides, and salts.

[3] Smil (1993).

[4] Sinton et al. (1996).

   [5] Additional strategies currently under study include options for pretreating coal to remove sulfur in advance of combustion (coal washing) or removing sulfur during combustion by burning the coal on a bed of limestone sorbent (fluidized bed combustion). Commercial applications of these technologies have been relatively limited to date but are expected to grow in the future. In the FGD process, the sludge is recovered and disposed of elsewhere. This must be done carefully if additional environmental problems are to be avoided. The cost of retrofitting power plants with FGD has dropped significantly in the West in recent years, from more than $220 per kilowatt in 1982 to less than $170 in 1996, with prospects for further reduction.

   [6] The earth's atmosphere is composed mainly of molecular oxygen (O_2) and nitrogen (N_2), with trace quantities of water (H_2O), carbon dioxide (CO_2), and other gases. Despite their low abundance, typically less than 1 percent of the atmosphere, H_2O and CO_2 play a critical role in determining the climate of the earth. Their importance relates to their capacity to absorb light at infrared wavelengths. If the atmosphere were composed solely of O_2 and N_2, which are transparent to radiation in the infrared, heat radiated by the surface of the earth could escape directly to space: the average temperature of the surface of the earth would be about 20 C below the freezing point of water. Water vapor and CO_2 play a role for the surface-atmosphere system roughly equivalent to that of the glass in a greenhouse. They allow visible solar radiation to penetrate to the surface while inhibiting emission of infrared radiation to space; hence the name, greenhouse gases. The analogy is not entirely accurate. The air in the greenhouse is warm, not only because of the optical properties of the glass, but, to an equal measure, because the walls of the greenhouse inhibit exchange of air with the exterior. Motions of the atmosphere play an important role in moving heat from the surface to higher levels where it can be radiated to space. In the absence of such motion, the surface would be almost 50 C warmer than it is today.

   The temperature of the interior of a building in winter is regulated by the degree of insulation and by the energy output of the furnace used to supply heat. The temperature of the exterior surface of the building adjusts to accommodate the energy released by the furnace; ultimately, heat supplied by the furnace must be communicated to the exterior through the walls and windows. In response to an increase in insulation, the heat radiated to the exterior remains fixed but the temperature of the interior rises reflecting the extra layers of insulation. So it is with the greenhouse in the atmosphere. An increase in insulation, a higher concentration of greenhouse gases, is expected to lead to an increase in surface temperature. The temperature at which the earth radiates to space is fixed, however, as long as the energy supplied by the furnace remains the same.

   The terrestrial furnace is fueled by energy absorbed from the sun. In turn, this depends on the albedo, or color, of the earth. Light-colored deserts absorb less solar radiation than dark tropical forests; clouds are particularly effective in reducing the energy supplied to the furnace. Under current conditions, the exterior surface of the earth must radiate at a temperature of about 20 C below zero to dispose of the energy absorbed from the sun. The radiating layer is located in the upper regions of the troposphere (the region of the atmosphere closest to the surface extending up to an altitude of about twelve km) and is regulated primarily by H_2O and CO_2. Clouds are important both in determining the energy input from the sun and the emission of heat radiation to space.

   If greenhouse gases were absent, the earth would be frozen over from equator to pole. Volcanic eruptions, though, would quickly result in a buildup of CO_2 in the atmosphere. The surface temperature would increase, initially in response to CO_2, but subsequently in reaction to a combination of CO_2 and H_2O as H_2O evaporated from a warming ocean. Water vapor is the most important greenhouse gas in the atmosphere today. Its importance, however, is ultimately linked to the presence of additional greenhouse agents such as CO_2.

The abundance of H_2O in the upper troposphere, the critical region for the contemporary greenhouse, is several orders of magnitude less than at the ground, reflecting the role of rain in wringing excess H_2O from air as it rises from the surface. Intense cumulus convective storms in the tropics are thought to provide the major input of H_2O to the upper troposphere. Water is carried upward in these storms not only in the form of vapor but also as hydro-meteors (small particles of ice and liquid) that evaporate as they enter the low vapor environment of the upper troposphere. It is relatively easy to account for the direct input of vapor to the upper troposphere; it is determined primarily by temperature. It is more difficult to describe the contribution from hydro-meteors. These particles are lofted in updrafts operating on spatial scales orders of magnitude smaller than the resolution of even the best of the models employed to simulate climate.

Predicting the response of H_2O vapor in the upper troposphere to a change in the concentration of greenhouse gases such as CO_2 is a formidable task. The related, and equally demanding, challenge is to anticipate the change in the thickness and spatial distribution of clouds. The current approach involves use of computationally intensive three-dimensional general circulation models (GCMs) to simulate the basic physics of the atmosphere. There are several problems. First, the spatial and temporal resolution of even the best of the GCMs is incapable of resolving all of the important scales of motion. Second, the climate of the earth depends not only on the atmosphere but also on the ocean. A number of models addressing climate change consider the ocean as a reservoir capable of storing and releasing heat locally but ignore its potential to move heat from one region to another. Others adjust fluxes of heat at the air-sea interface to provide at least an approximate representation of the role of the ocean in transporting heat. What is needed is a physically consistent coupled ocean-atmosphere GCM, but the computational requirements to resolve all of the important scales in this case are extreme, probably unattainable at least in the immediate future. Processes operating below the resolution of the models must be parameterized, that is, they must be described as functions of variables computed by the model. There is a serious question as to whether this approach can be justified, irrespective of the skill of the parameterization. Customarily the model is tuned to ensure consistency with the present climate. Whether the tuning is applicable under very different circumstances is an open question.

[7] IPCC (1992), (1995b).

[8] Mahlman (1992).

[9] Blanchon and Shaw (1995).

[10] Hulme et al. (1992).

[11] Hulme et al. (1992).

[12] Brown (1995).

[13] Bardeen (1996); Smil (1995).

[14] No single country has a monopoly on supply. The United States accounted for only 6 percent of world wheat production and 31 percent of wheat exports in 1995–96. Together, Australia, Argentina, and Canada exported more wheat than

the United States in the same period, and exports from the European Union were almost as large.

[15] Another incentive based system, an emissions permit scheme for sulfur dioxide, has been introduced on an experimental basis in fifty-seven cities, but its effectiveness is still unclear.

[16] The Clinton administration's 1993 Climate Change Action Plan proposed to meet the pledge made at Rio to reduce emissions mainly through voluntary measures. Not surprisingly, these have proved insufficient.

[17] Although the future of JI/AIJ as currently constituted is uncertain, in time some mechanism for leveraging private capital from Western countries into greenhouse mitigation in lesser developed countries may be unavoidable. The costs of worldwide abatement of greenhouse gases are potentially too high to expect each nation to squeeze mitigation gains solely from its own energy sector and land-use practices. Such an approach would ignore opportunities to exploit comparative advantages internationally to achieve overall efficiencies in global abatement and sequestration. The costs are too great to rely on more traditional mechanisms of government-to-government or multilateral transfers. There are serious obstacles, both institutional and political, to the introduction of the strategy for which there is the most compelling theoretical justification, tradable carbon permits. In the meantime, transnational investment mechanisms akin to JI/AIJ, modified perhaps to respond to the concerns of lesser developed countries, can make an important contribution to the objective of slowing the growth of greenhouse gases in the atmosphere.

[18] Peter Montagnon, "China May Need $1000Bn for Energy." *Financial Times,* April 5, 1995, p. 6.

[19] Sinton et al. (1996).

[20] Lu (1993); Sinton et al. (1996).

[21] Sinton et al. (1996).

8

Domestic Forces and Sino–U.S. Relations

KENNETH LIEBERTHAL

Bilateral relations among major nations are typically analyzed in terms that imply that each country acts as a unified body with identifiable national interests. But such portrayals are incomplete. Domestic considerations inevitably impinge on wide-ranging, complex relations among major powers over a period of years. Political leaders are naturally sensitive to domestic pressures and concerns, and they develop their policies within the constraints of the structures and styles of their own political systems. During periods

KENNETH LIEBERTHAL is Arthur Thurnau professor of political science and William Davidson professor of business administration, research associate of the Center for Chinese Studies, faculty associate of the Center for Russian and East European Studies, and faculty associate of the William Davidson Institute at the University of Michigan. He has written and edited nearly a dozen books and authored about four dozen articles. His books include *Governing China: From Revolution Through Reform* (1995) and *Policy Making in China: Leaders, Structures and Processes* (1988). He has consulted widely on Chinese affairs and has served as a consultant for the U.S. Department of State, the World Bank, the Kettering Foundation, and firms in the private sector.

of national crisis—or even of the sustained "crisis" that the cold war arguably created—such internal factors may exert less influence on policy making. But in more normal times, such as the post–cold war era, a "billiard ball" model of the international system, which sees each country as a solid object and all pressures resulting only from external contacts with other countries, is inadequate.

Ironically, while national leaders intimately understand the internal factors that constrain their own diplomatic choices, they only rarely fully appreciate those that affect their counterparts' actions. Typically, information is too imperfect to permit such understanding in more than the most unsophisticated fashion. Internal factors thus often have particularly pernicious effects on foreign policy: each leadership believes that its own internal constraints are so clear that the other side *must* understand them, and yet each discounts or ignores the other leaders' internal constraints because they are so difficult to understand with certainty. This subtle factor can contribute to substantial mutual distrust.

Leaders of major countries are, moreover, political beings. They have risen to power through their deep immersion in the political landscape at home. They may feel that they truly understand how politics works and may be particularly insensitive to the important differences that shape politics in the other country. Political leaders are, in short, the products of their systems, and they may never feel comfortable in trying to fathom the different premises that shape the thoughts and strategies in very different polities.

Ample research in the field of perception, moreover, makes clear that where leaders are insecure in their knowledge and grasp of crucial factors in other political systems, they tend to let broad images and untested assumptions relieve their uncertainty, enabling them to act with confidence. This is a reasonable strategy: leaders must produce decisions, and failure to decide is itself a kind of outcome (and often a very poor one).

The political systems in the People's Republic of China and the United States differ sharply in their fundamental assumptions about the way power is obtained and how it should be wielded. Each country has long seen the other in highly symbolic fashion, and the political processes of each country are complex and significantly different from each other. Little wonder that the two leaderships tend to be suspicious of analyses that point to underlying internal constraints on the other's actions. They feel that this type of argument may well be just a ruse to conceal purposeful, unwelcome political agendas.

During the annual negotiations for the renewal of China's most-favored-nation (MFN) status in the early 1990s, for instance, Chinese leaders began to feel that the American president was playing a "good cop, bad cop" game with them by asking each year for concessions "to help the president get MFN renewal through the Congress." Many Chinese had no real appreciation of an independent legislature. American leaders, in somewhat comparable fashion, found it difficult to give credibility to the repeated assertions by China that "the Chinese people would never permit Beijing to give up Taiwan." The U.S. image of a "Communist" country made no allowance for a genuine role for public opinion.

This chapter describes the major internal factors that affect Sino–U.S. relations in the mid-1990s. No analyses of and prescriptions for Sino-American ties should ignore these domestic influences.

Domestic Influences on American Policy toward China

U.S. policy toward China derives from the complex interaction of many features of the political landscape: the structure of the national government, fundraising by politicians, the activities of domestic interest groups, and so forth. The democratic nature of American politics, moreover, means that issues of great symbolic resonance can become entangled with seemingly unrelated facets of the American body politic, as many political actors try to utilize the symbol for their own purposes.

Over the past century China has often acquired great symbolic importance in the American polity—in the early decades, for example, as a potential reservoir of converts ("China for Christ in one generation" was a rallying cry for missionary activities of the period), during World War II as a bastion of freedom suffering from Japanese aggression, in the 1950s and 1960s as a Red Menace, and in most of the 1980s as a leading force for enlightened reform in

Communist systems. These and other developments during the twentieth century suggest that the dominant symbol *du jour* is especially important in structuring the politics of American policy toward China, and that such symbols can change dramatically and quickly.

We shall focus here on key aspects of the domestic pressures on China policy during 1989–1996, a period dominated by the 1989 Tiananmen massacre as the symbolic template for China in U.S. politics. This symbolic framework and the resulting American domestic dynamics made it difficult for the United States to develop and implement a carefully crafted, coordinated, bipartisan policy toward China based squarely on the long-term interests of both countries. This fundamentally negative period highlights the structural components and dynamics that can profoundly influence Washington's China policy, for better or for worse.

As the Tiananmen incident demonstrates, critical events that turn into powerful symbols may take place in China or elsewhere, beyond the control of the American government. But in more normal times, the U.S. president can play a major role in defining the image of China around which policy options are debated. During 1997 the U.S. government may seek to cultivate a different image of China, changing many of the specific political dynamics noted below. But the underlying message will remain true and important: domestic pressures must be taken into account to understand both the policies and the potential of the U.S. stance toward the People's Republic of China.

China as a Political Symbol

In early June 1989 tanks and armored personnel carriers rolled through the streets of Beijing, bringing to a shocking finale more than two months of student-led calls for greater democracy. One of the largest audiences in the history of American television witnessed that bloody repression. Those vivid images, in turn, made China into a negative symbol of great political weight for the American public. Americans see their nation as having been founded on the basis of opposition to European despotism, and they react sharply to visible acts of repression by a government against its own people. The televised pictures of the repression in Beijing therefore evoked a powerful U.S. reaction and produced major negative changes in popular views of China.

American politicians and political groups seek to define themselves in terms of strong images and views, in part because to do so helps to garner votes. A highly recognizable, emotionally powerful symbol itself thus becomes a political resource that can be used by various groups to promote their agendas. For these organizations, the changing realities of China may be less important than the value of keeping attention focused on the symbol and utilizing the resulting feelings.

At times the image of China has been so positive that its symbolic resonance has cast a glow over the entire U.S. policy process. The visits to China by Henry Kissinger and Richard Nixon in 1971–72 initiated such a period, during which China's positive image swept away the realities of the grotesque human rights abuses and other problems of the late Cultural Revolution era. The 1989–1996 period witnessed the reverse effect.

China's negative status after 1989 affected America's attitudes and policies toward the People's Republic in many ways. Candidate Bill Clinton in 1992 castigated President George Bush for "coddling the butchers of Beijing," a sentiment that affected policies in the initial years of the new president's administration. Even when Clinton recognized the importance of developing a construtive, basically cooperative relationship with China, he feared the political costs of following through on this approach. Concern over China's negative image, for example, contributed to the president's unwillingness in September 1995 to invite President Jiang Zemin to Washington for a state visit and made it difficult for Defense Secretary William Perry to host Defense Minister Chi Haotian for a visit, with full military honors, in April 1996.

During 1989–1996, at least four groups sought to use the China symbol to serve their own political ends. In each case, China could legitimately be linked to the kinds of problems the group was trying to address. But also in each case, the extent to which attention focused on China, rather than on other countries in which similar issues arose, reflected China's enormous negative symbolic importance after 1989.

Groups concerned with fair trade used China's rapidly growing trade surplus with the United States to press their case for trade barriers. The bilateral U.S.–China trade deficit mushroomed during these years from $6.235 billion in 1989 to $33.789 billion in 1995, but this number conceals underlying complexities.[1] In 1995–96, groups such as labor unions increasingly reached out to tap the broad uneasiness among American employees about job insecurity that they associated with the globalization of the international economy. Leaders of multinational corporations tend to view globalization as presenting major opportunities, but employees and small business people, seeing China as the next Japan in terms of threats to American jobs, tend to view this process as highly threatening. Many Republicans elected to Congress in 1994 reflected the views of small business people. Not surprisingly, the conservative Republican candidate Patrick Buchanan in 1996 directed his strongest protectionist rhetoric at China.

Human rights advocates have also fought to influence American foreign policy. China's actions in June 1989, particularly because they received such extensive television attention, created the kind of high-profile political symbol that enhanced the visiblity and impact of the human rights arguments well beyond their previous levels of success. These advocates thereafter focused enormous energy on highlighting continuing human rights abuses in China, and they won many supporters for their cause. During much of the 1989–1996 period, nearly all television coverage of China included mention of human rights abuses,[2] often accompanied by file footage from early June 1989.

Right-to-life advocates, a potent force in American politics in the 1990s, are another group that sees China as a villain, in this case because of its vigorous birth control efforts and the elements of coercion associated with that program. At the same time, opponents of abortion in the United States, along with the Christian fundamentalist movement with which many are associated, play an important role in Republican party politics. Although right-to-life advocates are primarily concerned with U.S. domestic politics, through their positions in Republican state organizations and their support of many successful Republican candidates, they are able to make their views on China known as well.

An additional set of groups, those favoring nonproliferation, have used the China symbol as well. During 1989–1996, these advocates highlighted every piece of evidence that pointed to China as a violator of international conventions on the proliferation of weapons of mass destruction and their means of delivery. Violations by other countries such as France and Germany received negligible coverage by comparison.

Overall, very few Americans cast votes or contribute money to political campaigns on the basis of U.S. China policy. Those whose votes and contributions are based on an individual issue tended during 1989–1996 to focus on issues such as human rights, the right to life, and so forth. But the importance of these single-issue voters reinforced the tendency of many members of early and mid-1990s Congresses to link their China related votes to these "hot button" issues. One highly knowledgeable member of Congress believes, for instance, that as of 1996, 120 members voted against China on virtually all issues because of their perception of its abortion policies.[3]

In addition, the party out of power in the White House has used China's negative image as a tool. Not surprisingly, Democrats in the Congress held Bush's feet to the fire on China issues, and Republicans in the Congress then did the same to Clinton. Each president therefore had to consider partisan congressional sentiment when thinking about China policy during this period. Members of the Clinton administration, for example, wanted to include China in America's Asia Environmental Initiative. But because the enabling legislation for this program was passed in the early 1990s and explicitly excludes China, the administration would have had to ask Congress to change this provision. Given the Republican penchant in Congress to use every China initiative to criticize the president, the White House proved unwilling to expend the political capital necessary to obtain this change. In this and many other ways, partisan politics affected American policy toward China after 1989.

Congressional Structure and Practice

The U.S. Constitution, through the separation of powers, gives Congress the initiative in some areas, such as trade, and forces the White House and Congress to bargain across a wide spectrum of issues. Especially during the 1989–1996 period, strong advocates of a tougher policy toward China in Congress kept the White House on the defensive in developing and executing its China policy.

The annual debate over renewal of China's most-favored-nation trading status became a major battleground after 1989.[4] The 1974 Trade Act mandates that consideration of renewal of MFN for China be taken up each year. It also, in a highly unusual stipulation, makes this a "privileged resolution" that any member of the House or Senate can take directly to the floor of the chamber for a vote by the entire membership. On almost all other issues, powerful committee chairs can effectively bottle up troublesome legislation and prevent it from reaching the floor. That is not true with MFN renewal.

During 1990–96, the annual MFN debate provided an occasion for all groups seeking to influence China policy to mobilize to attach conditions to MFN renewal.[5] Anticipation of the debate affected administration policy toward China during the preceding months. Human rights and other interest groups made sure that negative stories about developments in China were provided to the American media around the time of the MFN debate. The annual cycle thus actually played out over a period of months, leaving relatively little time for a more positive set of initiatives to take hold before the MFN issue again moved to the fore.

By 1995–96 congressional sentiment toward China reflected, in part, the substantial attrition of historical memory on Capitol Hill regarding the People's Republic. Well over half the members of Congress in 1997 joined the Congress since 1989. Because in January 1995 the Republicans became the majority party in both the House and the Senate for the first time since the 1950s, massive changes in congressional committee staffs—the individuals who often provide much of the continuity from Congress to Congress— also occurred. Congress in the mid-1990s thus to an unusual extent viewed the issue of China in terms of its symbolic value rather than in terms of real national interest, grounded in a knowledge of the history of the relationship.

Late 1995 and early 1996 polls by Worthlin Worldwide illustrate the resulting damage of these developments vis-à-vis the perspectives of members of Congress. In these polls, although only 46 per-

cent of the members of Congress regarded themselves as quite fa-
miliar with issues concerning the People's Republic, 66 percent
agreed with the statement, "We should demand that China improve
its human rights policies if China wants to continue to enjoy its current trade status with the U.S."[6] On an attitudinal scale of 0 (very
unfavorable) to 100 (very favorable), legislators gave China a ranking of only 38. The 1997 Congress, even more than the one that pre-
ceded it, has few members who have detailed knowledge of—and
interest in—concrete foreign policy issues.

Members of Congress expend a great deal of time and energy
on getting elected. This process requires raising adequate campaign contributions and finding issues that give their candidacy a
clear, powerful identity in voters' minds. Campaign finance reforms
now require candidates for Congress to raise small amounts of
money from a large number of donors, rather than depending on
a few large contributors to provide the financial backing for a successful campaign. The need to appeal to donors means that candidates must embrace high-profile issues of considerable symbolic
value. In many instances, it also requires that they be able to elicit
active support from interest groups outside of their own electoral
jurisdiction.

Nearly all congressional candidates win or lose on the basis of domestic issues, and a large number therefore use foreign policy symbols primarily to help position themselves on the local matters that
resonate with their constituencies. High-profile symbolic issues—
such as human rights and birth control with reference to China—
become important in this context. Once in office, members of
Congress tend to vote in a way that is consistent with their campaign
rhetoric. Concerned interest groups may add to the incentives to
follow through on one's campaign statements. China policy during
1989–1996 suffered as a consequence.

Given these pressures, Congress was inclined to take a tough line
toward China despite lobbying to the contrary by seemingly important groups such as big business. U.S.–China trade mushroomed
after China stimulated its domestic economic growth in 1992, and
key American businesses such as the Boeing Corporation became
ardent supporters of cooperative ties with China. But many members of Congress view large corporations as interested only in mak-

ing a profit, and they become irritated when these companies try to tell Congress how to handle moral issues such as human rights and birth control. Many members of the 1995–96 Congress, moreover, hailed from small business backgrounds and held a far more negative view toward free trade and foreign investment than that of their counterparts in multinational corporations.

The Executive Branch

Each president has shaped the executive branch to suit his own priorities and style. From 1992 to 1996, the Clinton administration focused primarily on domestic issues, with foreign policy generally fighting a losing battle for the president's sustained attention. President Clinton himself, moreover, placed a high value on protecting human rights, on fostering global nonproliferation regimes, on supporting democratization, and on increasing American exports—and his choice of officials for top foreign policy posts reflected these priorities.

On a more fundamental level, the Clinton administration during its first term more than any before it gave priority within the bureaucracy to functional offices in foreign policy decision making over the "territorial" offices that seek to make and coordinate policy toward a given country or region. Within the Department of State, for example, the offices in charge of human rights and of nonproliferation enjoyed enhanced power, while the Bureau of East Asian and Pacific Affairs and the "desk" in charge of Chinese affairs played a lesser role in relating these issues to China in particular. Put differently, issues such as human rights and nonproliferation were primarily in the hands of officials concerned with the issue on a global level, rather than those concerned with developing and coordinating a carefully balanced policy toward China itself. As a consequence, various executive branch departments felt relatively free to press China hard regarding their specific core agenda. The White House, which sought in principle to build a constructive relationship with China, did not expend the energy to bring this process under control. This situation worked against the emergence of a consistent, well-crafted China policy.

Indeed, by 1995 each key agency seemed able to pursue a distinct

China policy suited to its own top priorities: the Department of Commerce strongly promoted Chinese acceptance of U.S. investment; the United States Trade Representative's Office repeatedly threatened punitive trade sanctions over intellectual property rights and other issues; the Department of Defense promoted expanded military-to-military contacts; the Department of State's various bureaus castigated China for its alleged proliferation activities and human rights violations; and so forth. Chinese leaders saw a method to these inconsistencies: they suspected that the White House rhetoric in favor of constructive engagement was a smokescreen intended to blind China to America's real policy, which sought to hold back China's advance, weaken the country, and isolate it from the international arena.

A Multiplicity of Factors

A wide array of factors during 1989–1996 made it very difficult for the United States to base its policy toward China solely on long-term consideration of America's international interests. The separation of powers within the American government, the dynamics and funding of congressional elections, the structure of decision making within the executive branch, and the outcomes of elections together created a situation in which a carefully crafted, coordinated, bipartisan policy toward China that took into account the past history of the Sino–U.S. relationship lay beyond the reach of the American political system. China's status as an extremely negative political symbol in the wake of the events of 1989 sowed the seeds of this situation, and the dynamics of politics during 1989–1996 nurtured those seeds into a reality that sharply constrained America's ability to respond effectively and sensitively to the imperatives of the Sino–U.S. relationship.

Forces supportive of a different American approach to China also developed during these years and form a basis for a potentially different U.S. policy. Bilateral economic ties grew dramatically, and as of 1997 numerous American jobs depend on the continuation of Sino–U.S. trade ties. Business lobbyists such as the Emergency Committee for American Trade have grown in their sophistication, and key firms in core U.S. sectors such as aerospace, telecommunications, and automotive transportation view China as a location vital to their continued growth and vitality over the coming decade. Chinese students play an important role in the graduate departments of numerous American universities, and many scientific associations strongly support better Sino–U.S. cooperation as necessary for dealing with fundamental problems such as environmental protection.

Over the long run, the American domestic scene will provide supporters both for strong Sino–U.S. ties and for policies basically antagonistic to China. Those who feel they are losing out as a result of the globalization of the economy and other basic changes will want to take a tough stance toward China; the beneficiaries of such processes will support strong Sino–American relations. All these forces and others will find their voice within the democratic American political system. This very diversity of perspective provides some room for initiative by the U.S. president, barring some cataclysmic development in China that creates a symbol too powerful to budge.

It will take a combination of strong presidential leadership and an absence of powerful, attention-grabbing developments in China to change the symbolic template against which China policy in the United States has been made since 1989. But the interplay of internal factors will affect both policies and possibilities in America's official posture toward the People's Republic of China on a continuing basis.

Domestic Factors in China's Policy toward the United States

Chinese foreign policy is produced by a system very different from that in the United States. But like its American counterpart, it bears the imprint of the broad symbolic context within which policy is developed, the domestic issues the country confronts, and the bureaucratic process from which it derives. China lacks the formal separation of powers that is at the core of American policy making, and Chinese leaders obviously do not confront the vote-getting and fundraising pressures that are part of the daily lives of elected American officials. But China's leaders still cannot act completely independently of the people whom they govern and the characteristics of the system within which they operate.

At the most fundamental level, Chinese leaders and citizens view the international arena against the background of over a century of humiliation inflicted by stronger foreign powers. The resulting desires for national dignity and territorial integrity are very powerful. Just as Americans view themselves as champions of the fight against despotism, Chinese citizens and officials view themselves as victims of foreign hegemony and as champions of national sovereignty. This historical perspective, stemming from China's experience for more than five generations, significantly shapes and constrains China's foreign policy. It adds obvious weight to the problems created in Sino–U.S. relations when voices on the American side challenge China's sovereignty over Tibet and Taiwan and speak disparagingly of China's leaders and ambitions. American criticisms of China's human rights record, for example, often sound to China's leaders of the 1990s like arrogant moralizing, attempting to make them lose face despite their impressive achievements in raising the standard of living and reducing political repression in their country.

Social, Economic, and Political Change

The most fundamental domestic issues China confronts in the 1990s derive from the massive changes occurring in the country's economic and social systems, and the repercussions of those changes in various spheres of life and governance. Concerted efforts to restructure the system that Mao Zedong created have been under way for more than fifteen years, and it will be at least a decade before the country reaches some sort of steady state.

It is difficult to overstate the scope of the changes occurring in China or the speed with which they are taking place. Major shifts in the economic system have produced substantial redistribution of wealth, both between regions (the coast has widened its lead over the interior) and within localities. The nature of economic change has had a powerful impact on the value system embraced by the population, and cultural changes have been accelerated by the extraordinary spread of television, tapes, compact disks, and other foreign media products. The political system itself has undergone major transformation, including significant alterations in priorities, in the internal distribution of power, in the policy-making process, and in relations with the population. China is no democracy, but it also is no longer the totalitarian system of the Maoist era.

In Chinese eyes, the United States is associated with these massive changes. America is almost universally regarded by the Chinese as the most important country in the world. The United States critically affects China's access to the international arena in the diplomatic, economic, and security realms; American firms are major investors in China; more Chinese students study in America than in any other foreign country; and American consumer goods and cultural products flood into China through various channels. Perhaps most important, America has since 1978 vocally championed reform in the People's Republic. Not surprisingly, insiders in China note that Sino–U.S. relations go more smoothly when the domestic reformers have the initiative, and that the two countries' relationship encounters rougher sledding when those who want to slow down or even retreat from reform are in the ascendancy.[7] In this broad sense, Sino–U.S. relations are significantly influenced by the flow of domestic politics in China.

The reforms have produced changes in the dynamics of the political system that in turn have an impact on Sino–American ties. To spur economic growth and encourage initiative by officials, each level of the government (national, provincial, municipal, county, township, village) in effect permits the next level down to exercise enough flexibility and initiative to produce rapid local economic growth, on the proviso that this growth in turn ensures social and political stability. This approach is not embodied in law but rather describes actual practice. Constant negotiations among officials are one natural result, as each local leader tries to squeeze resources from higher levels while maximizing local operational flexibility.

Beijing has combined this strategy with financial incentives for government officials to enliven their local economies. These incentives are both negative and positive. Central government budgetary support for local government functions has declined significantly, while localities have developed an increased ability to retain revenues generated by taxes and fees they impose on local enterprises. This structural change in the budgetary system has had wide-ranging repercussions, among which two of the most important are local protectionism and corruption.

Local protectionism reflects the continuing extensive links between the government and enterprises, despite market oriented reforms. Essentially, many local governments now act partly as if they were the headquarters of local territorial corporations, intervening massively in the affairs of the local enterprises both to expand production and jobs and to increase local coffers. The local officials also use their extensive power to protect local enterprises from competition and to keep them in business.

This pervasive role of officials in local entrepreneurship has nurtured extensive corruption of the political apparatus. Beyond that, localities often shield their firms from effective application of environmental protection laws, because the local environmental officials are administratively under the thumb of local government leaders (that is, the entrepreneurs control the regulators in the local government). This whole focus on local economic development has, moreover, eroded any former sense of political élan, replacing it with a pervasive scramble for funds.

The Effect on Relations with the United States

China's political changes have affected Sino–U.S. relations. On the one hand, they have vastly increased the array of opportunities for American based firms to do business in China, and economic ties have expanded rapidly. Indeed, the rapid growth that the systemic changes have produced is itself having an impact on Sino–U.S. ties by making China the fastest growing market for U.S. exports in the 1990s.

But on the other hand, the very changes that have expanded economic opportunities for Sino–U.S. relations also pose nettlesome problems in the relationship. The new system is one in which Beijing often has difficulty in finding out what localities are actually doing and in getting them to comply with commitments made by the national leadership. Where Beijing has agreed to increase market access, various localities may devise means to protect their markets from competition from American products. Where Beijing has given assurances about stiffening its support for the protection of intellectual property, local governments may actively support theft of intellectual property in order to increase the wealth in their own areas. The court system, moreover, often cannot implement judgments if the local government is determined to thwart them. Where Beijing has set goals on environmental protection, localities often use tax rebates and other means to take the sting out of penalties that are levied against polluting firms. Thus, just as the reform program has expanded China's interactions with the international arena and increased the agreements entered into by China's leaders, this same program has reduced the ability of those leaders to ensure disciplined implementation of the international agreements they have signed.

The reforms have also produced problems in national-level organizations that intrude on the Sino–U.S. relationship. Under the reforms, for example, the People's Liberation Army (PLA) has become deeply involved in business pursuits rather than in concentrated preparation for war. According to knowledgeable Chinese sources, by the mid-1990s this situation caused top PLA leaders to become deeply concerned about the military's loss of fighting spirit and decline in discipline. In this context, the March 1996 large-scale military exercises against Taiwan served multiple purposes. They laid the basis for increasing the PLA budget, raised morale in the military, increased discipline in the PLA, and provided a justification for maintaining a large military force. The PLA convinced the civilian leadership to back this effort. This same mobilization, of course, brought Sino–U.S. relations to their nadir.[8]

Interviews with insiders make clear, indeed, that national-level policy making under the reforms has generally become more fragmented and specialized. Specialized functional agencies are now quite strong in decision making in both domestic policy and foreign policy. This situation in part reflects the evolution away from a political system dominated by a single strong leader such as Mao Zedong or Deng Xiaoping and toward a more collegial style of rule. More important, it is a natural consequence of the increasing array of issues with which the leadership must deal and the greater technical sophistication required for responsible decision making.

This increasing fragmentation and specialization of decision making has almost certainly produced greater flexibility and enhanced sophistication in China's handling of the complex issues that confront it. But these same bureaucratic trends also mean that China's international activities are not as tightly coordinated as they have been in decades past, as Foreign Ministry diplomats now lack both the bureaucratic reach and the technical expertise to ride herd on the specialists in, for example, foreign trade. The very top leaders can and do intervene decisively when they feel an issue warrants their attention, however, and major problems in U.S.–China relations typically do draw the attention of the highest levels.

The spring 1996 decision by China to turn to Europe's Airbus rather than purchase Boeing aircraft was, according to Chinese sources, made against the advice of the U.S. division of the Foreign Ministry. The key bureaucratic player in this decision was the Ministry of Foreign Trade and Economic Cooperation, which wanted to retaliate for stinging U.S. criticism of its performance regarding intellectual property rights. In this instance, China's top leaders were also irritated over a range of American initiatives and thus were inclined to "teach the United States a lesson."

These trends also mean that developments occur beyond the ken of the top leaders, who learn about them only when some incident heightens their visibility. Such developments can produce unintended problems in Sino-American relations. According to knowledgeable Chinese officials, for example, the PLA had sought to earn money through military sales to Iran—and had signed a Memorandum of Understanding with Teheran regarding future sales—when the Foreign Ministry acceded to a Bush administration request that China adhere to restrictions stipulated in the Missile Technology Control Regime (MTCR).[9] At the time, the Foreign Ministry was unaware of the memorandum with Iran. When the problem became known in Beijing, it created an internal crisis, with the PLA arguing that its proposed sales were routine and that the Foreign Ministry lacked the expertise to judge the issue.

After this incident, China set up new bureaucratic procedures requiring the PLA to report for review all foreign military sales that might violate international agreements. But in 1996 a new problem arose, as the United States accused China of selling ring magnets to Pakistan, in violation of American nonproliferation requirements. The actual sale to Pakistan involved such a modest sum (less than $80,000) that nobody had thought of including the small transaction in the new reporting system, and China says that it first learned about the problem from the U.S. government.

These problems in military sales highlight a phenomenon in which real world issues are moving ahead more rapidly than are the bureaucratic reporting and review procedures to supervise and control them. A similar phenomenon has occurred in the arena of intellectual property rights, where actual bureaucratic expertise to handle the issue both in Beijing and in key localities has developed more slowly than the quickly spreading scope and increasing complexity of the problem.[10] These difficulties call attention to a reality of China too often overlooked: despite the nation's very rapid economic progress, it is still a developing country that is struggling with the task of increasing its administrative sophistication to a level adequate to deal effectively with the demands being made on the government. Shortcomings in this effort at times bedevil Sino–U.S. relations.

In sum, although the reforms have not changed the basically authoritarian nature of the Chinese system, they have created a national political system that is far less disciplined, far more diverse, and far more difficult to monitor than was the prereform polity. Often Americans have assumed that violations of commitments made by Beijing reflect desultory efforts of China's leaders or even active duplicity on their part. Evidence typically is lacking to specify precisely the real intentions of China's top officials in any given instance. But the broad changes in the Chinese system have been sufficiently fundamental that they have without question reduced the overall ability of the country's leaders to implement rigorously the international commitments they make.[11]

Additional Sources of Friction

The reforms have produced dramatic economic growth and a general rise in the standard of living. These phenomenal economic achievements have, during the 1990s, had major psychological repercussions in China. During this decade, most Chinese have for the first time gained a sense of confidence that their country is assuming its rightful place as a major power in the world. After more than a century of failing to live up to its potential, there is a palpable sense that, to use Mao Zedong's famous phrase, "China has stood up." This sense of national pride is accompanied by some acute sensitivities. The Chinese not only look for evidence that the country's international status has risen, but also are quick to conclude that others fear this development and seek to hold China back.

The reforms have also produced another psychological result—a sense of malaise among many citizens. The rapid domestic changes have made substantial portions of the population feel disconcerted—worried about the lifestyles of the younger generation, jealous of the wealth of some, angry at the corruption they see around them, upset by the possibility of unemployment, resentful of the millions of peasants who have flooded into the cities to compete for low-end jobs, concerned about inflation, and so forth. The government is well aware of these popular anxieties, and feels hard pressed to maintain stability and popular support.

Both the surge in national confidence and the undercurrents of popular malaise have increased the pressure on China's leaders to defend the country's dignity and national sovereignty in their international dealings. In the early 1990s the leadership therefore created a new body, the Foreign Propaganda Leadership Small Group, to increase vigilance concerning the Chinese media's treatment of international issues. This deeply conservative, anti-American group had, by 1996, developed considerable momentum, significantly affecting the rhetoric used to discuss U.S. intentions and Sino–U.S. relations. Key members of this group also became very active in developing China's responses to American charges of human rights violations.

In addition, the National People's Congress, while falling far short of behaving as an independent legislative body, has nevertheless increased its stature in the Chinese system. By all accounts of knowledgeable insiders, the top government leaders, as of 1996–97, pay far more attention to the views expressed in the Congress than was previously the case. But this legislature, like many in developing countries, appears to have a conservative cast to its foreign policy views. China's leaders have responded, not surprisingly, with heightened nationalist rhetoric; they fear harsh internal judgment should they supinely accept foreign condemnation or compromise China's claims to Taiwan or other territories.

Within this context, Sino–U.S. relations are considered particularly sensitive, given America's preeminent role in the international arena and longstanding ties with Taiwan. China's leaders bridle at American criticism and are especially concerned that the United States might seek to constrain China's rise. The importance accorded to America could, ironically, provide a basis for a strong Sino–U.S. relationship if the United States were seen as supportive of China's aspirations. But from mid-1989 to 1996 these sensitivities made it difficult for China and the United States to find common ground.

Finally, the reforms have produced not only successes but also structural weaknesses that further complicate Sino–U.S. relations. The reforms have, for example, shifted the burden for funding deficit-ridden state enterprises from the national budget to the banking system, which in turn has relied on long-term deposits indexed against inflation to garner the capital for this effort. But as of 1996 nonperforming loans to state enterprises amounted to more than 15 percent of annual gross domestic product.[12] Currently Chinese citizens continue to put their money into the banking system because they lack other avenues for investment. Should China make its currency fully convertible, as the United States is encouraging it to do, many Chinese would undoubtedly change their savings into hard currencies and then invest the funds abroad. This could severely strain the entire Chinese banking system (and the system for keeping state enterprises afloat).

In similar fashion, unreformed state enterprises and their ministerial overseers in major sectors such as machine building insist that the political leadership provide substantial protection from foreign competition for the domestic market for years to come. They point to the threat of politically destabilizing unemployment if their demands are not met. Similar arguments are made by the agricultural sector. The results of such pressures can be seen in the relatively protectionist sectoral policy for automotive development adopted on February 19, 1994. These pressures effectively prevent China from accepting an invitation to join the World Trade Organization (WTO) on other than relatively lenient terms. To protect themselves,

China's leaders criticize the United States for insisting that China enter the WTO on terms more suitable for the successful exporting country that the People's Republic has become.

Generally speaking, there is no evidence to date that the losers in China's domestic reforms have blamed their problems on the United States. But there are many groups who feel that they have not fared well under the reforms, and numerous strains lie just beneath the surface. If domestic political stress increases over expanding the role of the market, downsizing and reforming state owned enterprises, or even redefining family values in the context of China's reforms, demagogic politicians could link these issues to America's influence and castigate China's cooperation with the United States, much as the Buchanan candidacy in 1996 managed to link underlying stresses in the U.S. population to China's changing position in the world economy. The possibility of an earthquake in Sino–U.S. relations stemming from domestic political strains in China will thus exist for the coming decade, if not longer.

Conclusion

America and China have wide-ranging ties at official and unofficial levels. As the other chapters in this volume make clear, great potential exists for future cooperation in Sino–American relations— cooperation that could have a defining impact on prospects for peace, security, and prosperity globally and in the Asia Pacific region. Domestic constituencies already exist in both countries to support this type of fundamentally cooperative relationship.

Yet from 1989 to 1996 in both the United States and China, internal political dynamics created serious obstacles to greater sensitivity and flexibility in seeking accommodation for the sake of building a trusting, cooperative relationship. Each country's domestic constraints, moreover, have been little appreciated in the other capital. The resulting rhetoric and policies have, therefore, typically been seen as mean spirited and intentionally antagonistic, rather than being understood as responses to domestic pressures and not particularly targeted at the other side.

The inability of each nation's leaders during this period to understand and empathize with the domestic political constraints confronting the other side and to act with sensitivity to their counter-parts' internal political needs presents a cautionary tale for those who seek to realize the positive potential inherent in Sino–U.S. ties. Too often, what has seemed obvious to each leadership in terms of its own domestic political needs has been opaque or at least very unclear to the other. The resulting insensitivity to internal political realities has limited both the ability and the desire of each leader-ship to accommodate the other.

Domestic developments will inevitably continue to affect Sino–U.S. relations into the coming century. The consequences of those effects will be determined by each leadership's ability to un-derstand the other's domestic pressures and to respond meaning-fully and responsibly to them. Regular meetings at the highest levels should therefore become a core feature of Sino-American rela-tions. Frequent personal contacts permit the leaders (and their top staff assistants) to gain a better feel for their counterparts' goals, style, and domestic political considerations. This understanding is necessary if they are to establish mutual trust and to craft effective, realistic policies that take into account the domestic political reali-ties that inevitably impinge on the relationship in each country.

Notes

[1] Two factors should be taken into account. First, as Julia Chang Bloch notes in chapter 6, the United States counts as exports from China all goods from Hong Kong that originate from China, but it fails to subtract the 16 percent or so that is added to the price by the Hong Kong firms engaged in the reexport. For its own exports, America classifies all goods that are reexported to China from Hong Kong as U.S. exports to Hong Kong only. Second, a substantial portion of China's ex-ports to the United States consists of products largely produced in Taiwan and Hong Kong, but for which final assembly (and a minority of the value added) takes place in China. Put differently, the enormous Taiwanese and Hong Kong investments in China since the late 1980s have had the somewhat misleading effect of driving down U.S. trade deficits with Taiwan and Hong Kong and shifting those deficits to the trade with China. These issues are discussed in Lardy (1994), chapter 4. Also, it should be noted that China has been America's fastest growing export market for most of the 1990s.

[2] This even included NBC's coverage of the opening ceremony of the 1996 cen-tennial Olympic games.

[3] Private communication with the author.

[4] "Most favored nation" is a misleading term. MFN in reality means being ac-corded nondiscriminatory tariff treatment, as reflected in the fact that the United States currently grants MFN status to over 170 countries. Not to accord MFN tar-

iff treatment is, therefore, highly unusual and severely discriminatory against the country concerned, effectively making it a "least favored nation."

[5] Ironically, MFN renewal occurred without difficulty immediately following the Tiananmen repression in June 1989.

[6] Worthlin (1996).

[7] This is both because reformers generally seek closer ties with the United States while more conservative elements consciously try to create problems in Sino–U.S. relations, and because the United States, for its own reasons, finds it easier to deal cooperatively with reformers.

[8] Taiwan, despite its international repercussions, is treated bureaucratically primarily as a domestic rather than a foreign policy issue in Beijing. The Foreign Ministry deals with the subject only very gingerly, as it avoids adopting a posture that could be interpreted as regarding Taiwan as other than a domestic issue. Special bodies have been created to handle the Taiwan issue: a Central Leadership Small Group on Taiwan, headed by Jiang Zemin and serving the Standing Committee of the Politburo; the State Council Office on Taiwan Affairs, headed by Wang Zhaoguo; the Central Office on Taiwan, a party body also headed by Wang Zhaoguo; the United Front Work Department of the Central Committee, which focuses on non-Kuomintang (KMT) groups in Taiwan; and the Straits Exchange Commission, headed by Wang Daohan. Of these, the most important body is the Central Leadership Small Group on Taiwan, and its composition is instructive. The key members include the heads of the Straits Exchange Commission, the United Front Work Department, the Ministry of State Security, the intelligence branch of the PLA General Staff Department, the State Council Office on Taiwan Affairs, and the Economic and Trade Commission of the State Council.

[9] The Missile Technology Control Regime is a group of states (originally fewer than ten but by 1996 numbering closer to thirty) that have agreed to certain restrictions on the transfer of missiles and their related technologies. China is not a member of the MTCR.

[10] This issue is well documented in a study by Oksenberg, Potter, and Abnet (1996). Michael Swaine (1996) provides the most detailed analysis available of national security policy making.

[11] Should the top leaders give enormous priority to rigorous implementation of a particular policy, they are likely to succeed if the policy's results can be easily measured. But this type of high-priority effort requires the expenditure of substantial political resources, and thus it can be done only very selectively. Inevitably, most issues in Sino–U.S. relations cannot receive such focused support from Beijing.

[12] By comparison, bad debt in the U.S. savings and loan crisis of the early 1990s totaled about 2 percent of America's annual GDP, and the stressed Japanese banking system as of 1996 was probably carrying bad debt on the order of 4 percent of Japan's annual GDP.

Address to The American Assembly

SAM NUNN
NOVEMBER 15, 1996

Ambassador Leonard Woodcock, Secretary John Whitehead, Professor Ezra Vogel, and executives of The American Assembly Stephen Stamas, Dan Sharp, David Mortimer, and Eleanor Tejirian are to be congratulated for convening this assembly to assess American policy toward China. The recommendations that emanate from you will surely receive great attention.

The United States and China at least temporarily have halted last spring's dangerous drift toward rivalry and acrimony with a number of encouraging developments.

- Secretary of State Warren Christopher enunciated a broad China policy in May and will visit China next week.

SAM NUNN was a United States senator from Georgia from 1972 to 1996. He chaired the Armed Services Committee and the Permanent Subcommittee on Investigations of the Governmental Affairs Committee, served as a member of the Committee on Small Business, and cochaired the Senate Arms Control Observer Group. In 1963 he served as legal counsel to the House Armed Services Committee and from 1968–72 was a member of the Georgia House of Representatives.

- The two sides have reached an interim solution to the dispute over protection of intellectual property rights.
- The president's National Security Advisor Anthony Lake has initiated a strategic dialogue with his Chinese counterpart, Vice Foreign Minister Liu Huaqiu. The Chinese have responded positively to these overtures.
- Chinese Defense Minister General Chi Haotian will be visiting Washington in December.
- It seems likely that state visits will resume next year after an eight-year hiatus.
- Tensions in the Taiwan Strait have eased.
- The leaders of both the United States and China apparently wish to develop a shared perspective on how our two nations can best cooperate to maintain global and regional stability. Both countries also seem to be attaching greater importance to securing China's entry into the World Trade Organization on terms that will strengthen a liberal world trade regime and serve the interests of both China and the advanced industrial democracies.

Despite the temporary improvement, no national security issue is in greater need of consideration than the topic of this fall's Assembly. China has become a central concern of American foreign policy. In all the areas of crucial interest to the United States, whether strategic, political, economic, or cultural, China is an increasingly important factor in determining whether the United States can attain its objectives. Moreover, in all these areas China's goals frequently overlap with American interests but partially depart from them, sometimes rather sharply. The task before the United States and China is to broaden and strengthen the areas of cooperation while narrowing and containing the differences.

This can only be done if the leaders and people of both countries are convinced that their national interests will be well served through greater Sino-American cooperation. This in turn requires that both countries clearly understand how their bilateral relations affect their broader objectives and strategies in world affairs. Let's consider a few examples.

First: Arms Control and Disarmament. Preventing the proliferation of weapons of mass destruction—nuclear, biological, and chemical weapons and their means of delivery—and reducing stockpiles of these weapons are American interests of the highest priority.

As a nuclear power and a permanent member of the Security Council, China can either assist or torpedo efforts to stop the proliferation of weapons of mass destruction. Its role is critical. China's attitude toward various arms control measures has certainly improved in the past decade. In the realm of nuclear proliferation, its recent commitment to cease nuclear testing and to support the Comprehensive Test Ban Treaty is an encouraging development. China seems to recognize its interest in reducing the dangers of nuclear proliferation globally and especially in East Asia.

Although it has recently given signs of greater sensitivity, China seems insufficiently concerned about the destabilizing consequences of its transfer of advanced technology and sale of materials related to strategic weapons in South Asia and the Middle East. Aspects of its military and technology relations with Pakistan and Iran are deeply troubling to the United States. American law may ultimately necessitate application of sanctions as a result.

In our dialogue with the Chinese at high levels we should point out that as a growing importer of oil from the Middle East, China has an increasing stake in the tranquility of the Strait of Hormuz and the Persian Gulf. Its pattern of arms sales do not seem to take this into account. We should also emphasize to Beijing that the U.S. Navy protects the waters through which oil tankers bring petroleum to China. China benefits from the stability our naval presence brings to the high seas.

Second: The Collapse of the Soviet Union. Both the United States and China must respond to the consequences of the collapse of the Soviet Union. While the new situation offers much promise, the present favorable opportunities could be lost through inattention or mismanagement. Let me list some examples:

- While the transformation of the Soviet Union has enabled the United States to forge new ties with the states of Eastern Europe, the Soviet collapse also has posed challenges to America's alliances in Europe and Northeast Asia. With the Russian threat now greatly diminished, the security frameworks erected in the cold war era must take into account new realities. Plans are underway to extend NATO eastward and to adjust our treaties with Japan and Korea. These measures are being contemplated in order to promote peace and stability. However, these changes must be undertaken in ways that do not raise new and deep security concerns in Russia about its western flank or in China about its eastern flank. The result could inadvertently stimulate the two to nurture a strategic relationship that neither prefers.

- Meanwhile, Russia's new situation also has offered China opportunities to improve its relations with Moscow. This is a welcome development. Previous Soviet-Chinese rivalry and military confrontation brought tension to the entire region. Improved Sino-Russian relations help promote regional stability. But economic considerations on the Russian side and opportunism on the Chinese side could prompt an undisciplined flow of weaponry and military technology to China from the military industries in Siberia and the Russian Far East, thereby accelerating China's military modernization. The result would be to provoke an arms buildup throughout Asia to balance China's growing strength.

- A resurgence of expansionist nationalism in Russia brought on by protracted chaos and economic failure would be as threatening to China as to the United States and its allies. China benefits from a stable and peaceful evolution of Russia, especially in the control and orderly dismantling of its nuclear arsenal. Erosion in Russian control over nuclear weapons and fissionable material poses particularly severe problems to China, the United States, and the entire world.

- In Central Asia, Mongolia, and the Russian Far East, China grapples with the uncertainties of the Soviet collapse. China faces some serious questions:

    —Will any of the new Central Asian nations stimulate separatist impulses among China's Islamic peoples?

    —Where is the Russian Far East headed, in light of Moscow's ebbing economic and political grasp over this region?

    —Will the migration of Chinese to Siberia continue and become a new source of tension between Russia and China?

    —How will the resources of the Russian Far East be developed in the next century?

We should discuss with Beijing all these broad strategic issues: how to ease Russia's political and economic transformation; how to create a framework of stability for the states of the former Soviet empire; and how to consolidate the current favorable alignment among the major powers of Asia. After all, for the first time in a century, China, Russia, Japan, and the United States have good relations with one another. No major fault line divides one major power from another. Answers to these questions will require constant dialogue among all the countries in the region in the years ahead.

Third: Regional Security Issues. In addition to its global strategic interests, the United States has enduring regional security concerns. These are to prevent a hostile power from dominating any one of the four regions in the world in which America's vital interests are engaged—Latin America, Western Europe, the Middle East, and the East Asian rim—and to assure that no nation threatens freedom of the seas.

None of these regions is more important to the United States than the Asia Pacific region, where the American people have fought three costly wars in this century and where the rapidly growing economies offer the United States its greatest expanding markets and its most serious competition. Needless to say, China also has a keen interest in maintaining stability in this region. Our overlapping interests have enabled China and the United States to cooperate in sustaining peace in Korea and ending nearly forty years of war on the Indochina Peninsula.

In addition to constructive Sino-American relations, the core framework for regional security arrangements is provided by the Japanese-American and the Korean-American alliances and the close security relations among the United States, Australia, and the six core members of the Association of Southeast Asian Nations (ASEAN). In my opinion, these relations objectively serve China's interests, although many Chinese strategists do not share this view.

Our treaties with Japan and South Korea and the specific arrangements developed under them—the status of forces agreements, the basing arrangements and force structures—took shape in an earlier era of American dominance. Much has happened in the subsequent years. Japan and South Korea have emerged as prosperous, full democracies. Through consultations, the United States and China must forge an understanding that adjustments to these treaties are not aimed at China but are intended to ensure that the alliances remain a cornerstone of regional stability.

Fourth: International Economic Interests. The United States has a major interest in maintaining steady international economic growth, uninterrupted by financial crises or disruptions in the international monetary system. We seek access to the markets of other countries, and we believe that the growth of imports into the United States should occur in an orderly fashion. For the most part, we defend an open international trade regime. We seek a level playing field, in which Americans have the opportunity to participate in the economies of other countries, just as their citizens enjoy that opportunity in the United States. All too often, however, the playing field is not level. Too frequently, foreign countries adroitly exploit their open access to American markets while limiting access to their markets or discriminating against American firms. Under such circumstances, the United States has no recourse but to rely on the trade law and its 301 provisions.

These sanctions should be employed with great care, but any American government that ignores the American people's strong desire for a fair playing field in world trade will have great difficulty conducting a sensible trade policy or foreign policy.

With one of the world's largest economies, its rapid increases in foreign trade, its substantial foreign currency reserves (nearly $100 billion), and its external indebtedness (over $100 billion), China's economic performance clearly affects American interests.

On the positive side, World Bank officials consider China's record to be exemplary. It has created a better institutional and legal environment to welcome foreign direct investment than most other countries in East Asia. It has taken measures to facilitate repatriation of profits. It is only one of three former non-market economies whose sovereign offerings are deemed creditworthy by international rating agencies. In America, China has not received adequate recognition for its accomplishments in joining the international economy.

On the negative side, roughly 40 percent of China's exports are ultimately consumed in the United States, but its government does not appear engaged in addressing its growing trade deficit with the United States through increased purchases from American vendors. While decrying American linkage of trade and politics, China is practicing its own form of linkage. Too often China has discriminated against American vendors on political grounds even though China enjoys easier access to the American market than to markets of other developed countries.

Further, China's laws governing commerce remain underdeveloped, and corruption is a growing problem. Many nontariff barriers still exist that restrict access to the China market. It protects certain "pillar" industries such as petrochemicals, telecommunications, automobiles, and construction materials. It is reluctant to open its service sector to foreign competition. It encounters difficulties in implementing its commitments to protect intellectual property rights. Without pressure from the outside and the threat of sanctions, it is not clear that China will summon the will to resolve these problems.

China makes these challenges much more difficult by turning our legitimate responses to their trade violations into a political contest of wills. If this pattern continues, U.S.–China commerce, instead of building political bridges, would tear them down.

Fifth: Problems of Interdependence. The United States also has a major interest in reducing a wide range of problems that transcend national boundaries: environmental degradation; international terrorism; illegal migration; narcotics trafficking; the spread of communicable diseases; pressure on world food supplies; and rapid population growth. These problems threaten the survival of vast portions of the world's peoples and introduce global instability. The growing income disparities between the haves and the have nots and the gap between those who benefit from our increasingly interdependent international economy and those who suffer from it are likely to generate increasing tensions in the years ahead.

Chinese-American cooperation cannot assure success in addressing these most fundamental problems that threaten all humankind. But Chinese-American animosity will surely make it more difficult to cope with these issues. Acting together, the United States and China can accomplish much. In confrontation, both will suffer.

Sixth: Democracy and Human Rights. The United States must also give expression to the values on which the nation was founded and that draw Americans together as one people. These beliefs have universal appeal. They are a source of American strength. Americans must not, cannot, and will not abandon their articulation abroad.

Put bluntly, the leaders of China believe that many political values that Americans espouse are inapplicable to their country under its present circumstances. They naturally resent efforts—either domestic or foreign—fundamentally to alter or challenge their authoritarian system. At great cost to China's stature abroad, they imprison leading political dissidents in defiance of international pressures.

The reasons for their obstinate posture on democratization and human rights are no doubt complex. In my view, democratic political reform would serve China's interests. I believe that the rule of law, broadly speaking, is essential for China's economic progress. China's leaders jeopardize their nation's long-term domestic stability by not moving more rapidly toward the rule of law and expanding the opportunities of their populace to participate meaningfully in their governance. And until they do so, a chasm will separate the United States from the leaders of China in this domain. China cannot expect United States and world acquiescence or silence in response to flagrant abuses of human rights.

This review of America's foreign policy interests reveals that a thick web of partly convergent and partly divergent interests now binds the United States and China. In recognition of this reality, a new, very fragile consensus on China policy is slowly emerging in Washington and among the American people. This fragile move toward consensus rejects the extremes of hostility toward China or a warm embrace on China's terms. It seeks cooperation with China while realistically accepting disagreement where values and interests diverge. If strengthened, this consensus has the potential to embrace several fundamental concepts.

First, the United States should continue to adhere to the Shanghai Communiqúe, the normalization agreement, and the August 1982 joint communiqúe on arms sale to Taiwan. The United States should remain firmly committed to the one China policy.

Second, China's role in world affairs is one of the major developments of our era. Sino-American relations merit high-level sustained attention of the United States government. Management of this relationship cannot be relegated in chaotic fashion to the lower levels of each department in the executive branch but must be co-ordinated at the highest levels of government.

Third, the United States has an interest in a prosperous, stable, and unified mainland that is effectively and humanely governed. A strong, secure, and well-led China can contribute to global economic growth and the maintenance of peace and stability in the Asia Pacific region, while a weak or isolated China would surely threaten the region's peace and prosperity.

Fourth, the United States should seek to work constructively with China to facilitate its entry, on mutually acceptable terms, into all the international regimes that regulate and order world affairs. China will be more likely to adhere to international norms that it has helped to shape. But China's entry must not be permitted on terms that jeopardize the purpose of those regimes.

Fifth, the United States is determined to retain a comprehensive, unofficial relationship with Taiwan. The American people feel deep moral obligations toward the people of Taiwan and admire their economic and political progress. The Taiwan Relations Act appropriately governs America's relations with this thriving democracy. The past twenty-five years also demonstrate that Taiwan flourishes best when relations between the United States and China are sound while Sino-American tensions harm Taiwan's well-being. The overarching American interest is in a peaceful reconciliation of Taiwan and the mainland. The United States does not seek permanently to detach Taiwan from the mainland. That said, Taiwan deserves a status in world affairs commensurate with its economic and political attainment. Realistically, Taiwan can best secure a greater international voice and stature through cooperation with Beijing and not through provocation of it.

Sixth, to attain all these objectives, the United States must retain a robust military presence in the western Pacific. Effective multilateral security arrangements in East Asia may eventually supplement the bilateral treaties, but at present, there is no substitute for the Japanese-American and Korean-American security treaties. These treaties are not directed against China. Rather they maintain stability, enhance the security of the entire region, and thereby deter an arms race or proliferation of weapons of mass destruction. Indeed, the treaties enable the current development of regional and subregional bodies such as the Asia Pacific Economic Cooperation (APEC) forum and the ASEAN regional forum.

Seventh, the United States—especially the private sector—should cooperate with China in its efforts to develop institutions necessary for its continued modernization: a legal system and the rule of law; a strengthened judiciary; an effective banking and revenue system; a civil service system; strengthened representative assemblies; competitive, democratic elections of local officials; civilian control of the military and police; and a vibrant press. Many Chinese, including some in the Chinese government, favor these reforms because they are necessary to curb corruption, sustain economic growth, attract foreign investment, and promote stability and human rights.

Eighth, the United States government must speak out firmly when the Chinese government violates universally accepted norms for protecting basic political and civil rights. I believe that unilateral U.S. economic sanctions on the Chinese government and people for human rights violations are counterproductive to the promotion of human rights in China and ill advised. The leaders of China must clearly understand, however, that their behavior in this area makes it difficult to generate political support in the United States for constructive initiatives in other areas.

This emerging consensus is very, very fragile. The recent stabilization of Sino-American relations and the prospects for improvement in the months ahead are vulnerable to disruption. They are particularly vulnerable to possible Chinese actions—such as mishandling of Hong Kong after July 1, 1997; arms sales that violate previous agreements; diversion of imported dual-use technologies and equipment from civilian to military use; flagrant human rights abuses; or a growing trade deficit; as well as other challenges that are inevitable.

Many observers caution that for deeper reasons, the new consensus cannot be sustained, citing the historical "love-hate" relationship between these two great countries. Some analysts claim that two civilizations as different as that of China and the United States simply cannot sustain constructive relations. Other analysts assert that political and ideological differences preclude a close, cooperative relationship between Washington and Beijing. Yet others claim that accommodations between the United States and China will necessarily prove to be temporary because of their differences in wealth and power and because the United States, as a global power and a leader of the industrial democracies, is a defender of an international system that it helped to create and that advances its interests.

Let us acknowledge and accept the dangers these observers offer. They remind us of the enormous challenges in fostering cooperative Sino-American relations. They caution us neither to harbor illusions nor to allow expectations to soar. But in the final analysis, what should we do with their warnings? Should our policy become fatalistic, devoid of hope that the United States and China can be partners in the building of a more stable and secure world? Should the United States look upon China as a potential enemy and therefore seek to weaken or divide it, thereby creating the reality we seek to avoid?

I believe the clear answer is no. To move in this direction would become a self-fulfilling prophecy. Forewarned of the difficulties, the leaders of China and the United States must persist in forging cooperative bonds between our two nations. I have identified some of the areas where cooperation is possible. In your deliberations, you no doubt will expand and deepen the list. But one conclusion is clear. In no small measure, the future well-being of the American and Chinese people depends on the ability of these two nations to cooperate. I remain hopeful that enlightened self-interest will prevail, as it largely has in the twenty-five years since Richard Nixon and Mao Zedong shook hands. The American Assembly is to be congratulated for exploring in greater depth how the progress of the past generation can be sustained.

Bibliography

Almond, G., and S. Verba. 1963. *The Civic Culture*. Princeton: Princeton University Press.

Avendon, J.F. 1984. *In Exile from the Land of Snows*. New York: Knopf.

Bardeen, W. 1996, "Grain Mandate of Heaven: The Struggle for Self-Sufficiency in Chinese Agriculture." Undergraduate thesis. Harvard College.

Blanchon, P., and J. Shaw. 1995. "Reef Drowning during the Last Deglaciation: Evidence for Catastrophic Sea-Level Rise and Ice-Sheet Collapse." *Geology* 23, no. 1.

Brown, L. 1995. *Who Will Feed China?* New York: W.W. Norton.

Brzezinski, Z. 1985. *Power and Principle*. New York: Farrar, Straus, Giroux.

Cheng, Chu-Yuan. 1965. *Scientific and Engineering Manpower in Communist China, 1949–1963*. Washington, D.C.: National Science Foundation.

Ching, F. 1984. *Hong Kong and China, For Better or For Worse*. New York: China Council of the Asia Society and the Foreign Policy Association.

———. 1996. *Hong Kong and China: "One Country, Two Systems."* New York: Foreign Policy Association.

Clough, R. 1978. *Island China*. Cambridge: Harvard University Press.

Cohen, R. 1987. "People's Republic of China: The Human Rights Exception." *Human Rights Quarterly* 9 (November).

Fletcher, J. 1978. "Ch'ing Inner Asia" and "The Heyday of the Ch'ing Order in Mongolia, Sinkiang and Tibet." In Twitchett and Fairbank 1978.

Funabashi, Y., M. Oksenberg, and H. Weiss. 1994. *An Emerging China in a World of Interdependence.* New York: Trilateral Commission.

Gold, T. 1986. *State and Society in the Taiwan Miracle.* Armonk, NY: M.E. Sharpe.

Goldstein, M. 1989. *A History of Modern Tibet, 1913–1951: The Demise of the Lamaist State.* Berkeley: University of California Press.

Grunfield, A.T. 1987. *The Making of Modern Tibet.* Armonk, NY: M.E. Sharpe.

Harding, H. 1992. *A Fragile Relationship: The United States and China since 1972.* Washington, D.C.: Brookings Institution.

Hulme, M. et al. 1992. *Climate Change due to the Greenhouse Effect and Its Implications for China.* Gland, Switzerland: World Wide Fund for Nature.

Hunt, M. 1966. *The Genesis of Chinese Communist Foreign Policy.* New York: Columbia University Press.

Huntington, S. 1993. "The Clash of Civilization?" *Foreign Affairs* 72, no. 3 (summer).

Information Office of the State Council. 1996. "Safeguarding Human Rights or Interfering in China's Internal Affairs? A Commentary on the Country Report on China of the Human Rights Report for 1995 Released by the U.S. Department of State," in *Newsletter [of the] Embassy of the People's Republic of China* no. 6 (March 29).

IPCC (Intergovernmental Panel on Climate Change) 1992. *Climate Change 1992: The Supplementary Report to the IPCC Scientific Assessment.* Cambridge: Cambridge University Press.

———. 1995a. "IPCC Second Assessment Synthesis of Scientific-Technical Information Relevant to Interpreting Article 2 of the U.N. Framework Convention on Climate Change." Available at World Wide Web site http://www.unep.ch/ipcc95.html.

———. 1995b. "Working Group I Summary for Policymakers (The Science of Climate Change)"; Working Group II Summary for Policymakers (Scientific-Technical Analyses of Impacts, Adaptations, and Mitigation)"; "Working Group III Summary for Policymakers (The Economic and Social Dimensions of Climate Change)." Available at World Wide Web site above.

Jacobson, H., and M. Oksenberg. 1990. *China's Participation in the IMF, the World Bank, and GATT: Toward a Global Economic Order.* Ann Arbor: University of Michigan Press.

Johnson, T., Li Junfeng, Jiang Zhongxiao, and R. Taylor. eds. 1996. *China: Issues and Options in Greenhouse Gas Emissions Control.* Washington, D.C.: World Bank.

Keidel, A. 1994. "China GNP per Capita." World Bank Report no. 13580-CA. Washington, D.C.: World Bank.

Kent, A. 1995. "China and the International Human Rights Regime: A Case Study of Multilateral Monitoring, 1989–1994." *Human Rights Quarterly* 17 (February).

Kissinger, H. 1979. *The White House Years.* Boston: Little, Brown.

Lardy, N. 1994. *China in the World Economy.* Washington, D.C.: Institute for International Economics.

Leiberthal, K., and M. Oksenberg. 1988. *Policymaking in China: Leaders, Structures, and Processes.* Princeton: Princeton University Press.

Liu Huaqiu. 1995. "Evaluation and Analysis of China's Nuclear Arms Control Policy." In *Xiandai Junshi* [Contemporary military affairs], November 11, 1995, no. 226, in Foreign Broadcast Information Service, *Daily Report: China,* no. 246.

Lord, W. 1996. In Conable, B. et al. *United States-China Relations: Current Tensions, Policy Choices.* New York: National Committee on United States–China Relations.

Lu Yingzhong. 1993. *Fueling One Billion: An Insider's Story of Chinese Energy Policy Development.* Washington, D.C.: Washington Institute Press.

Maddison, A. 1995. *Monitoring the World Economy, 1820–1922.* Paris: Organization for Economic Cooperation and Development.

Mahlman, J. 1992. "Mathematical Modeling of Greenhouse Warming: How Much Do We Know?" *Energy and the Environment.* Singapore: World Scientific.

Nathan, A. 1996. "China and the International Human Rights Regime." Draft paper prepared for the Task Force on Constructive Engagement with China, Council on Foreign Relations, January 22, 1996.

National Research Council. 1992. *China and Global Change: Opportunities for Collaboration.* Washington, D.C.: National Academy Press.

Oksenberg, M., P. Potter, and W. Abnet. 1996. *Advancing Intellectual Property Rights: Information Technologies and the Course of Economic Development in China.* Seattle: National Bureau of Asian Research.

Orleans, L. 1961. *Professional Manpower and Education in Communist China.* Washington, D.C.: National Science Foundation.

Packenham, R. 1973. *Liberal America and the Third World: Political Development Ideas in Foreign Aid and Social Science.* Princeton: Princeton University Press.

Poppele, J. 1994. "The CFC Challenge." *China Business Review,* July–August.

Ren Ruoen and Chou Kai. 1995. "China's GDP in U.S. Dollars Based on Purchasing Power Parity." World Bank Working Paper no. 1415. Washington, D.C.: World Bank.

Richardson, H. 1984. *Tibet and Its History.* Boulder: Shambala Books.

Robinson, R., and D. Shambaugh. 1994. *Chinese Foreign Policy: Theory and Practice.* Oxford and New York: Oxford University Press.

Ross, R. 1995. *Negotiating Cooperation: The United States and China, 1969–1989.* Stanford: Stanford University Press.

Schlesinger, A. 1992. *The Disuniting of America.* New York: W.W. Norton.

Segal, G. 1993. *The Fate of Hong Kong.* London: St. Martin's.

Shirk. S. 1977–78. "Human Rights: What about China?" *Foreign Policy* no. 29 (winter).

Sinton, J. et al. 1996. *China Energy Datebook.* Berkeley: Lawrence Berkeley Laboratory.

Smil, V. 1993. *China's Environmental Crisis: An Inquiry into the Limits of National Development.* Armonk, NY: M.E. Sharpe.

Solomon, R. ed. 1981 *The China Factor: Sino-American Relations and the Global Scene.* Englewood Cliffs, NJ: Prentice-Hall.

State Council. 1994. *China's Agenda 21: White Paper on China's Population, Environment, and Development in the 21st Century.* Beijing: China Environmental Science Press.

State Statistical Bureau. 1995. *Statistical Yearbook of China, 1995.* Beijing: China Statistical Publishing House.

Stein, R.A. 1972. *Tibetan Civilization.* London: Faber & Faber.

Swaine, M. 1996. *The Role of the Military in National Security Policymaking.* Santa Monica, CA: Rand Corporation.

Tien, Hong-mao. 1996. *Taiwan's Electoral Politics and Democratic Transition: Riding the Third Wave.* Armonk, NY: M.E. Sharpe.

Tucker, N. 1994. *Taiwan, Hong Kong, and the United States, 1945–1992.* New York: Twayne Publishers.

Twitchett, D., and J. Fairbank, eds. 1978. *The Cambridge History of China,* vol. 10. Cambridge: Cambridge University Press.

Wackman, A. 1994. *Taiwan: National Identity and Democratization.* Armonk, NY: M.E. Sharpe.

Welch, H. 1968. *The Buddhist Revival in China.* Cambridge: Harvard University Press.

Wills, G. 1993. *Lincoln at Gettysburg.* New York: Simon and Schuster.

Wills, J. 1974. *Pepper, Guns, and Parleys: The Dutch East India Company and China.* Cambridge: Harvard University Press.

World Bank. 1996. *China Development Briefing.* Issue 3, October.

Worthlin Worldwide. 1996. "Attitudes toward the People's Republic of China." April 26, 1996.

Yasuaki, O. 1996. "In Quest of Intercivilizational Human Rights: 'Universal' vs. 'Relative' Human Rights Viewed from an Asian Perspective." Occasional paper no. 2. San Francisco: Center for Asian Pacific Affairs, Asia Foundation, March.

Zhou Dadi and Li Junfeng. 1995. "Chapter 5: Case Study of China." *Perspectives on the Institutional Needs of Joint Implementation Projects for China, Egypt, India, Mexico, and Thailand.* Berkeley: Lawrence Berkeley Laboratory.

Final Report of the Eighty-Ninth American Assembly

At the close of their discussions, the participants in the Eighty-ninth American Assembly, on "China-U.S. Relations in the Twenty-First Century: Fostering Cooperation, Preventing Conflict," at Arden House, Harriman, New York, November 14–17, 1996, reviewed as a group the following statement. This statement represents general agreement; however, no one was asked to sign it. Furthermore, it should be understood that not everyone agreed with all of it.

Sharing a Common Future: Building Cooperation, Reducing Differences

China's emergence as a great power in the next century will redefine the world's economic, political, and environmental dynamics. An active U.S. policy is needed to meet that challenge. Imagine by way of illustration two possible dramatic alternatives for the year 2010:

Scenario One: U.S. exports to China are booming, as is Chinese trade with the United States; large groups of Chinese and Americans from all circles of life are in close contact; China and the United States are cooperating closely in international organizations

aimed at controlling proliferation and protecting human rights; U.S. firms have supplied
large quantities of capital and technology to China's efforts to clean up its air and water;
Shanghai has joined Hong Kong as a major international center of commerce and cul-
ture; and direct trade and cultural relations across the Taiwan Strait have brought new
levels of security and prosperity to both Taiwan and the China mainland. The relaxed
atmosphere has led to the steady liberalization of the Chinese political system, especially
at the local level.

Scenario Two: U.S. troops in Asia have been significantly augmented to respond to grow-
ing Chinese military threats. As Chinese and U.S. warships confront one another in the
Pacific, the Japanese public is clamoring to expand its military and debating whether to
go nuclear; huge Chinese purchases for its strategic petroleum reserve have destabilized
world oil markets, at the same time as large Chinese weapons sales to Iran have raised
fears about an Iranian threat to the security of oil supplies in the Persian Gulf; Hong
Kong has become an economic backwater from which large numbers of skilled people
and large quantities of capital have fled. Political repression within China has intensi-
fied.

While these scenarios are only illustrative, the stark differences between them make clear how high are the stakes and how grave the
risks for both China and the United States. These include the possibility of a new cold war in Asia that would put at risk China's economic modernization efforts and undermine the attempt to balance
the U.S. budget, the loss of critical cooperation on a variety of
global and regional issues, and a strain on the East Asian security
involvement to the detriment of all countries in the region.

Yet, while the stakes are high, Sino-American relations have not
been treated with commensurate seriousness. High-level contacts
have been infrequent. Official exchanges have often dwelt principally on reciprocal litanies of complaint. Mutual distrust has been
the result. The United States has adopted an approach of engagement, yet Beijing worries that the intent is to weaken China internally and to isolate it internationally. China seeks the benefits of
international cooperation and trade, yet it appears indifferent to
some international norms. The positive influence of the United
States on China is limited, but a lack of proper attention could propel us toward the dire Scenario Two.

Disagreements and Misperceptions

The United States and China have real differences. The United States, as an established power, has helped shape the world order. China, as a rising power, has less commitment to and less experience with existing rules.

The United States is a pluralistic nation, federalist in structure, shaped by immigrants who came here seeking freedom. China, ethnically more homogeneous, has a long tradition of centralism, and, because of painful experiences in its contacts with the West, is preoccupied with internal stability and sovereignty.

But there are also serious misperceptions. Few Americans have an accurate understanding of the complexity of the internal situation in China or of the extraordinary pace and consequences of its rapid change. The images of the June 1989 killings around Tiananmen Square remain more vivid for most Americans than the transformation that economic reforms are helping to bring about in the lives of most Chinese, including the hundreds of millions of people who have been lifted out of poverty. Few Americans are aware, moreover, that this economic growth has contributed to a rise in decentralization, grassroots political reform, and expression of diverse opinion; nor do they realize that despite continued repression of political dissidents and independent union organizers, and restriction of religious freedom, ordinary Chinese enjoy much greater freedom of movement, job choice, life style, and access to information.

Few Chinese, on the other hand, have an adequate understanding of the enormous good will that Americans feel toward their country or appreciate the degree to which the United States would welcome China as a strong and prosperous partner in building a stable international order. Neither country adequately understands the relevant political dynamics of the other.

Facing Historic Transitions:
Post–Cold War and Post–Deng Xiaoping

Both the United States and China find themselves at points of historic transition that complicate the effort to develop fruitful relations with one another.

With the end of the cold war, the U.S. government has been heavily preoccupied with long-neglected domestic issues and has not yet developed a coherent policy for coping with the challenges of the post–cold war world. Many Americans no longer see any need for the United States to continue to play a leadership role in the world, nor to work with governments of whose policies it disapproves.

As China approaches the post–Deng Xiaoping era, its government is in the throes of a political succession. New leaders—technocrats who lack the strong broad political base of their powerful predecessors—are emerging. Reforms of banking, state enterprises, government finance, and the welfare system are still in experimental stages. Nationalism and xenophobia are on the rise. China desires U.S. support and cooperation in its modernization efforts, yet a history of humiliation at Western hands, combined with growing strength, makes China extremely sensitive to any hint of condescension or reluctance to accord it the status it considers its due.

In this situation, the United States needs to be clear about its long-term national interests and how their fulfillment can be advanced or impeded by China's policies.

• The United States seeks a generally free global trade regime. Yet, no effort to regulate global trade and investment can succeed if China, the world's fastest growing economy, is not a part of it. No sustainable improvement of human rights is likely unless China's economy is increasingly prosperous and open to the outside world. China wants access to the U.S. market, investment funds, and technology. The United States wants access to China's market, the greater predictability that the rule of law and increased transparency would afford, and Beijing's help in refining and enforcing equitable, multilateral rules for the global economy. In this realm converging interests abound, yet disputes have proliferated.

• Preventing the proliferation of weapons of mass destruction is a major security interest in the post–cold war world and a focus of

U.S. policy. No attempt to regulate their transfer—not least the transfer of those from the former Soviet Union—can succeed without China's active involvement. Beijing's ratification of the Non-Proliferation Treaty and its recent commitment to the Comprehensive Test Ban are encouraging signs; periodic reports of nuclear technology and other transfers to Iran and Pakistan are disquieting and threaten to trigger sanctions under existing U.S. law.

• The United States cannot expect to maintain a stable equilibrium and avoid an arms race in Asia unless potential conflicts in Korea, the Taiwan Strait, and disputed territories in the South China Sea are resolved peacefully—a task in which Beijing's cooperation is indispensable. More broadly, preserving peace in the Asia Pacific region requires cooperation among all powers on emerging issues. Thus a positive relationship between China and the other powers of the region, including the United States, is indispensable.

The U.S. role in the Asian balance depends heavily upon the preservation of our alliances with Japan, South Korea, and others. The United States is currently adapting the contours of our defense cooperation with Japan and Korea to post–cold war security and political circumstances. Consultations with Beijing will be required to assure that such adjustments are properly recognized as maintaining important elements of regional stability rather than as harbingers of a renewed effort to contain or encircle China.

• The United States has an abiding interest in human rights and political pluralism. These are values on which our nation was founded, and they remain a source of unity and strength. We cannot abandon the affirmation of these values as an integral element of our foreign policy. Chinese officials often express resentment at what they regard as our interference in their domestic affairs. Yet there is widespread recognition that economic growth may often generate pressures for political pluralism. The Chinese government has welcomed efforts by foreign nongovernmental organizations (NGOs) to strengthen the legal system, establish the social infrastructure necessary for the rule of law, and establish more transparent rules to govern trade and investment. Greater tolerance for pluralism and the development of a more responsive government would further narrow the chasm that separates the United States from China in this domain.

• Regional and global attempts to address environmental problems would be ineffective without China's active cooperation. China's rapid economic growth is fueling a dramatic rise in its energy demands. China is second only to the United States as the world's largest emitter of greenhouse gases. Furthermore, China cannot successfully combat international drug trafficking and organized crime activities in its territory, or illegal immigration, without effective collaboration between the United States and China.

• Building cooperation on many other transnational issues will also require Beijing's assistance, since it plays a significant role in a host of international organizations and possesses a veto in the UN Security Council.

A renewed dialogue between Beijing and Washington should be directed primarily at exploring ways of enhancing cooperation and reducing differences in all these spheres.

Developing a More Cooperative Overall Relationship

We have a new window of opportunity. The American election is over. Visits of Secretary of State Warren Christopher and National Security Advisor Anthony Lake to China in 1996 and the visit of Chinese Defense Minister Chi Haotian to Washington in December prepare the way for possible reciprocal state visits—the first since Tiananmen—in 1997. Tensions in the Taiwan Strait have eased, and the leaders of both countries have expressed their desire to cooperate and to fashion a new framework for their relations, in order to expand cooperation and limit differences.

In dealing with China, our highest priority should be to establish a new overall relationship of greater mutual confidence, grounded on a new post–cold war rationale of working together on global, regional, and bilateral issues in a pragmatic way that advances our mutual interests. By viewing individual problems within a broader context, it should become easier to find successful solutions and to reduce the remaining differences. If the United States can focus first on building cooperation in areas where our interests converge, we may be able to reduce suspicions and increase mutual confidence so that it will become easier to make progress in solving more difficult problems.

The growth of trade between the two countries and increased

investments by U.S. companies in China provide some of the foundations for building the new relationship. Care must be taken to remove uncertainties and impediments to their growth.

Building this overall relationship will require exchanges of high-level officials to engage in comprehensive and constructive private discussions about their respective views of the world. The United States should affirm its interest in a prosperous and stable China and emphasize that it prefers to work with a China that is becoming strong rather than to pursue futile illusions that it can somehow keep China weak. The United States should set a proper tone for this relationship by treating China and its leaders with the status appropriate to a major power. The United States should support China's participation at meetings of the G-7 in the same status as Russia, and should encourage Chinese membership and active participation in international organizations.

At the same time, the United States should make it clear that for China to become a true international leader—commensurate with its past history and future importance—it is essential for China to respect and support international norms of behavior. The United States should make it clear that it expects reciprocity as it attempts to accommodate China's needs; the extent to which the United States can accommodate China's needs will depend on the extent to which China takes U.S. concerns into account.

Taiwan

For more than four decades, issues relating to Taiwan have been the most difficult and potentially explosive in U.S.–China relations. They remain the principal issues that, in the worst case, could cause open conflict.

Stability in the region depends on gradual, mutual accommodation between the People's Republic of China (PRC) and Taiwan. The United States should continue to stress to the PRC that Asian stability and Sino-American relations are founded on a peaceful approach to the resolution of this issue. The United States should:

- make clear to Taiwan that the United States will oppose unilateral efforts to seek independence, and
- give high priority to restoring increasingly productive crossstrait relations.

To this end, the United States should adhere to the Shanghai Communiqué, the normalization communiqué, and the August 1982 joint communiqué on arms sales to Taiwan. At the same time, the United States must retain a comprehensive, unofficial relationship with Taiwan as provided by the Taiwan Relations Act. This framework enables Taiwan to sustain democracy, prosperity, and security in an atmosphere free of coercion.

Regional Security Issues

Even as the Asia Pacific region enjoys unprecedented prosperity made possible by the sustained peace that has prevailed throughout most of the region over the past two decades, the durability of this peace is being called into question. Historical precedents certainly give cause for concern about the ability of the international system to accommodate peacefully a new major power such as China. The absence of effective regional security institutions, such as those that exist in Europe, compounds the difficult task of peacefully assimilating a much more powerful China into the region. Certain Chinese actions, including missile exercises in the Taiwan Strait, and the building of a military installation on Mischief Reef in the South China Sea, have further contributed to a growing regional concern that China increasingly may be prepared to use force to achieve its policy objectives.

While working to develop Asian regional institutions to deal with these problems, the United States should take the following steps:

- engage in a sustained strategic dialogue with China and U.S. allies to reduce Chinese suspicions and promote the mutually beneficial preservation of regional peace and stability in Asia;
- increase military contacts at all levels to expand mutual understanding of intentions and capabilities, thus promoting mutual trust and stability;
- maintain U.S. force capability and bilateral alliances in the region at current levels to sustain the credibility of our commitments while taking into account any dramatic changes in the regional situation that could justify cuts (e.g., the peaceful reunification of the Korean Peninsula);

• make clear that it supports the peaceful resolution of territorial disputes in the South and East China Seas, and views as unhelpful any unilateral actions that alter the *status quo* and threaten the principle of freedom of navigation in international waters.

North Korea

The United States and China share a number of important interests with respect to North Korea: the desire to avoid a conflict, opposition to a nuclearized Korean Peninsula, and an interest in deterring North Korea from military adventures. Even with respect to the continued deployment of U.S. troops in Korea following reunification, there is not an inherent clash of interest as long as the United States does not seek to deploy troops north of the Thirty-Eighth Parallel.

The United States should make a concerted effort, in coordination with its Korean and Japanese allies, to improve the quality of its dialogue with China about North Korea, and to try to allay mutual concerns about U.S. and Chinese intentions in the post-reunification period. To date, China's actions concerning Korea, although consistent with U.S. interests, have not received due recognition. A more explicitly coordinated approach would help alter perceptions in some quarters that U.S.–Chinese interests are necessarily divergent.

Nonproliferation

Building on the considerable progress that has already been achieved in dealing with proliferation over the past fifteen years in this field, the United States should:

• continue to work with China to secure its accession to new nonproliferation regimes and improve its compliance with existing ones;
• assure China that as it is asked to abide by international rules, it is entitled to have a seat at the table at which the rules are being drafted;
• seek to turn areas of current confrontation with China into arenas for cooperation. For example, the United States and China

have a common interest in preventing either a nuclear arms race or the actual use of nuclear weapons in South Asia. The administration should initiate a broader, more strategic dialogue with China that seeks to base our respective policies on our common interests in this region. In addition, in view of the damage to the relationship that would occur if sanctions were triggered by Chinese transfers of weapons of mass destruction covered by U.S. law (such as the alleged transfer of M-11 missile components to Pakistan in 1992), the administration should work with Beijing to better meet its nonproliferation commitments.

Economic & Commercial

China's stunning economic growth has deep implications for the United States. Exports to China have grown rapidly, but U.S. companies have encountered a variety of market access obstacles. Imports from China have risen even more rapidly, benefiting American consumers, but also creating adjustment problems for U.S. producers and workers.

- The United States should seek to normalize fully its commercial relations with China and to facilitate Beijing's entry into international economic regimes. To that end,
- The United States should actively lead in multilateral efforts to bring China into the World Trade Organization (WTO) on terms compatible with the existing WTO regime. This will require flexibility in negotiating transition arrangements. The U.S. should expect Beijing's commitment among other things to the principles of national treatment, transparency, and nondiscrimination; increased market access for foreign products and services; a standstill with respect to performance requirements and agreement to their eventual elimination; substantial and continuing tariff reductions and the steady elimination of nontariff barriers; and a gradual phaseout of subsidies to national industries.
- At the same time, the U.S. president should seek legislation to extend to China permanent most-favored-nation trading status. The current annual review damages Sino–U.S. relations and creates uncertainties for U.S. businesses in China.

- The United States should seek support from China's other large trading partners in its efforts to improve market transparency and to negotiate away impediments blocking access to China's market.
- China should understand that lax enforcement of agreements reached with the United States undermines a stable bilateral economic relationship. Both the United States and China should refrain from linking trade with unrelated issues.
- The United States should promptly lift post-Tiananmen economic sanctions on China that have become counterproductive or place an unnecessary burden on U.S. business. These include restrictions on trade and development assistance to China, Overseas Private Investment Cooperation (OPIC) coverage on U.S. businesses operating in China, and the ability of China to participate in the U.S.–Asian Environmental Partnership. The administration should work with China to remove the obstacles to bringing into force the 1985 Agreement on Peaceful Nuclear Cooperation.
- The United States should look for ways to provide stability to world markets while helping China meet soaring demands for energy and food. China's environment, in tandem with its rapidly growing energy and food consumption, ought to be areas of intensive cooperation with the United States. China's energy consumption is growing at close to 8 percent per year while domestic sources of coal continue to supply the bulk of China's energy demand; increasing numbers of cars and trucks are causing a growth in demand for oil of close to 15 percent per year. This soaring demand for oil, which cannot be satisfied by domestic sources, may be drawing China closer to oil-producing countries in the Persian Gulf and Central Asia. Its grain purchases are large enough to affect world prices. Close cooperation can assure stability in world supplies with minimal disruption to the environment. This will also enhance commercial opportunities for U.S. firms in these areas.

Human Rights

The United States has a strong abiding interest in the way all countries, including China, treat their people. China's pursuit of policies that promote meeting human needs and respect for humanitarian values, political freedoms, and the rule of law will enhance stability, reduce corruption, and create the conditions for stronger economic growth, with positive consequences for American economic stakes in the country. At great cost to China's stature abroad, the Chinese government has imprisoned individuals for the nonviolent expression of political and religious beliefs and for attempting to establish independent trade unions. While not the only important issue in the relationship, encouraging improvements in China's human rights environment will remain a priority of U.S. policy toward China. More progress is likely to be made on resolving differences over human rights when the overall relationship between the two countries is sound.

- New ways must be found to engage the Chinese government in a constructive, goal oriented dialogue on human rights and the rule of law that builds on China's own interests in achieving progress in these areas. The threat of imposing sanctions is not a useful tool in advancing respect for human rights in China, and in fact is often counterproductive. Without necessarily resorting to sanctions, especially serious violations of universally accepted human rights require a strong response.
- Discussions on human rights should be made an integral part of the strategic dialogue between the two countries. Maximum engagement implies maximum frankness, but this does not imply public diatribes. In discussions on human rights, the United States should make clear that its goal is not to undermine the Chinese government. It should be willing to listen to China's criticisms of U.S. human rights failings and should acknowledge the progress that has been made in the expansion of economic and, to a lesser extent, political freedom and the meeting of human needs.
- In taking human rights seriously, the U.S. should consider what is good for the majority of the Chinese people and the underlying forces that tend toward improvement: economic growth, growth of nongovernmental institutions, and expansion of democratic institutions.
- Egregious violations of rights in individual cases should be used as illustrations of larger systemic problems.

- China should be encouraged to sign and ratify the international human rights covenants and other human rights instruments, and to facilitate monitoring by international humanitarian organizations such as the International Committee of the Red Cross.
- A bilateral human rights forum between nonofficial organizations of the two countries should be established.
- Greater attention should be paid to using multilateral forums. Human rights concerns can be pursued within the established human rights framework of the United Nations, though this does not necessarily mean sponsorship of or lobbying for a resolution critical of China in the U.N. Human Rights Commission. China's participation in G-7 meetings would provide additional opportunities to address human rights concerns.

Hong Kong: Both the United States and China have important economic and humanitarian interests in Hong Kong's continued prosperity and stability. Hong Kong has been a bastion of civil and commercial freedoms in Asia, including freedoms of the press, speech, and assembly. The United States should take an informed interest in the territory's transition to Chinese rule. A successful transition in Hong Kong will heighten prospects for a peaceful resolution of Beijing's differences with Taiwan.

There is growing concern within the United States that, while China's leadership has committed its prestige to a smooth transfer of sovereignty, political aspects might be mismanaged. Given the extent of media attention, missteps will be magnified, and these could harm U.S.–China relations. The United States should emphasize the importance to China of taking steps—both before and after July 1, 1997—to increase confidence in its commitment to honoring the terms of the Joint Declaration and the Basic Law. Such steps might include proceeding cautiously with passage and implementation of the law against subversion, permitting continued human rights reporting on Hong Kong within the United Nations framework, and reaching agreements with the United States on its consular presence and ship visits. At the same time the United States should emphasize to Taipei that it will closely monitor Taiwan's actions with regard to Hong Kong.

Tibet: The United States should make clear that it does not challenge Chinese sovereignty over the area and that its concerns over the situation in Tibet are concerns of a human rights and humanitarian nature. It must refrain from any actions that suggest or raise expectations of Tibetan independence. The United States should encourage China to engage in a dialogue with exiled Tibetan leaders aimed at greater autonomy and the preservation of Tibet's unique culture and religion, and should stress the importance of greater access to Tibet by foreign diplomats and journalists.

Revitalizing the U.S.–China Relationship

Some Americans believe that China's policies across the board run counter to U.S. interests and that efforts to moderate Chinese behavior by cooperation will be unproductive. This Assembly rejects this view, but recognizes that its existence complicates a smooth implementation of the policy we advocate.

To revitalize the U.S.–China relationship, the U.S. president must take the lead. The president and his cabinet must articulate publicly as soon as possible a carefully reasoned, broad-ranging policy. That would not only give Americans a clearer understanding of the objectives, benefits, and costs of the China relationship, but would also strengthen the political support for a long-term policy and provide a basis for clearer and more consistent communication and engagement with China. This will require the president to:

- engage actively with Congress to build bipartisan support;
- maintain a schedule of regular meetings with the Chinese leadership that is not derailed by transitory friction; President Jiang Zemin should be invited to the United States for a summit meeting in the first half of 1997;
- direct a range of high-level exchanges, including the military;
- encourage direct congressional engagement with the Chinese, including visits to China.
- At the same time, it is imperative that a compelling case for a revitalized approach to China be articulated to the media.

A healthy U.S.–China relationship will not only depend on government-to-government relationships, but also on the contributions of a range of private organizations, both businesses and nongovernmental organizations. These are important because they can:

- support the development of needed institutions in China, for example the law, the court system, legal aid, alternative dispute resolution organizations, local elections, independent parliamentary bodies and judiciary, Chinese NGOs, and a freer and livelier press;
- lend expertise where it can be helpful as China seeks to improve its capacity to govern effectively;
- provide additional channels of informal dialogue on important issues;
- support experimental projects that enable China to deal more effectively with specific problems, such as the environment; and
- help inform the U.S. public and promote educational and cultural exchanges.

Four decades ago, when the United States and China had no trade, no diplomatic relations, and faced the ominous possibility of military confrontation, the United States decided to devote major resources to the training of students and professional specialists capable of understanding and interpreting the behavior of the PRC. Today, with the two nations engaged in massive trade and political relations, the public commitment to the training of young Americans has, ironically, been increasingly neglected. As the United States and China confront the opportunities and challenges of a new, twenty-first century encounter between great and powerful world actors, it is crucial that the United States rededicate the public and private resources needed to provide the nation with a stable and adequate supply of trained and politically independent professionals.

Mutual suspicions between the United States and China are too deep to be erased by a few visits or a series of newly announced programs. Domestic political considerations in the United States may make new initiatives to improve relations difficult. On some issues, Chinese leaders' reluctance to pay the costs of participation in international organizations may prevail over their desire to participate. Yet with such high stakes, the United States and China must take risks and exercise patience to set the relationship on a sound basis for the next century. The risks of trying and failing are negligible compared to the risks of not trying at all.

Participants
The Eighty-Ninth American Assembly

*MICHAEL H. ARMACOST
President
The Brookings Institution
Washington, DC

A. DOAK BARNETT
Professor Emeritus
Johns Hopkins/SAIS
Washington, DC

JULIA CHANG BLOCH
President
The United States-Japan
 Foundation
New York, NY

CARROLL BOGERT
International Correspondent
Newsweek Magazine
New York, NY

BEAU BOULTER
Former Congressman
Attorney-at-Law
Washington, DC

**MARCUS W. BRAUCHLI
China Bureau Chief
Wall Street Journal
HONG KONG

RAYMOND F. BURGHARDT
Foreign Service Officer
Bureau of East Asian and
 Pacific Affairs
U.S. Department of State
Washington, DC

RICHARD C. BUSH
National Intelligence Officer for
 East Asia
National Intelligence Council
Washington, DC

RONNIE C. CHAN
Chairman
Hang Lung Development
 Group
HONG KONG

MIKE CHINOY
Hong Kong Bureau Chief
CNN
HONG KONG

*JEROME A. COHEN
Director, Asia Studies Council
 on Foreign Relations
Professor, New York University
 Law School
Partner
Paul, Weiss, Rifkind, Wharton
 & Garrison
New York, NY

CURTIS C. CUTTER
President
ChinaMetrik
Washington, DC

DOUGLAS N. DAFT
Senior Vice President
President, Middle & Far East
 Group
The Coca-Cola Company
Atlanta, GA

KARL EIKENBERRY
Country Director for China,
 Mongolia & Hong Kong
Office of the Secretary of
 Defense
Washington, DC

JEFFREY L. FIEDLER
President, Food and Allied
 Services Trades Department
AFL-CIO
Washington, DC

CHAS. W. FREEMAN, JR.
Chairman
Projects International, Inc.
Washington, DC

*WILLIAM P. FULLER
President
The Asia Foundation
San Francisco, CA

PETER F. GEITHNER
Former Director, Asia Programs
The Ford Foundation
Larchmont, NY

HARRY HARDING
Dean
Elliott School of International
 Affairs
The George Washington
 University
Washington, DC

CHARLES O. HOLLIDAY,
 JR.
Executive Vice President and
 Chairman
DuPont Asia Pacific
Tokyo, JAPAN

KAREN ELLIOTT HOUSE
President, International
The Wall Street Journal
Dow Jones & Company, Inc.
New York, NY

††ARTHUR W. HUMMEL,
 JR.
Former Ambassador to PRC
Consultant, Lecturer
Chevy Chase, MD

**JOHN KAMM
President
Asia Pacific Associates, Inc.
San Francisco, CA

ROBERT A. KAPP
President
United States-China Business
 Council
Washington, DC

JAMES A. KELLY
President
Pacific Forum/CSIS
Honolulu, HI

DAVID M. LAMPTON
President
National Committee on U.S.-
 China Relations
New York, NY

TERRILL E. LAUTZ
Vice President
The Henry Luce Foundation,
 Inc.
New York, NY

HERBERT LEVIN
Executive Director
America-China Society
New York, NY

KENNETH LIEBERTHAL
Arthur Thurnau Professor of
    Political Science
William Davidson Professor of
    Business Administration
University of Michigan
Ann Arbor, MI

ABRAHAM F. LOWENTHAL
President
Pacific Council on International
    Policy
Los Angeles, CA

WHITNEY MacMILLAN
Chairman Emeritus
Cargill Inc.
Minneapolis, MN

MICHAEL B. McELROY
Chairman
Department of Earth &
    Planetary Sciences
Rotch Professor of Atmospheric
    Sciences
Harvard University
Cambridge, MA

LAURENCE T. MURPHY
President Emeritus
Director, Asia Center
Distinguished University
    Professor
Seton Hall University
South Orange, NJ

†SAM NUNN
United States Senate
Washington, DC

JOSEPH S. NYE, JR.
Dean
JFK School of Government
Harvard University
Cambridge, MA

MICHEL OKSENBERG
Senior Fellow
Asia/Pacific Research Center
Stanford University
Stanford, CA

SUSAN O'SULLIVAN
Regional Officer/China East
    Asia & Pacific
Bureau of Democracy, Human
    Rights & Labor
Washington, DC

DOUGLAS PAAL
President
Asia Pacific Policy Center
Washington, DC

DWIGHT H. PERKINS
Harvard Institute for
    International Development
Harvard University
Cambridge, MA

A. KEN RICHESON
Vice President, Public Affairs
IBM World Trade Asia
    Corporation
Tokyo, JAPAN

ALAN D. ROMBERG
Principal Deputy Director
Policy Planning Staff
U.S. Department of State
Washington, DC

ROBERT S. ROSS
Department of Political
    Science
Boston College
Fairbank Center for East Asian
    Research
Harvard University
Cambridge, MA

**STANLEY ROTH
Director, Research & Studies
   Program
United States Institute of Peace
Washington, DC

ORVILLE SCHELL
Dean
Graduate School of Journalism
University of California,
   Berkeley
Berkeley, CA

†BRENT SCOWCROFT
President
The Scowcroft Group
Washington, DC

ELEANOR B. SHELDON
Former President
Social Science Research Council
New York, NY

RICHARD H. SOLOMON
President
U.S. Institute of Peace
Washington, DC

DAVID K.Y. TANG
Managing Partner
Preston, Gates & Ellis
Seattle, WA

††ANNE F. THURSTON
Independent Scholar
Washington, DC

††EZRA F. VOGEL
Director
Fairbank Center for East Asian
   Research
Harvard University
Cambridge, MA

RAYMOND J. WALDMANN
Vice President
International Business
The Boeing Company
Seattle, WA

WILLIAM J. WARWICK
Chair & CEO
AT&T (China) Co., Ltd.
Basking Ridge, NJ

†JOHN C. WHITEHEAD
Chair
AEA Investors Inc.
New York, NY

ALFRED D. WILHELM, JR.
Executive Vice President
Atlantic Council of the United
   States
Washington, DC

*PAUL D. WOLFOWITZ
Dean
The Paul H. Nitze School of
   Advanced International
   Studies
Johns Hopkins University
Washington, DC

EDEN Y. WOON
Executive Director
Washington State China
   Relations Council
Seattle, WA

††JOHN YOUNG
Executive Director
Committee of 100
New York, NY

314

NANCY YOUNG
Partner and Chair,
International Practice
  Group
Richards & O'Neil, LLP
New York, NY

FAREED ZAKARIA
Managing Editor
Foreign Affairs
New York, NY*

Discussion Leader
**Rapporteur
†Delivered Formal Address
††Panelist

††MADELEINE H. ZELIN
Director
East Asian Institute
Columbia University
New York, NY

MICHAEL ZIELENZIGER
Tokyo Bureau Chief
Knight-Ridder Newspapers/
San Jose Mercury News
Tokyo, JAPAN

About The American Assembly

The American Assembly was established by Dwight D. Eisenhower at Columbia University in 1950. It holds nonpartisan meetings and publishes authoritative books to illuminate issues of United States policy.

An affiliate of Columbia, the Assembly is a national, educational institution incorporated in the state of New York.

The Assembly seeks to provide information, stimulate discussion, and evoke independent conclusions on matters of vital public interest.

American Assembly Sessions

At least two national programs are initiated each year. Authorities are retained to write background papers presenting essential data and defining the main issues of each subject.

A group of men and women representing a broad range of experience, competence, and American leadership meet for several days to discuss the Assembly topic and consider alternatives for national policy.

All Assemblies follow the same procedure. The background papers are sent to participants in advance of the Assembly. The Assembly meets in small groups for four or five lengthy periods. All groups use the same agenda. At the close of these informal sessions participants adopt in plenary session a final report of findings and recommendations.

Regional, state, and local Assemblies are held following the national session at Arden House. Assemblies have also been held in England, Switzerland, Malaysia, Canada, the Caribbean, South America, Central America, the Philippines, and Japan. Over 160 institutions have cosponsored one or more Assemblies.

Arden House

The home of The American Assembly and the scene of the national sessions is Arden House, which was given to Columbia University in 1950 by W. Averell Harriman. E. Roland Harriman joined his brother in contributing toward adaptation of the property for conference purposes. The buildings and surrounding land, known as the Harriman Campus of Columbia University, are fifty miles north of New York City.

Arden House is a distinguished conference center. It is self-supporting and operates throughout the year for use by organizations with educational objectives. The American Assembly is a tenant of this Columbia University facility only during Assembly sessions.

CLIFFORD M. HARDIN	Missouri
KATHLEEN H. MORTIMER	New York
ELEANOR BERNERT SHELDON	New York
CLARENCE C. WALTON	Pennsylvania

Index